Forward Positions

Forward Positions

The War Correspondence
of Homer Bigart

COMPILED AND EDITED BY BETSY WADE

WITH A FOREWORD BY HARRISON E. SALISBURY

THE UNIVERSITY OF ARKANSAS PRESS · FAYETTEVILLE · 1992

This book was designed by Chiquita Babb using the Garamond and Bodoni typefaces.

The paper used in this publication meets the minimum requirements of the American National Standard for Permanence of Paper for Printed Library Materials z39.48-1984. ♾

Library of Congress Cataloging-in-Publication Data

Bigart, Homer, b. 1907.
 Forward positions: the war correspondence of Homer Bigart / compiled and edited by Betsy Wade; with a foreword by Harrison E. Salisbury.
  p. cm.
 Includes references and index.
 ISBN 1-55728-257-9
 1. Bigart, Homer b. 1907. 2. War correspondents—United States—History. 3. Reporters and reporting—United States—History. 4. War in the press—United States—History. I. Wade, Betsy. II. Title.
PN4784.B54A3 1992
070.4'333'092—dc20   92-4784
                CIP

For Else Holmelund Minarik Bigart,
as Homer Would Want It

———————

Contents

Illustrations

Foreword

By Harrison E. Salisbury

T HE first time I saw Homer Bigart he was the solitary figure in the windy acres of the Ministry of Information press room in Malet Street on the edge of Bloomsbury. We had just arrived in London, Homer on January 19, 1943, and myself on February 4. We had come to cover the war.

The glimpse of Homer transmitted the essential characteristics of the man who would become *the* war correspondent of his time. He was alone, a slim, almost frail figure hunched over his Olivetti, slowly punching with two or three fingers, often pausing, often X-ing out words, often consulting notes, often looking out into space before resuming. He gave no sign that he saw me nor the oak-stained walls of the University of London lecture hall that had been converted into a press working space. He was alone in the corridors of his mind.

That late afternoon Bigart was the only reporter still writing his dispatch on the latest R.A.F. raid over Germany. The care, the precision of his reporting, the extraordinary attention to detail, the slowness with which he constructed his stories, and the luminosity of his prose were already making him legendary.

I watched him for a few minutes from the rear of the room. It was an image that would remain in my mind for fifty years. To anyone who observed Bigart it was plain that it was no accident that he emerged as a brilliant recorder of war, setting it down with an eye as precise as Goya's. Inevitably, he became a role model for successive waves of reporters in the age of wars that was to follow 1945.

Bigart was a man who worked with the skill of a diamond cutter, dipping again and again into the cornucopia of information he had assembled before sitting at his typewriter. Long since, his colleagues had become accustomed to his tedious questioning, going over a point again and again, repeating and repeating, asking explanations of the obvious, never satisfied. It could be very boring. But when the answers mortised together into the plain but intricate structure of Homer's prose his edifice of words stood out like a tower on a treeless plain.

Nothing better revealed Bigart's technique than the experience of Neil Sheehan, who worked with him in Vietnam in 1962, a neophyte learning his craft at Bigart's side. For several days the two went out together on American operations. Each day Bigart questioned the commanders on their objectives, the number and training of their troops, the experience of higher officers, what was known of enemy dispositions and terrain, what they hoped to achieve.

After this ponderous exercise, Bigart and Sheehan would helicopter to the scene of action. After the operation (which seldom went off as planned) Bigart would subject the field officers to more endless questioning. Sheehan had never heard so many questions, but Bigart did not write a word. Finally, returning from a third day of tedium, Sheehan turned to Bigart and complained. "All that time and no story," he said. Homer blinked his owlish eyes. "Really," he said. "There's no story?" "Well, what is it?" Sheehan asked. "What do you mean?"

"It doesn't work, kid," Bigart said. "It doesn't work any more."

Only then did Sheehan understand what they had been doing. Bigart had been making a painstaking assessment of the basic military operation. That was the point of his repetitious questions. He was measuring results against expectation and had come to a stunning conclusion: the American intervention had reached dead end. "It doesn't work any more." This was pure Bigart. It took some years before General Westmoreland and the others, Presidents Johnson and Nixon, came to the same conclusion.

––––––––––

On that late gray London afternoon in February when I first glimpsed Bigart he had yet to fling himself on the ground to dodge an incoming shell. By this time the blitz was over, although London still went through the Luftwaffe's night raids to the accompaniment of a stunning antiaircraft barrage. Bigart was then thirty-five years old and earning eighty-five dollars a week. He had been working at the *Herald Tribune* since 1927, when he caught on as a night copy boy at the age of twenty. It took Bigart five years to become head copy boy and something of a martinet, and a year later he became a not-too-promising reporter, handicapped by slow writing and a bad stutter. In his working career he did not overcome the stutter, but he learned to employ it as a device for asking repetitive and apparently aimless (or even stupid) questions, catching his subject off guard and opening up angles no one else had.

By the time Bigart arrived in London he was a first-class journeyman with no foreign language, no foreign experience, no combat experience, no more knowledge of war or foreign affairs than he could glean from the headlines. He was still excruciatingly slow in composing a story, but he had begun to develop a writing style that avoided clichés and superfluities. He was deft with detail, possessed of a mind that viewed the world with skepticism and limned its creatures with sardonic wit. The *Herald Tribune* boasted a covey of writers more brilliant than Bigart, more sophisticated, more literary but none with his organized simplicity, unpredictable turns of phrase, and ability to cut through chaff.

––––––––––

A month after setting foot in England, Bigart had his first taste of combat. He flew in a B-17 bomber of the U.S. Eighth Air Force on a daylight raid over Wilhelmshaven, a submarine base on the German north coast. Half a dozen American correspondents flew that day, including Walter Cronkite of the United Press, Gladwin Hill of the

Associated Press, Andy Rooney of *Stars and Stripes,* and Robert Post of *The New York Times.* Post was lost on the mission.

Bigart, Cronkite, and Hill were badly shaken by their experience. As the pilots used to say in London, the flak was so thick you could walk on it. News that Post was missing did not ease their nerves. Cronkite couldn't get his story started. Finally, as his editor at U.P., I fed him a typical wire-service overline: "I flew through hell today." Walter eyed the words with some doubt but finally modified the phrase and used it to lead his story. It won him a clean sweep of the play in England (but not in the U.S. papers because Glad Hill's story for the A.P. was cleared by the censors ahead of Walter's).

Walter was slow in writing his story, but Bigart was slower. A single command car that seated four passengers had been assigned to take the eight of us back from Molesworth to London. We waited for Bigart and waited. Everyone's nerves jangled. Hill got a talking jag. Finally Bigart appeared, apologizing to Cronkite: "I just couldn't get started. What did you lead with?"

Cronkite quoted his "I flew through hell" lead. Bigart looked at him for a long time. "You wouldn't!" Bigart said reproachfully. His own lead was broomstick plain:

"Our target was Wilhelmshaven. We struck at Fuehrer Adolf Hitler's North Sea base from the northwest after stoogeing around over a particularly hot corner of the Third Reich for what seemed like a small eternity."

––––––––––

The Wilhelmshaven raid set the pattern of Bigart's career as a war correspondent. Physical peril was the price of the game. At that moment Eighth Air Force losses were running at 25 percent per mission, a one-in-four chance that you would not return. Some missions lost as many as thirty-six or thirty-seven planes out of forty starters. But Bigart had concluded that if you covered a war you went where it was. You did not count the odds. His superiors tried to rein him in—never successfully. Bigart was not a showoff. He did not court danger. He took every precaution. He was quick as anyone to seek cover, but he never let danger bar him from a story.

Bigart grew to be a fatalist, or so he said. The bullet had not yet been cast that would take his life. If a shell had your name on it you could not escape it. The more knowledgeable he grew about war, the more careful he was.

By June 1943, Bigart had left London and was off to North Africa. He first saw ground combat in Sicily, and in Italy he saw it at its most deadly serious. His willingness to push forward in the face of enemy fire began to manifest itself and was reflected in the immediacy of his prose. This was not fearlessness. Bigart was never without fear. But in battlefield reporting peril was a given.

And Bigart began to display another trait that would distinguish his war reporting. His temperament did not permit him to be a mindless cheerleader. He had discovered that war could easily be defined as an endless succession of blunders. He had no patience with patriotic gore. He reported the agony of the Anzio beachhead as it was—and the miscalculations, the meaningless deaths, the false optimism of the communiqués, the mindless sacrifice of men. He got into trouble as he was to get into trouble again and again.

Bigart's blunt words brought down on him the wrath of the Allied commander, Sir Harold R. L. G. Alexander, who responded to bad news much as did his namesake Alexander the Great. Alexander the Great beheaded the messenger who brought bad news; Alexander, the commander, blamed the correspondents and Bigart in particular, who had reported that Anzio had turned into a disaster. Bigart stood by his message that the Anzio tragedy was caused by high military muddle and mistakes. It was Bigart's first major controversy but far from his last.

Before Bigart reached Vietnam he had experienced more warfare than all but a few of the commanders he met, and he evaluated their performance with bluntness and a professional eye. He could not abide cant. He found his place with the mud-covered men in the fox-holes and not with the boot-polished men of headquarters.

————————

Bigart possessed a quality that distinguished him from most of his competitors. Some of his peers did not immediately realize that their quiet, often tiresome, stuttering companion was a deadly competitor; that behind a facade of slow-wittedness and slow writing was concealed a man who could never be satisfied with anything but first place. Nothing was too much trouble, no expenditure of energy too exhausting to achieve that aim. The task Bigart assigned to himself was far more demanding than any ever imposed by an editor.

Never was this quality more manifest than in Korea when Bigart was pitted shoulder-to-shoulder against a competitor of fierceness equal to his own, Marguerite Higgins, a colleague on the *Herald Tribune*. It was not a happy experience. Neither gave an inch. That either survived the battle dangers to which they exposed themselves to be the first with the best story seemed a miracle to other correspondents.

After it was over Bigart conceded that he was not happy with his conduct. "No way can I make my behavior toward her appear in a favorable light," he confessed. He said that he felt Higgins had come close to getting him killed by making him take chances that he knew he shouldn't have, in order to meet her competitive drive.

———

Of all the wars Bigart covered Korea was the ugliest, the most dangerous, most exhausting, coldest, most lacking in transport and communications, staffed by the harshest censors and most hostile commanders (largely because the war went so badly). Few generals in Korea would have found fault with the dictum of William Tecumseh Sherman, who believed war correspondents should be shot.

When Bigart left Korea in January 1951, he was called by *Newsweek* "the best war correspondent of an embattled generation."

Bigart went on to other wars—some bigger, some smaller—and finally once more to Vietnam, now as a *New York Times* correspondent. He hated all of them. War was ugly, frightful, terrifying. It possessed no redeeming qualities in his eyes.

When the Vietnam war was lost it did not surprise Bigart that the generals blamed the media, print and electronic, for their failure nor that the public took up the same cry. He had long since learned that if a reporter gets nothing but bouquets he must be missing part of the story—the important part.

Introduction

HOMER Bigart spent a career of forty years as a reporter for two New York morning newspapers—first the *Herald Tribune,* gone since 1966, and *The New York Times.* For twenty of these years, from 1943 to 1963, he was primarily a war correspondent. Early on, during the ground war in Italy in 1944, his dispatches began to crop up in his colleagues' reporting and anecdotes as the benchmark against which they measured their work. He won two Pulitzer Prizes on the *Tribune,* and after he went to the *Times* in 1955 it was common to hear of a new hotshot in the newsroom: "He's good, but he's no Bigart."

Bigart's writing—simple and clear, with a rich, precise but not florid vocabulary—was produced slowly and typed with a manual stutter to match his rather effective vocal stammer. He hit the spacebar several times while he waited for a desired word to come. Once he joked that what took him so long was putting in the punctuation. The truth was he used a period more than anything else.

A distinctive style of reporting fueled the writing. One reporter acidly called it Homer's "all-American dummy act." It was no act, but rather the demeanor of a naturally reticent, semi-solemn man with a stammer that activated at crucial words; behind the stammer, he was totally concentrated on getting more of the story than any of his competitors. Bill Borders, a *Times* news editor, told a *Times* historian he had learned a great lesson from Bigart. If a gang of reporters was staring at a corpse in the street with a knife in the back, "trying to figure out what to say that wouldn't sound dumb," Borders said, it would be Bigart who would ask the police officer: "What's the cause of death?" To which the reply would be, "Arsenic poisoning."

Joseph Lelyveld, also a Pulitzer Prize winner and later managing editor of the *Times,* said that as a beginning reporter he was sent to the other Philadelphia, in Mississippi, the area where three young civil rights workers had been killed. He decided to interview a probably courageous minister—Lelyveld said he had recently preached on the text "Thou shalt not kill." After the interview, the minister asked about the person he met the week before who had also introduced himself as a *Times* reporter. This could hardly be so, the preacher said: "I had to explain *everything* to him!" Lelyveld, who retold this story at a memorial for Bigart, received hearty applause; almost everyone recalled fidgeting while Bigart asked just one more question.

Murray Kempton, a Pulitzer Prize columnist, wrote that Bigart once agreed to drive him home from a racial disturbance in Pennsylvania if Kempton would wait while he talked to the town clerk—for a long time, as it turned out—about his memories of a simpler life. "When we left at last," Kempton wrote, "Homer apologized with the explanation that you might have to come back to this place and could need this sort of stuff. He would always know more than the rest of us because he could never think that he already knew enough."

In 1973, the year after he retired, Bigart was honored by his successor generation with the A. J. Liebling Award from *More* magazine. David Halberstam, who was the *Times* correspondent in Vietnam soon after Bigart in 1962, and J. Anthony Lukas presented the award at the *More* "counter-convention" in Washington. The citation spoke of Bigart's "four decades of single-minded attention to his craft, a persistent skepticism toward all forms of power and tenacious pursuit of social injustice long before such reporting became fashionable."

Homer was not secretive about what drove him for those four

decades, or why he did what he did. He was hungry, he said. He just wanted to get the damned story.

He began at the *Trib* about the time of his twentieth birthday, October 25, 1927. The son of a sweater manufacturer and his wife in Hawley, Pennsylvania, he had a fragment of a college education from Carnegie Tech, which considered him not suited to the architecture program. His family was Presbyterian, which may account for his sometimes Calvinist view of those in temporal power. He grew up with two sisters, Gladys and Margaret. Margaret had an early and accurate measure of the significance of his work and maintained a giant-format scrapbook of her brother's clippings.

Bigart's first job was as a copy boy. He couldn't seem to break out of this lowliest of newsroom jobs and feared he would become the oldest living specimen. While he bided his time, he began a newsletter, *The Copy Boy's Call.* He took journalism courses at New York University until the crash in 1929, when he gave up school, got an apartment in Brooklyn, and began to send money home. As long as I knew him, he was taking care of relatives in Pennsylvania, fretting about roof repairs and such. He had a reputation as a tightwad, but his relatives would dispute that.

Bigart had risen to be the *Trib's* head copy boy before he finally got a reporter's post in 1932. Those days, his writing was laborious, and he did not win great favor with the city editor, Stanley Walker, whose name is usually preceded by the word "legendary." According to what Bigart told Richard Kluger in interviews for his research on his superb 1986 history, *The Paper, The Life and Death of the* New York Herald Tribune, he didn't do very well either with Charlie McLendon, the less-than-legendary city editor who succeeded Walker in the mid-thirties.

The first byline that survives in Bigart's file is from May 1934. It appears on a nearly endless story on the installation of a Catholic auxiliary bishop at St. Patrick's Cathedral. When he was a copy boy, Bigart had made extra money covering religious stories, where slowness was not a huge impediment. He did get sent out of town, to conferences in Williamstown, Massachusetts, St. Louis, and New Orleans, to a coal dispute in Pennsylvania, and even to a Triangle Club show at Princeton.

In 1939, Walker's night city editor, L. L. Engelking, rose to city editor. He was a man who loved the language, and, as Kluger says, had a compassion that invited "extraordinary effort by his reporters." Bigart got better assignments and his work improved. In March 1940, he undertook the classic New York color story: the St. Patrick's Day parade, conducted that year in "slush and swirling snow" and reviewed by Mayor Fiorello H. La Guardia, who stayed the course, and District Attorney Thomas E. Dewey, who did not.

"The snow lay an inch deep in the folds of the Mayor's large black felt hat," the story said, "by the time the County Kerry boys went by singing 'The hat me dear old father wore.'"

Bigart pinned the weather and the politicians to the board for all to read:

"Apparently the Mayor had less confidence in the proverbial luck of the Irish than his fellow-reviewers, for he came better equipped against the weather. He wore a fireman's raincoat. Lieut. Gov. Charles A. Poletti gloated because he had brought his rubbers.

"'Haven't you any brains?' he scolded Mr. Dewey. 'Why didn't you wear rubbers?'

"'No brains, no rubbers,' conceded Mr. Dewey glumly as he looked around for an exit."

Later in 1940, Bigart was assigned to the First Army's far-flung maneuvers in New York State along the Canadian border. That story, the first in this collection, contains elements of his characteristic mock-serious style. Other dispatches from this assignment to what was then Pine Camp, now Fort Drum, show budding expertise on arms and the military.

In 1943, when he was thirty-five, after an apprenticeship so long it would be considered beyond endurance today, he was sent to England to cover the war. It was that or be drafted, he said.

His gosh-I-don't-know-a-thing approach must have been well developed on his first overseas assignment, covering the Eighth Air Force fliers who conducted the daylight bombing raids on Europe. One dispatch notes wryly that among the eight correspondents who trained to ride on bombing missions, he was voted the one least likely to return.

In mid-1943, he was sent to Allied headquarters in Algiers and from there to Sicily, where he covered ground combat for the first time. On January 22, 1944, he landed with the troops at Anzio, south of Rome, where the entire precarious beachhead was exposed to enemy fire. He remained there sixty-two days, through three German efforts to push the Allies back into the sea. This experience, and the dispatch displaying his disgust at the complacency he found back in Naples, set a pattern for his coverage of the rest of World War II, and thereafter.

By the time Bigart slogged his way on to Rome and to southern France in the last summer of the European war, his work was nationally known, although hard to pigeonhole. He wrote about combat as it happened, and he tried to avoid merely covering the day's communiqué from that day's headquarters, which was usually the cautious editor's choice for the lead story in the paper. Nor did Bigart, although he carried a bedroll and traveled with the infantry, compete with Ernie Pyle in personal, life-of-a-dogface coverage.

Kluger explains well the evolution of the kind of work Bigart did. Bigart told him he seldom saw a copy of the *Trib* in World War II and did not know how his work was displayed, but by the same token, he was not pecked to death by editors' cables telling him to go do something different. So he kept doing what he was doing, detailing the work and achievements of ordinary soldiers to inform both their sometimes ill-advised commanders and the citizens at home.

Reading his dispatches makes clear the difference between combat reporting from forward positions, replete with fear, fatigue, colors, and odors, and rear area communiqués on the day's events. But it is also true that one correspondent, at one spot, can seldom assess grand strategy. So Bigart's file might or might not lead the paper on a given day, but wherever it was printed, it was the dispatch other correspondents wanted to match.

Like thousands of the soldiers he traveled with in Europe, Bigart shifted to the war in the Pacific in 1945, covering it to the end, walking in the rubble of Hiroshima, observing a Japanese Cabinet minister's cane fall to the deck at the signing of the surrender.

Five years later, Bigart covered his second war, in Korea. At the end of that assignment, *Newsweek* wrote: "By almost unanimous agreement of colleagues there—and of many stateside readers—Bigart left the Korea battlefront as the best war correspondent of an embattled generation."

Eyeing the precarious state of the *Trib*, he shifted to the *Times* in 1955. By 1958, I was on a copy desk that handled Bigart. It was a wonderful experience. I learned from editing him never to "just make hooks"—copy editor's paragraph marks—or stop paying attention. He was just as likely to bowl some pun past you, or some hidden barb. "After yesterday's thrilling bombing of the Presidential Palace," one dispatch from Vietnam started. When he was in Vietnam, I also suffered nagging doubts, for obvious reasons, that there *was* such a place as Phuoc Long. The map department, and later Bigart's letters, reassured me. If you met a word you didn't know—I remember "prizing a shirt off a man's back"—you had better look it up before changing it or bear terrible scorn from the author.

His dispatches were almost always shapely, and his coverage of long-running stories such as the Eichmann trial, where the time differences meant that a new day would start before the final edition closed in New York, showed the result of careful planning and even plotting. Bigart left for the trial in Jerusalem with a letter from his family lawyer in Hawley, I. Reines Skier, that eventually won him what everyone else wanted—an interview with Eichmann's defense lawyer. Just a lucky break, Bigart said. Hardly.

His two Pulitzer Prizes on the *Trib* were awarded for his work on the end of the Pacific war in 1945, and for Korea, a prize he shared with five other correspondents, including Marguerite Higgins of the *Trib*. This book does not need to retell the Bigart-Higgins war, which was epic, and grave, although old-timers still laugh about it. But since Bigart cannot now speak for himself, I want to add a few words on this issue, which threatened in some quarters to become more famous than Bigart's work or Higgins's.

Too lowly to have known him when I was on the *Trib*, I introduced myself to Bigart at the *Times* on the basis that a classmate of mine had briefly been in one of Batista's jails with him while he was in Cuba tracking down Fidel Castro in 1958. It was a case of hero-worship at first sight, and I planned a role for myself as his Boswell. So I pestered him to retell old tales and took notes constantly. I once asked: "Homer, there are two stories about what you said when they told you Marguerite Higgins had a baby. One is that you said, 'Wonderful, who's the mother?' And the other is that you said, 'Well, did she eat it?' Which one is correct?" Typically, Bigart replied: "Yes."

But in 1966, when Higgins died of leishmaniasis contracted in Asia, Bigart was at the *Times,* brooding at his desk in the front row. He said: "You know, they keep coming to me to ask me to say something terrible about her. But you can't say something terrible about someone who dies dreadfully." Still later, he said to Kluger that in retrospect he was unable to defend his treatment of her: He had desperately wanted her out of Korea because, he told other correspondents, competing with her forced him to take chances where he found himself jeopardizing his life. But a newspaper with two war correspondents who are competing daily to outdo each other is not going to recall one on the other's complaint, so the battle went on and the bitterness ended only with one rival's death.*

Whatever his mordant tendencies, it was impossible to get Bigart to comment unfavorably on the work, personality, clothes, or sex habits of any reporter who followed him in an assignment. They might have been check-dodgers, thieves of notes, or spouse-beaters, but you'd never hear it from him. He seemed to have a reasonable estimation of how difficult it must have been to pick up his threads. By the same token, it was not wise to introduce him as a Pulitzer Prize winner. "Two-time," he would reply. "Two-time Pulitzer Prize winner." And tuck his chin in and grin at his newspaper cliché.

His diffidence, his puns, his aphorisms, and his acid barbs made him a favorite of his colleagues, but when his wit is assessed, and the puns, denunciations on Higgins, and stories that hinge on his stammer are set aside, what remains are his aphorisms, which are pretty fine. Tex McCrary says that Bigart, while covering the Eighth Air

*For those who want to pursue the matter, Kluger's *The Paper* has good detail on Korea and on Higgins's career before and after. This book also contains twelve pages on Bigart, derived from the archives as well as long interviews Kluger and his collaborator, Phyllis Kluger, held with Bigart in retirement.

Force in England, counseled the chief public information officer, John Hay Whitney: "Why don't you buy the *Herald Tribune:* You'll have more fun than riding or in bed." Of picking teeth: "One of mankind's greatest satisfactions." When I told him that some reporters had held an orgy that was apparently a bore, he replied: "All orgies are bores." When McLendon was named city editor of the *Trib,* he said: "If this was a bank, there'd be a run on it."

A lot of his comment concerned drinking, traditionally a crucial diversion for reporters and editors. "The problem with Lagos," he said on his return from Nigeria, "it's too hot to drink anything but beer." "Gough's saloon is indeed a low place," he said of the watering hole nearest to the *Times,* "but newspapering is a low profession." As for guests who objected to the conversation there and at Bleeck's, the *Trib* reporters' joint, because it was all shop talk: "People who don't like shop talk shouldn't go to newspaper saloons."

Bigart never wrote a book, and his magazine articles, book reviews, and other diversions are fewer than ten in number. When he was on strike as a Newspaper Guild member, in 1962–63, he wrote news copy for CBS, but he never moved to jump the print journalism ship. His old colleague Don Cook says that Bigart was never at home in other than a newspaper setting. It may have been more basic: He told the *Times* history project interviewer, Mary Marshall Clark, "With me, there had to be a deadline; otherwise it would never get done."

When he was in Vietnam, I wrote him that when I encountered great art and great music, Bix Beiderbecke for instance, I despaired of ever doing anything enduring while working for a newspaper, even an eminent one. "As you say, the newspaper business is an inadequate vehicle, but it will take a profound psychological shock to make me ever want to rise above it," he wrote. "I have no burning message." And at another point, in a more practical mood: "You shouldn't listen to Biederbecke if it depresses you."

In the years it has taken to get this book between covers, I have had with me a quotation from James W. Carey, eminent in journalism education as thinker and conscience. In 1973, just after Bigart retired, Carey told a conference on education for newspaper journalists: "I take it to be a remarkable fact that each year I read more of

Homer Bigart than I do of Plato and yet today twenty-five hundred years after Plato wrote, there is more critical work on Plato each year than there is on Bigart. In fact, there is nothing published on Bigart."

This book will at least assure that students of writing and journalism, newspaper historians, Bigart admirers, and, perhaps the most important, those young people who also are hungry, and who also just want to get the damned story, will be able to read Bigart work that is otherwise only cartons of clippings that now crumble at my touch.

Betsy Wade
April 1992

World War II, Europe

Army Exercises, New York State, August 1940

1st Army Gets
Night Off Under
Eyes of M.P.s

Troops Are Orderly; Many
Take Canadian Ship on
Thousand Islands Cruise

ARMY HEADQUARTERS, OGDENSBURG, N.Y., Aug. 10, 1940—A good part of Lieut. Gen. Hugh A. Drum's First Army came to town this sultry evening and gave the Ford Street night spots their best play since the Veterans of Foreign Wars convened here on the Fourth of July.

The men started trickling in from the "war zone" soon after the noon mess and by dusk porch sitters at the Seymour House could look up State Street and count more troops than natives. Police Chief Herbert S. Myers called out his entire force of 17 patrolmen and three sergeants.

Practically the whole army had the night off except for the military police, who had their heaviest duty since the maneuvers began. Five roving patrols of M.P.'s and state police toured the city and surrounding country, while hundreds of other M.P.'s patrolled Canton, Gouverneur, Potsdam and Winthrop.

Army Well Disciplined

No force of American troops has appeared more orderly and better disciplined than this army of General Drum's. There has been no serious trouble since the army arrived, and it now appears that the curfew enforced in some towns within the maneuver area was wholly unnecessary.

Canada is still forbidden ground to First Army officers and men, although Canadian authorities have told General Drum that the Dominion's hospitality awaits any soldier who crosses the frontier with "a pass signed by a competent authority." One of the rigidly enforced rules is that no officer or enlisted man may wear civilian clothes and the First Army command does not want a lot of American soldiers on the soil of a belligerent nation. . . .

The military policing of the 1,300-square-mile maneuver area is accomplished by more than 1,000 M.P.'s. . . . Some agents of the Federal Bureau of Investigation are also reported in the area keeping watch on possible fifth-column activities. . . .

The taverns and night clubs in St. Lawrence County are being closely watched by state police and agents of the state liquor authority. Those that sell liquor to a soldier after 11 P.M., Saturdays excepted, will have their licenses revoked.

So far none of the night spots has been marked "off limits," although two honky-tonks have been advised to tone down their entertainment. Two resorts were closed by police a few weeks before the troops arrived, and officials are now studying plans to eliminate a kind of hostess curb service that has sprung up recently. (Aug. 11, 1940)

Troopship to Britain, January 1943

Troopship Trip
To Britain Like
Pre-War Tour

Reporter Gets All Set for
Jitters and Discomfort;
All He Finds Is Boredom

LONDON, Jan. 19, 1943—American troops by the thousands are arriving in the British Isles after crossings that are only a little more uncomfortable and not much more eventful than a trans-Atlantic voyage at the height of the prewar June tourist rush.

This correspondent came over recently in a fast ship. He had carefully schooled himself for a nervous breakdown by imagining all sorts of horrors: packs of submarines under foot; the sky darkened by the Luftwaffe after the second day out; breakfast of kippers, boiled potatoes at noon, brussels sprouts at night.

You did not bring anything to read, because you figured the guns would be going off incessantly and the destroyer escort dumping high explosives over the side, so naturally it would be very hard to concentrate. You would go to bed fully clothed, of course, and in your lifebelt. Sleep would be impossible. Every one would be deathly sick. You decided it might be a good idea to sit up in a liferaft at night, winning the friendship of a plump seagull.

So by embarking time you were a raw bundle of nerves, and it was of slight comfort to know that the large body of American soldiers and men on board were in the same state of jitters. At any rate they were very subdued, the ship being so quiet that you couldn't escape hearing the puns being dropped by your cabin mate, a youth who said he suffered from claustrophobia, which you agreed was an interesting condition on a crowded transport.

Several hours elapsed from boarding time to sailing time, a ghastly interval during which you drank all the brandy you had hoarded against sea sickness.

You managed a little sleep, and when you hit deck next morning, the flat American coast was going down over the stern. A patriotic emotion was appropriate, but the odds were that the lump in your throat was a bit of undigested sourdough roll. Yet breakfast wasn't hard to take. The salt cod, prunes and tea were palatable, and there was more butter on the table than you had seen during the last month of spartan living in America.

The ship had sounded awfully hollow in the night, but now you discovered that the decks below were packed with troops who had slept in double and triple tiers of bunks and hammocks. There was a moderate sea, and the boys down on E deck, quartered near the crew's kitchen, were already turning a little green. After a few days of rough weather the Yanks started grousing about the food, and then you knew that everything was normal.

The days passed and nothing happened. Everyone relaxed. A hillbilly orchestra of Texas troops gave nightly concerts in B deck square. Crap games broke out wherever two or more soldiers were gathered together. In the officers' lounge the poker stakes got astronomically high. There were no deck sports, but pingpong was played in the hall outside the main dining room.

No one was allowed on decks during blackout hours. Even interior gangways were generally pitch dark, and with flashlights forbidden, the descent to dinner could be quite an adventure in a rough sea. You could smoke only in the lounges and not on deck, and you had to carry your life belt everywhere.

There was no bar and you were traveling in very sober company, few of the men having had enough forethought to bring their own. The canteens did a flourishing business in soft drinks, cigarettes at 70 cents a carton, candy, cookies and toilet articles. They did not carry salt-water soap, so there was no use taking a bath. Lifeboat drills were held daily at 3:30 P.M. Signs and colored lights in halls and stairways directed the various units to their muster stations. All cabins were emptied a few minutes after the horns blew.

Until they were more than halfway across, few soldiers had the remotest idea where they were going. The port of debarkation was a secret, kept even from the officers. For all they knew they might be bound for North Africa, England, Ireland, Scotland or Wales. It was not until the eve of arrival that unit commanders got their orders how to proceed from the port of arrival to American stations scattered throughout the British Isles.

As we approached Europe rumors became more fantastic. Someone had it straight from the engineer that a big pack of submarines was trailing the ship. Another said the whole German Navy was loose in the North Atlantic—Major So-and-so heard it on the wireless.

Then you woke up one morning and the ship was very steady and you knew she had entered the harbor. You had arrived. You had crossed the submarine-infested Atlantic without sighting even a por-poise. A hell of a thing to have to confess to your grandchildren.

The boys were very happy to see the British Isles. "When I get on shore," said an infantry captain from Utah, "I'm going to get a hand-ful of dirt and eat it."

The green fields looked like propaganda. (Jan. 21, 1943)

Eighth Air Force Bombs Germany, February 1943

Bigart's first war assignments involved the air raids on Europe from the bomber bases in England. He told Richard Kluger, author of *The Paper,* that each night in London he would await a cryptic phone message, then take the train to interview pilots returning from daylight raids.

In time the military decided that correspondents should be prepared to go on the raids, and early in February, the Eighth Air Force gave a week's briefing and training in use of oxygen masks and the like to eight correspondents.

Bigart's close brushes with death became legend, but he said later that he was never really afraid because he did not believe any of the shells had his number on it. But the casualty rate in the raids on Germany surpassed the average hazards to a war correspondent. After he retired, Bigart told Mary Marshall Clark of the *Times* history project that it was terrible to say but he was probably still alive because of the death of Robert Post, the correspondent of *The New York Times*, who was lost on the raid that Bigart recounts below. The bad publicity, he said, "squashed that idea that it was going to be sort of a steady job going on air raids."

In an interview with Karen Rothmyer, author of *Winning Pulitzers*, Bigart said that the original target on this raid was Bremen, but it was clouded over, so the bombers hit the U-boat pens at Wilhelmshaven. Prof. Russell Strong, who maintains the records for the 306 Bomb Group Association, confirmed that the destination was indeed the Focke-Wulf factory at Bremen, but that midway, the mission went for the secondary target, Wilhelmshaven. The dispatches never hint this was a second choice.

Reporter Rides Fortress
In Wilhelmshaven Raid

With Flak Bursting and Nazi Fighters Swarming,
He Is Too Excited to Have Time to Be Afraid;
R.A.F. Hammers Nuremberg, Sets Big Fires

America Flying Fortresses and Liberators bombed the docks and U-boat lairs at Wilhelmshaven yesterday, while British bombers raided enemy installations at Dunkerque and Cherbourg. Earlier, the Royal Air Force had made a midnight attack on Nuremberg. The Americans lost seven bombers over Wilhelmshaven; the British nine over Nuremberg.

By Homer Bigart
By Telephone to the *Herald Tribune*
Copyright, 1943, *New York Tribune,* Inc.

AN AMERICAN BOMBER STATION, SOMEWHERE IN ENGLAND, Feb. 26, 1943—Our target was Wilhelmshaven. We struck at Fuehrer Adolf Hitler's North Sea base from the southwest after stoogeing around over a particularly hot corner of the Third Reich for what seemed like a small eternity.

I could not quite make out our specific target for obliteration, the submarine pens, because at our altitude the installations along the Jade Busen (Jade Bay) seemed no larger than a pinhead. But the street pattern of the Prussian town stood out in perfect visibility and so did the large suburb of Rustringen, down the bay.

Our Fortress, "Old Soljer," piloted by Captain Lewis Elton Lyle of Pine Bluff, Ark., led the squadron. I was up in the nose with the bombardier, Second Lieutenant Reinaldo J. Saiz of Segundo, Colo., and the navigator, First Lieutenant Otis Allen Hoyt of Dawn, Mo. We were lucky. Just before our arrival a heavy cloud formation cleared the northwest tip of Germany, drifting east and disclosing Wilhelmshaven to our bombsight.

And there was no Focke-Wulf on our tail when we started our bomb run. We had a good run and we were squarely over the town. I watched Saiz crouch lower over his sight. I heard him call "Bombs away."

Our salvo of 500-pounders plunged through the open bomb bay. From where I stood I could not see them land, but our ball turret gunner, Staff Sergeant Howard L. Nardine of Los Angeles, took a quick look back and saw fires and smoke.

Frankly, I wasn't so much interested in the target. What intrigued me was the action upstairs. Flak was bursting all around the squadron just ahead and to our left. The shells were exploding in nasty black puffs, leaving curious smoke trails of hour-glass shape.

Enemy fighters were darting in all directions. "Hoss" Lyle said there must have been 35. They were out for stragglers and they let us alone.

There was a flak burst about 200 yards off our starboard wing, but that was the nearest we came to the casualty list.

Once our bombs were dropped Hoss Lyle pulled some evasive action. He had us shifting like the Notre Dame varsity, changing course so often that the Focke-Wulfs sitting there against the horizon never had a chance to set us up for a frontal attack. That's the way they like to come in on a Fortress—from 11 o'clock or 1 o'clock position. They seem to like the big glass nose of a B-17.

[In air-force parlance, "o'clocks" are used for compass points.]

You see them far ahead, mere specks in the sky, and they are on to you in a minute. He's doing about 400 miles an hour and you are not exactly standing still, so you have only a few seconds to put the bead on him and press the trigger.

Our squadron is back without loss, but the other formations had a few casualties.

The Liberators took a nasty going over. Coming home we saw a Liberator trying to shake off a whole swarm of fighters. He was racing for a cloud bank over the North Sea, with Messerschmitts hot on his trail. He disappeared in the cloud; and that was the last we saw of him.

Initiation for Reporters

It was a fairly easy initiation for the six newspaper correspondents who got themselves assigned to the 8th Bomber Squadron in the fervent hope of seeing Berlin by daylight from American bombers.

The worst moment came early in the attack. I saw a ship ahead of us go down in a dizzy spin, with two parachutes opening in its wake. For an instant I almost wished I was back in Brooklyn.

Yet the whole trip was so theatrical that you forgot to be scared. The technicolor was excellent, the action fairly gripping and the casting superb. Only the scenario needed cutting. I got awfully tired of looking at the North Sea, a disagreeable piece of scenery in February.

Our first view of the Continent was a low and desolate sand strip, which I identified as one of the Frisian Islands. The Frisians are heavily defended, but the flak was surprisingly light and inaccurate. We were close to the Dutch border, and far to the south I thought I saw the broad mouth of the Zuyder Zee shining in the sun.

Before we reached the mainland, the enemy was upstairs waiting with a reception committee of Focke-Wulfs and Messerschmitts. For about an hour thereafter I heard the gunners drone, "Fighters at 6 o'clock; fighters at 3 o'clock; fighters at 9 o'clock."

All our gunners were shooting at one time or another but the enemy stayed just out of range of our .50-caliber guns.

Peeling off after an attack on another ship, a fighter dove in front of us. Our bombardier gave him a spray, but he was going so fast I couldn't tell whether he was a Focke-Wulf or a Messerschmitt.

With Wilhelmshaven behind us we followed the Jade Busen down to the sea. There appeared to be a lot of flak ships in the roadstead and further up we passed over an island that fairly bristled with guns directly below. We were over that island for what seemed like an intolerable spell.

The Focke-Wulfs didn't follow us far. They were replaced by heavier twin-engined jobs, Messerschmitt-110's, which hung around like vultures until we were halfway to England, waiting to pounce on a cripple. The pink tip of Helgoland was far to the northeast when the Messerschmitts finally decided to go home.

This was "Hoss" Lyle's 13th operation, and he told me it was "a piece of cake" compared with jobs on Lorient and St. Nazaire, for Reich Marshal Hermann Wilhelm Goering has his best fighters around Abbeville and on the Brest peninsula.

"Hoss" is 26 years old and one of the smartest pilots in the air force. He intends to stay with the Army after the war.

"Old Soljer" has an able crew. Our co-pilot, Captain Jacob Wayne Frederick of Wakarusa, Ind., Purdue '38, is a veteran of equal experience with Lyle. Frederick was 26 years old today and the crew serenaded him all the way home.

The rest of the cast were: Third gunner, Technical Sergeant Michael ("Big Stoop") Hlastala, 23, who is 6 1/2 feet tall and comes from Uniontown, Pa.; waist gunners, Sergeant Henry George ("Hank") Schneiderman of Freeport, Ill., who was celebrating his 25th birthday, and Sergeant Harvie Cecil Collins of Hoxie, Ark.; tail gunner Staff

Sergeant Gilbert Agnew Murray, 24, of Oakland, Calif., radio operator, Technical Sergeant Richard J. ("Snuffy") Smith of Boston.

I did not tell the crew that during our training course a few weeks ago I was chosen as the man least likely to return from a mission.

Trained for Work

Mr. Bigart and the five other American reporters who went along on the Wilhelmshaven raid underwent recently a week of intensive training with the Eighth American Air Force.

The flying correspondents, whom air officers came to call the "Writing 69th," were subjected to physical examinations for high-altitude flying. During their training week they took a condensed version of the regular three-week refresher course at a combat replacement center somewhere in England. (Feb. 27, 1943)

Assessing Raid Coverage, March 1943

A week after the Wilhelmshaven raid, Bigart went back and looked deeper into the fabric of the story. This early test of his wry, self-effacing side was linked to his concerns about trying to evaluate something like a bombing raid. He also used the occasion to send home the bomber crew's words of distress, which would hardly have fit in the earlier dispatch.

He twitted Walter Cronkite, too, about his famous lead, in a way that would be visible only to his colleagues. It is unlikely that any of them knew, but *The New York Times* had used the Cronkite dispatch, as well as Hill's A.P. piece, on the Wilhelmshaven raid.

So here is Bigart a few days later.

Raid on Wilhelmshaven:
A Lesson in Perspective

Reporter Finds That Time Mars the Ringside-Seat Reactions; That Facts He Wants to Write Are Ones He Seldom Gets During Attack

LONDON, March 6, 1943—Several days have passed since our bombers were over Wilhelmshaven and although this correspondent remains a little flak-happy, warmth is returning to the body and blood to the brain and he is beginning to wonder how he happened to write such drivel as appeared in the paper the next morning.

I suspect that the other three reporters who completed the mission feel equally depressed. True perspective is rather hard to maintain in the hours immediately after an assignment in which your own neck was directly involved. You are apt to feel you had a ringside seat at the most crucial engagement since Waterloo or that final Yankee-Cardinal game at the Stadium.

This is known as the "I have just returned from a suburb of hell" reaction. To relieve this condition, it is necessary for the patient to hurl himself at the nearest typewriter, rap out a tingling yarn of a flak-filled heaven, of epic dog fights and derring-do.

Equally important to avoid is the "it was nothing, really" state of mind. You get that way hanging around the interrogation room, hearing our crews assure the intelligence officer that the enemy opposition was very sorry indeed. The German anti-aircraft was inaccurate, they relate, and the fighters untrained. Our seven missing bombers were lost simply because they drifted out of formation—they were asking for it.

I am particularly susceptible to this attitude because I hate writing a story. So when I got back from Wilhelmshaven and heard "Hoss" Lyle, my pilot, describe the operation as something incredibly simple, I began wondering whether the episode was worth writing down for posterity.

So instead of going to work, I killed an hour or two in the Intelligence library, reading the dossier on Wilhelmshaven, which seemed to consist chiefly of excerpts from standard tourist guides. I contributed a little of intelligence of my own (writing "Oh, yeah?" and "Ha-ha" in the margin opposite Baedeker's classic crack, "The road to Bremen is dull"), and was about to retire to the mess hall when the thought dawned that perhaps the boys on the cable desk might have an academic interest in my return.

I went to the shack and with the exercise of superhuman will power I uncovered the portable. Imagine my chagrin when, mulling over the notes, I discovered just enough material for two terse paragraphs of factual reporting.

It was not until then that I realized a truth that should be communicated to every student of journalism: A good deal of experience is needed to qualify as a competent aerial observer.

A few weeks ago, listening to Royal Air Force crews of the Mosquitos that bombed Berlin by daylight, I was impressed by the scant information they brought back. I thought it was the usual British reticence. Now I realize they told us everything they knew.

For the information you want is the information you seldom get. You want to write about raging fires, shattering explosions and rivers of German blood. Well, when the enemy is driven from the sky and when his very effective "defense in depth" rings of flak guns are silenced, maybe you can hang around long enough over the target to see something worthwhile. It can't be done just now in daylight, because if a Fortress tried to tarry long over Wilhelmshaven it would come down an extremely dead duck.

In that fleeting moment of the target run the only reliable reporter is the camera. Its story won't be ready until the next day. I was fairly alert, mentally and physically, during the bomb run of our Fortress, "Old Soljer," and I believe I kept a reasonably steady eye on the tiny pattern of streets which our navigator said was Wilhelmshaven. I used to think that I was pretty good at map reading, but not any more. If I were the pilot I would have mistaken Wilhelmshaven for an Oldenburg whistle stop, gone on to Bremen and be sitting right now in a German prison camp.

So I don't feel quite ready to enter into the debate of the effectiveness of daylight precision bombing. I would like to report, however, that our contribution to the aerial offensive against Germany is very modest. We are using nowhere near as many Fortresses and Liberators as we would like to use. Moreover, the weather over here is not often suitable for that kind of show. There has been on an average only one raid a week during the winter.

Our crews are out of the top drawer but need a little more high altitude training before they come over. And it would be a good idea if the aircraft companies could have a representative, preferably the president, take an occasional ride on a combat mission. Then the modifications suggested by the men who fly over Germany would be made with greater speed.

Crews like having civilians along. They are sick to death reading about the whining and backbiting of people back home. They are truly concerned about civilian morale in the States and nothing would please them more than to have a Senator or a labor leader or a political commentator appear at the base in flying clothes and sweat out a mission with them.

This could be arranged on a strictly nonpartisan basis. For example, Mrs. Franklin D. Roosevelt and Westbrook Pegler might ride in the nose of the lead ship.

A mission to Germany is a nasty experience. Apart from the very real danger to life and limb, there is the acute discomfort of enduring sub-zero temperatures for hours at a stretch and taking air through an oxygen mask. The altitude can affect your sinews, your kidneys, even the fillings of your teeth. You are very tired when you return. If you are a delayed-action type, you are likely to feel slightly under par for a couple of days. I must be crazy, but I should like to go again. (March 7, 1943)

Sicily, July 1943

––––––

Bigart met ground war in Sicily. John O'Reilly, known as Tex, had covered the entire Tunisian war for the *Trib,* and in June 1943, when he heard an invasion of Sicily was imminent, he sent for reinforcements. Bigart was dispatched from London. O'Reilly went ashore in the landings on July 9–10, with Bigart staying in Allied headquarters in Algiers. Then they switched places.

O'Reilly, later famous for light-hearted features, quickly recognized Bigart as a formidable competitor, even if they worked for the same paper. It was O'Reilly, in talking to a *Saturday Evening Post* correspondent heading into Italy, who first applied the phrase from "As You Like It" to Bigart: "Stay away from Homer," O'Reilly said. "He's always trying to build his reputation at the cannon's mouth."

A critic said once of a journalism anthology: "How can it be any good? It hasn't got Homer covering Sicily on muleback." Here are some of the best from Sicily, combined into a rough journal.

Nazis in Sicily Pursued Hotly By Americans

––––––

Herald Tribune Reporter Helps 'Take' Hamlet in Drive Along North Coast

WITH THE AMERICAN 7TH ARMY IN SICILY, July 25, 1943— American forces were in hot pursuit of the Germans today as the enemy retreated along the narrow coastal road which leads to the Strait of Messina. The division with which this correspondent is traveling knocked out several tanks and guns, wrecked an ammunition train, took a seaside town and crossed a dry river bed without halting its pursuit.

In the early part of this engagement today the Americans lost 80 men in dead and wounded. There are 10 fresh graves, blanketed with red geraniums, in the cemetery beside the limestone cliff of Celafu. . . .

The division has been meeting increasingly tough German opposition. This morning the Germans threw everything they had into a desperate holding action on a rocky headland. Cliffs dominating the coastal highway erupted clouds of dust as shells from the enemy's mobile 88-millimeter all-purpose guns came whining across the hills. There were snipers in every crevice.

The German position was well organized and well defended. Throughout last night American artillery shelled their pillboxes and emplacements. . . . At dawn the Germans retired.

An American colonel reached the crest of the ridge just as two Mark IV tanks were ducking behind a promontory a mile to the east. At that distance they looked like black beetles squeezing through a narrow crack. . . .

From the hilltop the coastal town's single street appeared lifeless under the blazing sun. Somebody had stuck a white flag in a second-story window. There was no movement in the town.

Reporters Enter Town

At noon the colonel ordered all batteries to cease firing and instructed Jack Loisie, reporter for the Army newspaper "Stars and Stripes," and myself to go down into the town. A patrol had reached the village an hour before and, finding no road mines, had pushed on toward the river. We swept the surrounding hills with field glasses, found no hint of snipers and advanced cautiously. An infantry colonel went along with us.

Howitzers which had been testing their range by lobbing shells into a lemon orchard behind the town fell silent. The town was deathly silent. On the western outskirts the colonel stopped our jeep and went ahead on foot to investigate a bridge, then he waved us across and we took the town.

There wasn't much to take. The town consisted of a dozen stone houses fronting the dusty road. A shell had opened the front of one house, baring the squalor of a typical Sicilian home. The inhabitants had fled.

Three middle-aged men emerged from the house flying the white flag. All grinned and raised two fingers in the V salute. . . .

We were able to reach the promontory where the Mark IV tank smoldered in the ditch. The road was littered with German camping effects, including soap tins, shaving brushes, bags of tough little biscuits and bedrolls of quite good material. There was no sign of German dead, for the Germans are very diligent in disposing of their killed.

Even after today's battle it is hard to realize that this is war and not just a summer maneuver. One reason is that our casualties in land fighting remain extremely small. Furthermore, war is associated with mud, foul weather and hostile civilians. There is none of that here. The weather has been perfect and the civilian conduct exemplary.

In fact, the Sicilians are too friendly. Their attitude strengthens the impression that this island is a forgotten portion of Southern California, instead of a segment of enemy Italy. (July 29, 1943)

Writers Almost Ride Into Nazis' Area in Sicily

Reporters Unwittingly Pass U.S. Infantry and Find Foe Just Around Bend

July 25, 1943—After a 50-mile retreat along the north coast of Sicily from Palermo strong Axis forces are making a stand on Cape Raisigelbi, a few miles east of Cefalu. Here the coastal road, pinned against the blue Tyrrhenian Sea by the sheer brown cliffs of the Madonie Mountains, is under fire from German 90-millimeter guns. . . .

The Axis stand, coming after two days of headlong retreat, during which the sizable ports of Termini and Cefalu fell without fighting to the Americans, began last night. Throughout today the division has made only slight progress beyond Cefalu.

Occasionally a 90-millimeter shell sends dust flying in the parched fields outside Cefalu, but the town, sheltered behind its limestone cliffs, presented so peaceful an appearance this Sunday afternoon that a party of war correspondents raced right through it in the belief that the Americans had captured San Stefano, some 20 miles east.

For six days we had been trying to catch up with the Americans. We learned that Army public relations is considerably slower than the infantry, but finally we got started and traveled the dusty highway across Sicily to reach Palermo.

This morning we set out for the front. A few burned-out Italian tanks and German half-tracks along the road were the only signs of conflict on this beautiful highway to Messina. So we raced on through Termini and Cefalu, hardly noticing that the military traffic had slowed to a trickle and that we were passing columns of foot soldiers, hot and grimy after a day in the foxholes just ahead.

Nobody stopped us at Cefalu. A mile down the coast two plumes of water rose lazily from the placid sea. Then, while rounding a curve, we heard the deafening roar of an American battery emplaced along the railroad. Our driver suddenly remembered a date he had in Palermo.

We had got ahead of the infantry. An artillery major informed us dryly that the Germans were just around the bend. Our infantry had gone into the hills on a flanking mission, and there the main column was canalized on the narrow coastal strip between sea and cliff.

We got out of there in a hurry. As we raced back for the shelter of the town, a shell stirred the dust 500 yards from the road and the blast reverberated from the great cliff of Cefalu. We had caught up with the war. (July 31, 1943)

Sicilian Mules
Aid Americans
At San Stefano

Supplant Helpless Jeeps in
Ridge-by-Ridge Conquest
of Range Guarding Town

July 31, 1943—San Stefano has fallen to the Americans. It is a crowded, filthy little town of 7,000 population, an ancient patch of stone houses dominating both the coastal road to Messina and the important lateral highway to Nicosia. Here the Germans made their first stand in the long retreat from Palermo.

. . . The Axis forces which had fled Palermo, Termini, Imerese and finally Cefalu after little fighting really dug in at San Stefano. They blew up bridges over a dozen deep gulches west of the town. They planted thousands of tank and personnel mines in the dry flats of the San Stefano River. Hillside farms with their ponderous masonry made perfect pillboxes. Road blocks of solid concrete made the highway impassable for guns.

A frontal assault would have been extremely costly. The Americans had but one alternative—the painful, tedious, scouring of the mountain range south of town. The lateral trails were hopeless, even for a jeep. . . . A reversion to frontier warfare was essential, and presently both the American and German lines were relying almost entirely on the Sicilian mule. Even the mules found the going tough, and two of them died trying to lift the American heavy mortars across the Nebrodie peaks.

But the Americans had the most artillery, the most men and the most mules, and the Germans were ousted from ridge after ridge.

Early Thursday night the Americans took a village five miles south-west of San Stefano. All night long the Germans poured a murderous artillery fire into the village from the surrounding hills.

The Americans were low on food and water. They had set out with only one day's rations and they were gone. Private John Suppe of 21-41 48th Street, Astoria, Queens, paid $2 for four loaves of bread, two onions and four olives—that was all the food the village could spare. That night no one slept. Huddling under the stone arches of the village, the troops could see the sharp flashes of the German mortars an instant before the shells came down. A man who had lost his child in the bombardment went screaming through the street unmindful of the shrapnel that beat like rain against the cobbled road. . . .

Slowly the Americans closed on San Stefano from the south. Their rations were gone but Sicily offers good forage in midsummer, so the boys were able to strip some of the vineyards and an occasional lemon orchard. They belonged to a division which had fought and marched without pause for three solid weeks with an unbroken record of victorious advances. Their morale was superb.

At 2 P.M. today Lieut. Col. Irving L. Schaefer of Montrose, Calif., led a hundred men into San Stefano. The Germans had retired at 9 A.M. and were retreating down the coastal road, harassed by a destroyer's guns far at sea.

. . . Even then the town was precariously held. A battalion of infantry was moving up from Tusa, but the road was heavily mined. The long bridge across the San Stefano River had been demolished and in the dry bed of the river German personnel mines had been sown thicker than grass.

Column Strikes Mine Field

This correspondent saw men die as the column, advancing single file across the rocky bed, walked right into the mine field. The German mine is a vicious little instrument. It springs three to six feet into the air, exploding with a sharp report similar to rifle fire. A half dozen of these shots had us leaping into a ditch. We thought enemy snipers had opened fire on the head of the column. Then we heard someone yell from the opposite bank: "Stay where you are; the whole damn river is mined."

. . . We decided to make a wide detour, scrambling along the river bank until we were a couple of hundred yards upstream. We crossed at a German outdoor latrine, reasonably confident that this particular meadow was free of mines. . . .

On the outskirts of San Stefano a dead German lay by the roadside. His comrades had covered the body with a white shroud, but it had slipped from his face. His blond head was matted with blood and dust and he was staring open-mouthed at the blue Tyrrhenian Sea.

. . . We found Colonel Schaefer at police headquarters getting his hair cut. He told us the mayor had fled and that all but 3,000 of the townspeople had been evacuated with the Germans. . . . In spite of heavy damage from our guns the civilians were friendly. Some had already broken into the Fascist headquarters, where they smashed portraits of Benito Mussolini. From the balcony of the Municipio (city hall) we could see for many miles the long stretch of coast toward San Agata. There was no trace of the Germans.

When we left the townspeople showed us a mine-free patch across the river. As we descended the fertile slope below the town, the peasants filled our arms with grapes and figs. (Aug. 6, 1943)

How U.S. Raiders Fought Off
Panzers Storming Sicily Peak

Bigart, Landing With Amphibious Forces, Tells
of Gallant All-Night Stand on Mt. Crioli
and Relief With Occupation of Brolo

Aug. 12, 1943—A tough and gallant band of Americans was relieved at 8 o'clock this morning on the thorny summit of Mt. Crioli, where it had made a last-ditch stand against encirclement by the 15th German Panzer Division.

We had landed in yesterday's predawn darkness on a beach near Brolo, seven miles behind the formidable German line at Cape Orlando, on Sicily's northern coast. Our objective was to cut the coastal highway, trapping German armor to the west and preventing its withdrawal to strong natural positions just east of the town.

This same force, led by Lieut. Col. Lyle W. Bernard, 33 years old, of Highland Falls, N.Y., had conducted a similar amphibious operation against the high ground at Agata, 15 miles to the west, only three days before. It was natural to assume that yesterday's operation would be considerably rougher. The odds were 10 to 1 against catching the enemy by surprise again.

Yet yesterday's landing was effected with few casualties. . . . The story began early Tuesday evening. Colonel Bernard's men left their bivouac in an orchard overlooking the sea and columns of dust arose from the sere brown meadows as the troops marched down to a pebbly beach and into the mouth of invasion craft. They were dog tired. . . .

The black holds of the invasion ships were jammed with tanks, half-tracks and ducks (amphibious trucks). It was hellish hot. The men scrambled up the iron ladder to the cooler deck. Colonel Bernard gave a little talk.

"Take this objective," he pleaded, "and we'll be in Messina in a week."

The colonel told a few jokes, unprintable here but suited to the occasion. Faces relaxed. Forward, someone shouted an inaudible order and the men squatting on the deck saw some soldiers duck into a galleyway. A sudden panic seized the group. A dozen infantrymen tried to crawl beneath a piece of tarpaulin, others crouched behind a mast. Then someone laughed, and the laughter spread uncontrollably. The cry that cleared the decks was "Chow!"

. . . Zero hour was 2:30 A.M. At 1 o'clock Colonel Bernard, a slight, wiry man with brown mustache and humorous blue eyes, called a halt to the briefing, lit his pipe and read a letter from his 3-year-old daughter. . . .

Everyone went below and boarded the tanks and ducks. There was a dim blue light in the middle of the hold and we were allowed to smoke until the prowgate was lowered.

First Wave of Ducks Away

The minutes dragged. A soldier became sick. Finally the gate opened.

"Away, ducks," a low voice said, and the duck slid quietly down the ramp and into the sea.

The moon had gone down, but the sky was bright with stars. The black mass of Mt. Crioli blotted the stars directly ahead.

There was no sound from the shore, no flash of gunfire. The first wave of ducks, carrying mine sweepers, wire cutters and a covering detachment of infantry, had gone in some minutes before, and they had apparently done their work without arousing the shore sentries.

Now the shoreline was visible and we could see shadowy figures running about on the beach. Our duck scrunched through the sand and came to a gentle halt near the orchard rim. A big gap had been cut in the barbed wire and we started running down a lane toward the hill.

. . . Tense and breathless, we huddled in front of the first house in Brolo, our ears straining for the sound of enemy traffic. . . . From far down the road came the slow clanking sound of heavy treads. "A tank," someone cried. We dived behind a stone wall, waiting for what seemed an eternity. The clanking grew steadily louder and finally materialized as a German half-track.

"Shoot, you stupid clown," yelled an officer from the roadside.

"Can't," drawled the soldier. "Some of our men across the road are directly in the line of fire."

He waited until the half-track was 50 yards down the road, then cut loose. The half-track came to an abrupt halt. A German leaped over the stone wall and approached some figures beneath the trees.

"Herr Lieutenant," he began. He was answered with a burst of small-arms fire.

By this time the Germans in Brolo were thoroughly awake. . . . Covered with sweat, we continued our climb. We could hear the unloading of ducks on the beach—none of our vehicles had reached the road. Something had gone wrong. The railroad culvert marked on the map was not wide enough and 30 precious minutes were wasted while engineers prepared an exit over the tracks.

On top of Mt. Crioli we caught eight Germans sound asleep. They were lying under a tree, sharing a single blanket. . . . At 11:40 A.M. enemy troops could be seen mounting a gun in an orchard east of the town. Another hour passed. . . . Then the German drive opened. It was directed simultaneously against both ends of our beachhead along the coastal strip. Protecting our medium tanks and mobile artillery was only one company of men. Colonel Bernard sent another company down the mountain as reinforcements. . . .

We shortened our lines and dug our slit trenches deeper. An enemy artillery barrage could drive us off the mountain. But the night passed without enemy heavy fire. The Germans sent a few score rounds of 75's and 88's into the meadow, but casualties were slight.

In the morning we looked down into Brolo and saw American troops inspecting bodies in the street. Unknown to us, we had been relieved during the night. (Aug. 16, 1943)

Fall of San Pietro, December 1943

On September 8, 1943, the Italian forces quit the war, surrendering to the Allies. Thus the prolonged battle for the village of San Pietro was fought against the Germans only. John Huston, using astonishing combat photographers' film, made a memorable documentary, "The Battle of San Pietro," but this Bigart dispatch is just as graphic, and in its way, as strong a statement on the cost of war.

San Pietro a Village of the Dead;
Victory Cost Americans Dearly

Germans Gone, Leaving Italian Town to Lifeless Soldiers and Animals, Wrecked Vehicles and the Wounded Patiently Awaiting Aid

WITH THE 5TH ARMY, Dec. 18, 1943 (via London) (Delayed)—We crossed the valley to San Pietro through fields littered with dead. The village, rising in terraces on the southern hump of Monte Samucro, loomed out of the blue haze of battle smoke like an ancient ruined castle, and even from the creek bed we could see that not one house in that tight little cluster of buildings had escaped ruin.

The Germans had cleared out—that much had been established later yesterday when patrols penetrated the outskirts without drawing fire. But we heard that enemy snipers were still clinging to their bunkers in the ravine north of the village and, since San Pietro was likely to receive further pastings from German artillery, no infantrymen ventured into the death trap. Instead a force led by Lieut. James Epperman of Hot Springs, Tex., skirted the town and took up positions on the high ground just beyond.

We followed a unit of medical-aid men into San Pietro. In the wrecked buildings, sprawling on blood-drenched rubble, were American as well as German wounded. Three times during Wednesday's initial attack American assault parties had penetrated San Pietro. Each time they had been driven off with severe casualties.

Early today litter bearers had cleared the lower building of wounded. In darkness they groped through narrow alleys choked with rubble, shouting into open doorways and listening intently for some response.

From the wine cellar of a house, sheared off nearly to the ground by weeks of shelling, came a faint cry for help. On the straw-covered earthen floor lay three wounded Americans who had been there two days and nights, too weak to get back to friendly lines. One had been wounded three times on successive days. In Wednesday's assault he received shell fragments in the right hip and lay helpless in a dugout just outside the village. Next day the Germans renewed their shelling and his right hip was subject to a near miss. Yesterday, while crawling toward a wine cellar, another fragment pierced his right hip.

He had used all his sulfa tablets. A comrade, less seriously hurt, gave him more. Without sulfa he would have died of shock. His condition is good, and he will receive the Purple Heart with Oak Leaf Cluster.

With him were two other privates mangled by shell fragments. One had sulfa and, despite grave injuries, will live. The third youth found the stuff too nauseous. He will lose a leg.

At noon, as we cleared the eastern base at Monte Rotunda and struck out across the valley, the battlefield was strangely still. A thick haze lay stagnant above the pass and a wan sun bathed the scene in sickly light. There was not a sound except our own cautious footsteps as we crossed the pasture, still uncleared of mines.

Near the forward aid station we met Capt. Ralph Phelan of Waurika, Okla., who had done such a heroic job evacuating wounded from within the range of snipers. Phelan warned us not to enter San Pietro. The town, he said, was full of booby traps and subject to intermittent shelling.

He showed us a path up the steep bank of the creek, where three days previously Maj. Milton Landry's men formed for their bloody, futile assault on San Pietro. We emerged on the field, so thickly pocked with shell holes that there must have been a hundred bursts within an acre of bare rocky ground.

The assault waves had met an intense and deadly hail of artillery at the very line of departure. On the far side of the field sprawled some dead. One boy lay crumpled in a shallow slit trench beneath a rock. Another, still grasping his rifle, peered from behind a tree, staring with sightless eyes toward the Liri plain. A third lay prone where he had fallen. He had heard the warning scream of a German shell. He had dropped flat on his stomach but on level ground affording no cover. Evidently some fragment had killed him instantly, for there had been no struggle. Generally there is no mistaking the dead—their strange contorted posture leaves no room for doubt. But this soldier, his steel helmet tilted over his face, seemed merely resting in the field. We did not know until we came within a few steps and saw a gray hand hanging limply from a sleeve.

Lose Medical Aid Patrol

Somehow we became separated from the medical aid patrol. We crossed another field scattered with abandoned rifles, cartridge belts, blood-stained bandages and other debris of battle, and reached a pass curving along the walled terrace. It was along this wall that American remnants which had survived a dash across the field crept in a desperate attempt to gain the village.

We heard a sudden rushing noise that made us stop, involuntarily. It was only a brook that tumbled down a wall and crossed our path beneath strands of enemy barbed wire. The brook was kind to us. It had carried away the dirt which covered a German Teller mine.

The mine lay just to the left of the path. A thin strand of trip wire ran from it directly across our trail. Don Whitehead, Associated Press reporter, was scrambling over the barbed wire. One of us saw that the trip wire was draped over the bottom strand. We were very careful getting across the barrier.

[Mr. Whitehead in his dispatch credited Mr. Bigart with noticing the trip wire and shouting a warning.]

Path Becomes an Alley

Now the path widened and became a cobbled alley. We passed the first house. A rifle was in position near the doorstep. Looking within we saw an American man lying beneath a heap of straw.

There were three other dead in the shallow gully house. Every approach to San Pietro, every ravine and sunken path offering shelter from machine-gun fire had been covered by German snipers.

The cobbled lane wound steeply up the slope into the heart of San Pietro. The village was a ghastly sight. Pounded for three weeks by American guns and bombed many times from the air, this village of 500 peasants was reduced to one great pile of shattered stone. Whole blocks were obliterated. The street pattern was almost unrecognizable for the narrow lanes were buried under five feet of rubble. A high wall, towering above the lesser buildings, showed where the Church of St. Michael and the Archangel had stood. The choir loft hung crazily above an altar almost buried under the masonry.

Prayer for Peace

In an alcove against the wall stood the statues of St. Michael and beneath the statue of St. Peter was the inscription, "By the devotion of Americans from San Pietro." A young woman who had followed us into the church explained that natives had emigrated to America and that her uncle Pietro Rossi had a farm near Syracuse.

She showed us a large iron crucifix which she said had "passed many miracles." In September the natives had prayed for peace and a few days later the armistice had come. The crucifix had survived the great earthquake of 1915 but the bombardment was a hundred times worse than the earthquake. Now the figure of Christ was headless, the Madonna of the Waters had lost an arm.

The Germans had evacuated San Pietro last Thursday afternoon. The steep slopes on both sides of the village were honeycombed with bunkers strongly walled with sandbags and roofed with stone. With flanking heights the Germans could have held out for weeks. They had taken a terrific toll from units attacking frontally and down the valley from the east. But now the Italians held Monte Lungo, to the west, and repeated German counterattacks had failed to budge the Americans from the crest of Monte Samucro above the town.

Grenadiers Become Panicky

So the 15th Panzer Grenadiers became panicky and left six German wounded in the town. A medical-aid sergeant stayed with them. They begged for food and water when the Americans arrived.

The German wounded were evacuated early this morning. As a precaution against a counterattack, Corp. John Ahrens of Middle Village, Queens, set up a machine gun at the head of the main street, while medical-aid men went to work. Corp. Peter Vagia of 1740 Melville Street, the Bronx, said that one German with a shattered shoulder cursed his comrades for deserting him.

Since dawn the German guns have been silent and now San Pietro's survivors have emerged from caves and gathered around the Americans. There were about a score of middle-aged men, a few women and children, all very dirty and unkempt, but showing no signs of hysteria. One old man ran behind the medical patrol, pointing toward a collapsed building and mumbling, "Many dead, many dead." But the patrol was concerned with the living.

Stored Vats of Water

Near a ruined cathedral two German trucks lay buried beneath a collapsed wall, and across the street were piles of enemy ammunition in cans. Great vats of water had been stored in one building and in an adjoining house we made a curious discovery. The floor was strewn with letters addressed to an American soldier and on a table was a baseball glove. Evidently the Germans had taken letters from an American prisoner. But the baseball glove was unexplained.

Above the village piazza the street narrowed and became nothing more than a steep lane between ghostly shells of houses. Occasionally we found a home with some of the lower rooms well intact. In one, Medical Aid Private Benjamin Shelleck of 10 Sunset Road, Bay Shore, L.I., and Pvt. Albert Schempp of Pittsburgh were dressing some wounded Italians. One of the natives had retrieved a case of wine from the ruins and toasts were offered to the American victory.

In another house, strongly built and with the lower floor undamaged, we found what apparently had been the enemy's command post. A copy of the "Voelkischer Beobachter" dated Dec. 6 lay on the table. It was the edition published in Posen, indicating that one of the officers recently passed through eastern Germany, probably en route from the Russian front.

Find Hulks of Tanks

Dead mules and pigs lay amid the debris in the eastern section of the village. Rounding a curve on the edge of the town we found two charred hulks of the only American tanks to reach San Pietro during Wednesday's abortive attack. They had been knocked out by German antitank guns before they could support the infantry advancing across the valley from the south. Farther up the road were other tanks, disabled by mines.

We went back across the fields, reaching the safety of Monte Rotunda, just as the German 88's began shelling San Pietro. At the command post Lieut. Col. Aaron Wyatt of Tarrytown, N.Y., said the battle had been the grimmest since the Volturno crossing.

The assault was led by Major Landry of San Antonio, Tex., who told us how two sergeants, Nolan Peele of Robstown, Tex., and Frauston* of El Paso, rounded up remnants of the company's cruelly mauled men in the initial attack and attached them to other companies preparing a new thrust.

"It's awfully hard to try to attack more than once in one night," Landry explained. "The men were desperately tired, and they suffered losses grim enough to demoralize anyone.

"All the officers were dead or wounded. The German outpost laid low until the Americans were well within the trap, then opened with automatic fire. In the company all officers were killed or wounded. Sergeant Frauston, assuming command, gathered 32 survivors and led them back.

*no first name in clipping

Refused to Give Up

"They could have melted into darkness, lying low until dark and then come straggling back to the regiment with the story of how they were cut off without officer leadership in no-man's-land. No one would have blamed them. They had been in the line 27 days.

"Many had 'fox hole feet'—their arches were cracked and swollen from wearing wet shoes for days without a change. Yet such was their morale that they reported to the nearest officer and were ready when the attack was resumed a few hours later."

Wednesday's casualties were so heavy that Capt. William Farley of St. Louis, the regimental surgeon, ran out of litter squads. A call for volunteers brought 25 replacements from antiaircraft and coast artillery units. They included several who had never been to the front.

That night they made two trips into no-man's-land, bringing back wounded, despite snipers and shell fire. Among the volunteers were Pvt. Robert Guertin Manville of Rhode Island, who had fought the Japanese in Java and the Vichy French in New Caledonia. "I figured some day I'd need the medics, so I joined," he said.

Final Counterattack

In attempting to cover their withdrawal from San Pietro the Germans threw a final vicious counterattack against the Americans attacking on the east. Just after dark Thursday night enemy troops swarmed from pillboxes on Monte Samucro's southern slope and struck hard at the right flank of a battalion led by Lieut. Col. Howard K. Dodge of Temple, Tex.

Back at the American command post the regimental commander heard the sudden clatter of small arms fire. Through the telephone he could hear the confused shouting of riflemen trying to stem the assault. He heard one infantryman groan: "My God, when are we going to get artillery support?"

"At first we thought it was merely the usual enemy patrol probing our position and we didn't dare to fire for fear of endangering our men," the colonel said. "But when the firing increased in intensity we ordered a barrage. It came within a few minutes and fell smack where we wanted it. It must have caught a lot of the Germans, for we could hear them hollering and moaning in a draw just beyond our lines."

The attack lasted four hours. Three times the Germans tried to crack the American lines. Their last attempt nearly succeeded. Company I, commanded by Lieut. David R. Fields, was badly chewed up by mortar and machine-gun fire and a breakthrough was prevented in the nick of time by the arrival of Company E, led by Lieut. Eben C. Bergman, who quickly organized a stonewall defense. Not one inch of ground was abandoned.

Company K, which shared the brunt of the attack, fought valiantly under the cool leadership of Lieut. Henry C. Bragaw of Wilmington, N.C., whose name has been put up for battlefield promotion. Bragaw, a mild-mannered horticulturist with a strawberry-colored handlebar mustache, steadied his men when the weight of the attack shifted from the right to the center and fell furiously against his line.

On his right Bergman's men saw the German wave fall back in disorder. They were too tired to cheer. On the previous afternoon they had supported the abortive tank attack on San Pietro and their casualties were sore. No sooner did the survivors of the tank attack return than they were pressed back into action to save Company I.

Dawn saw a noticeable lessening of enemy artillery fire. The Americans who had tried to attack San Pietro across an open valley from the south were able to recover their dead and wounded, cut down by machine guns and snipers' bullets Thursday.

A force atop Monte Samucro, commanded by Maj. David Frazior of Houston, Tex., advanced and seized the extreme northeastern rim of the crest. Frazior's battalion had beaten off a dozen desperate counterattacks in five days, leaving the slopes littered with at least 500 dead and wounded Germans. His battalion took 40 prisoners.

Laughed at Nazis

Outstanding among Frazior's men was Lieut. Rufus J. Cleghorn of Waco, Tex., a barrelchested football player from Baylor University.

Exulting in battle, Cleghorn clambered to the highest rock of Samucro's pinnacle and howled insults at the Germans, pausing now and then to toss grenades. For variety, Cleghorn occasionally put his weight against a huge boulder and sent it rolling down the slope. He roared with laughter as the Germans attempted to dodge the hurling boulders.

The supply problem was terrific. Every available rifleman was needed in the line, so cooks and clerks donned packboards and carried food, clothing and ammunition up the mountain. Each man carried a 42-pound can of water, plus two bandoliers of ammunition, mail and Sterno cans. They filled their pockets with hand grenades. Ahead of them was a grueling three-hour climb of a 1,000-foot slope so steep that the men had to crawl hand over hand up the guide ropes.

Capt. William R. Lynch of Huntsville, Tex., estimated that Frazior's battalions had thrown 2,000 hand grenades—more than a division would expend in normal combat. They used more than three times the normal amount of mortar shells.

It is very cold these December nights on Samucro's peak, and the uniforms and overcoats issued to the men were none too warm. Yesterday Army cooks carried warm combat suits to the troops and a can of Sterno to each man. (Dec. 20, 1943)

Anzio Censorship, February 1944

On January 22, 1944, Allied forces were put ashore on the west coast of Italy south of Rome, to establish a beachhead at Anzio. Bigart, who went in on the first day, was on the beachhead for more than two months.

Alexander Tells Why
He Curbs News in Italy

General Says Pessimistic
Dispatches Were "Rot";
a Reporter Answers Him

Herald Tribune editor's introduction:

The following dispatch reports for the first time the full story of General Alexander's charges against American and British correspondents on the Anzio beachhead and contains one correspondent's answer to the charges.

WITH THE 5TH ARMY ON ANZIO BEACHHEAD, ITALY, Feb. 14, 1944—In a remarkable interview today Gen. Sir Harold R.L.G. Alexander, commander in chief of Allied armies in Italy, accused war correspondents of "blowing hot and cold" in their dispatches from the Anzio beachhead, thereby damaging morale back home and comforting the enemy.

Alexander said he had been notified by superiors that stories emanating from the beachhead "alarmed the people." He found the reporters guilty of an abrupt reversal from over-optimistic accounts during the first week of the invasion to over-pessimistic accounts of the last two weeks.

He has penalized the correspondents by denying to them the use of radio facilities for filing their stories to Naples. Not until the reporters follow a policy line will the radio be restored to them.

[A delayed Associated Press dispatch from the Anzio beachhead published in Thursday's *Herald Tribune* stated merely that General Alexander said he had been upset by reports that press dispatches had alarmed the home public and quoted him as saying: "There's no basis for pessimistic rubbish." It made no mention of the "policy line" laid down by him for beachhead correspondents.]

Believer in Democracy

A stanch believer in democratic processes, General Alexander would be the last to deny reporters an opportunity to reply to his charges.

In the first place any accurate factual day-by-day account of this adventure could hardly avoid giving an optimistic impression of the first eight days and a sobering one thereafter.

If the stories blew hot and cold that is exactly the way the battle ran. As Alexander himself says, the first round went decisively to the Allies. The troops achieved a surprise landing on beaches practically undefended. Every break went to the Allies. The port of Anzio fell intact. There was an unusual run of fine weather—rough seas hindered the landing of supplies on only two days. With negligible loss the initial objectives were taken quickly. By the end of the second day the organization of all the units that landed in the first wave was virtually complete. There was no confusion. It was nothing like Salerno.

And that was what we wrote. No one, to the knowledge of this correspondent, ever predicted the fall of Rome in 24 hours or ever believed the German line of communications could be cut without tough fighting.

Then on Sunday, Jan. 30, there was a dramatic change in the Allied fortunes. The attack on Cisterna di Littoria was repulsed with heavy losses.

A few days later there was another sharp reverse in the sector north of Carroceto. A considerable British force, cut off by enemy infiltrations, was extricated in hard fighting. Some equipment was lost. Casualties were heavy.

The initiative went to the Germans. We reported it.

We tried to report that the situation was tense and critical. We still believe it was.

General Alexander's remarks recall the criticism leveled at reporters during the Salerno operation. At that time correspondents assigned to Allied Force headquarters in Algiers were permitted to give the public a true picture of how delicate the situation was. This was resented by the 5th Army commanders, who asserted that at no time was there any danger of being pushed into the sea.

Basically the issue is this—shall the public receive accurate day-by-day reports of the changing fortunes of battle or shall we maintain an "even tone," speaking only vaguely of reverses?

We six correspondents who landed with the troops and who stayed on under rugged conditions have been exceedingly careful lest our dispatches give information of military value to the enemy.

But the quarrel is not over battlefield security. Apparently there are still some military advisers who feel the British and American public do not yet realize that war involves risks, that the breaks do not always go to the Allies. They are afraid that the public cannot stand the shock of bad news and that it must be broken to them gradually over long periods of time and preferably after some victory.

General Alexander made it very plain that the reporters must adhere strictly to a policy line laid down by his headquarters and applied to stories when they reach Naples. The stories are censored for fact before they leave the bridgehead and then recensored for policy at Naples. . . .* (Feb. 19, 1944)

---

*The remainder of the story transcribed the Alexander remarks.

Green Troops at Anzio, March 1944

Green Men Get
First Taste of
Anzio Shellfire

Replacement Unit Huddles
Low in Truck on Way to
Front Across Open Field

WITH 5TH ARMY BEACHHEAD FORCES, ITALY, March 7, 1944—The truckload of replacements turned off the black-surfaced road and went bounding along a muddy track to the battalion bivouac. It had to traverse a half mile of naked fields that tilted northward to where enemy batteries sat.

The green men must have had a premonition. They had seen dead cows and sheep beside the road and they were crouching down to the floor of the truck when the first shells came in, rattling like a runaway coal truck.

The 105's fell short, showering the truck with mud and dirt. They exploded in clouds of bluish smoke or pillars of dishwater gray.

We knew the truck would draw fire, for we had been on this road before. We tried to get our own driver to pull up behind a farmhouse until the truck drew ahead a few hundred yards.

When you come under artillery fire, you obey one of two impulses: you step on the gas and get out of there or you jump out of your car and plop into a ditch. Our driver was seized by the first impulse so we leaped ahead and overtook the truck. Since there was no room to pass it, we had to crawl along behind and give the Nazi gunners a fatter target.

It was one of those grim March days that hold no hope of spring. The brown plain reached toward mountains still covered with snow. A raw wind marshaled steely bands of clouds across the sky and rippled the flooded fields.

On such a day you expect death more than on bright days. You think that if only you can survive this day, then tomorrow will be sunny and you'll be one day nearer to the end of the war.

The shells came down in pairs, landing just to the right of the truck. Luckily there was little dispersion—the shells burrowed too deep into the mud. One burst 10 yards from the truck, yet nobody was hurt.

With painful deliberation the truck dragged over the crest of a slight rise and, gathering momentum, rolled down the rutted track. A knoll gave a defilade and presently the terror faded from the faces of the new men. There always has to be a first time, but the men had not expected it so soon.

At the bivouac the men climbed down and stood on shaky pins. A platoon sergeant looked them over. There is a fiction that front-line sergeants are ruthless butchers who send recruits out on hopeless missions before they have been properly introduced. But it is the sergeant who gets it in this war. He is particularly liable to get it when he goes out in the line with a unit heavily larded with men who have never seen action.

The new men saw shell craters in the woods and started to grope for their intrenching tools. The sergeant saw that they were nervous, and told them to go ahead and dig themselves in for the night. (March 9, 1944)

"Green Men" is one of the many Bigart dispatches that prompted a *Herald Tribune* editorial. "Reading Mr. Homer Bigart's report from Anzio yesterday," the editorial on March 10 said, ". . . even those who have, in the old phrase, never heard a shot fired in anger can share something of the sudden, overwhelming reaction that must come upon men when they recognize the significance of those time-polished words. . . .

"A veteran might have noticed, as Mr. Bigart noticed, that the soft mud in which the German shells landed prevented the fragments from scattering widely. But for the green men there was only the knowledge that someone was seeking their lives with weapons of savage power.

"That is a bitter knowledge—one that cannot be absorbed from books or orientation courses. . . . Yet it is the one thing that sets the soldier apart from all the ways of peace, that initiates him into his deadly trade. . . ."

Assessment of Anzio, March 1944

Reporter Says Allies at Anzio Tried Too Much With Too Little

NAPLES, March 26, 1944—It is a depressing experience to return from the Anzio beachhead, where front-line misery rivals World War Flanders, and find in a city 60 miles behind the lines a complacency and lack of realism worse than that prevailing in New York.

Beachhead correspondents have been criticized for overpessimism. They have been told they do not know the full facts—they fail to grasp what is quaintly known as "the big picture."

That is true enough. For 62 days we have been cut off from good news about other theaters, where apparently the war is going well. We missed the cheery rumors that always are circulating among the rear echelons, where any suggestion that the war might possibly last through next Christmas is met with laughter and lofted eyebrows. It was the same in November, when some of us started writing about the winter line.

If at Anzio we missed the big picture, we also shed some delusions carefully nurtured by months of comfortable living as headquarters correspondents. At headquarters the bad news was glossed over. If we failed to take a town in one attack we would get it next time, so why worry? At headquarters there was always good food, amusements and security, and every one, of course, was chock full of confidence and quite happy about the situation.

Now after two months of costly fighting with little or no ground gained, one would expect to find a slight note of realism seeping into discussions about this campaign. It is disheartening, therefore, to hear correspondents who have never been within 20 miles of the front speak glibly about our success in keeping elements of 18 to 20 German divisions employed in southern Italy and around the Anzio beachhead.

Panic Plan Failed

They seem to regard this as ample justification for heavy losses among some of the finest American and British divisions.

Well, the main purpose of Anzio, as everyone knows, was not to attract more German divisions to southern Italy. Gen. Sir Harold R.L.G. Alexander explained on Feb. 14 that it was hoped the surprise landing would panic the Germans into a withdrawal from Cassino, breaking the long deadlock on the southern front.

That, of course, failed. It failed because the lesson of Salerno had not been learned. Again we were attempting too much with too little.

Critics have been quick to blame the Allied ground commander at Anzio for failure to push inland during the first week and seize the Alban Hills south of Rome. This commander was a careful tactician who refused to sacrifice the American Third Division and British troops in so foolhardy a proposition. He knew how many men he had on the beachhead and how many Germans were ahead.

Which Lost Battalion?

In those critical first four weeks our force was so small that even the most modest hundred square miles of beachhead were thinly defended against German pressure. Cooks, clerks, drivers and engineers shouldered rifles and marched into the line, plugging gaps that existed because so few infantrymen were available.

Against such a defense the Germans had great success in infiltration.

So many units were cut off that a grim joke went around—"Did you hear about the lost battalion?" "Which one?"

To this observer it seems awfully late in the war to attempt so dangerous an operation without first securing such preponderance of strength that the outcome is never in doubt once the landings have been secured.

The slowness and cost of the Italian campaign carry valuable lessons that never will be learned so long as the people in the rear continue to sit out the war in comfortable complacency. (March 27, 1944)

Taking Cassino, May 1944

On May 20, 1944, the *Trib* had two dispatches on the ruination of war, one from the author Maurice Hindus in the Crimean city of Sevastopol, besieged by the Germans for eight months in 1941–42 and not retaken by the Russians until May 1944, and Bigart's on the town of Cassino and its abbey, which follows. The editors twinned them on page one under a joint headline.

Two Cities That Were—Sevastopol and Cassino; Hindus and Bigart See and Describe the Ruins

Cassino, Once Thriving, Is Transformed Into Scene of Unrelieved Grimness

WITH THE 8TH ARMY IN CASSINO, ITALY, May 19, 1944—Cassino is a bleak, gray, smoking ruin which, with a little sulphur added, would be more grim than a Calvinist conception of hell.

The city, when we entered it at 12:30 P.M., was silent. For the first time since January, no shells crumped down amid the skeleton walls of the few score buildings still erect.

I have seen all the devastated towns on the road to Rome—Capus, Mignano, San Pietro, San Vittore and Cervara. But not even ghostly San Pietro compares with the utter ruin of the key citadel of the Gustav line.

This once prosperous district center of 15,000, roughly midway between Naples and Rome, is a phantom place of windowless shops and crumbled hotels. Not one Italian crawled from the ruins to cheer the British troops pressing onward for the battle against the Adolf Hitler line. Even in San Pietro part of the population had remained, but here in Cassino none could have endured the four hellish months of siege. The few safe shelters—shallow tunnels and caves along the bleak chalk slopes of Monte Cassino—were exclusively for the young fanatics of the First Parachute Division.

Kenneth L. Dixon of the Associated Press; George Silk, a *Life* photographer, and I were the first reporters to enter the western part of town, where German paratroopers threw back the American 34th Division in the midwinter offensive and stalled the New Zealanders in the March assault.

Yesterday two British reporters approaching the abandoned German defenses along Highway 6 were killed by a mine when they stepped off the road to avoid a sudden spate of enemy mortaring. Today we were lucky—not one shell landed within Cassino during our three hours in the town.

The uncanny stillness, broken only by the rumble of bulldozers wrestling with drifted rubble, intensified rather than lightened the uncompromising grimness of the scene. From the desolate cathedral on the southern outskirts of Cassino we looked across stagnant pools of water to where the ruined shops and houses rose tier on tier against the steep bare slopes of Abbey Hill. The terraced olive orchards rising almost to the monastery were reduced to successive levels of blackened stumps. Not one flower, not one blade of grass lived in the gardens of the town.

The Germans had diverted the Rapido River, blasting the levee above Cassino so that a considerable stream flowed between the cathedral and the central square, flooding the gutted buildings on the edge of the town and swamping the fields in front of the Hotels Continental and De Rosa, the outposts of their line.

Trees Are Defoliated

Twisted trees, defoliated by the fragments and concussion of thousands of bombs and shells, reached dead limbs out of the pools covered with greenish slime. Across the swamp the scene was solid gray—the gray honeycomb of ruins, then the gray slope of Monte Cassino merging imperceptibly with the steely sky. Only the jagged black outline of the abbey wall, topping the crest 1,300 feet above Cassino, showed where sky and horizon met.

British sappers had thrown a road across the bog. Before crossing we looked inside the cathedral crypt, which served as a command post and first-aid station for the advance spearhead of the three Allied assaults. First the 100th Battalion of Hawaiians had quartered its wounded there during the opening days of the siege. Then the chapel was intact, but soon enemy guns were reducing it bit by bit. Burial vaults, high up in the walls of the nave, were ripped open. Skeletons disturbed after centuries had rolled down on the startled troops.

After the Hawaiians departed the New Zealanders took over, remaining through the bloody futility of the March assault. When the British forces took over late in March there was nothing left except the underground vaults where fresh corpses lay. The British endured a month of ghastly stench, hanging sticky paper from the walls to arrest the spring invasion of flies. From this loathesome dungeon no one dared move during the daylight hours, for all approaches were swept by machine-gun fire from the Hotel Continental across the bog.

Hotel With a Guest

Few tourists will remember the Continental, a three-story limestone building of perhaps 30 rooms. Baedeker ignores it. But it was the only hotel in town that had a guest.

The guest squatted black and ugly in the vaulted lobby. Ever since Feb. 3, when the Americans penetrated the heart of Cassino, this Mark IV tank had slept there, rousing at intervals to poke its nose into the street and fire at the crypt or the buildings in the center of town.

One American patrol got inside the hotel, starting room by room to mop up the Germans before a counterattack set them back. They claimed the destruction of the tank but it looked quite formidable today when viewed from a four-foot pile of rubble at the massive lobby entrance. Its career ended definitely on March 15, when waves of Allied bombers threw great drifts of debris against the hotel wall, imprisoning the tank until the British closed in on the last German strongpoints early yesterday.

A German Bazooka

Sixty yards to Via Casilina in the direction of Rome was the Hotel De Rosa, another enemy stronghold somewhat less badly smashed than the Continental. Rooms along the rear wall were bulwarked with sandbags, and in front of the side entrance were heaps of discarded clothing and a battered German bazooka.

This was the last building on Highway 6, but across the fields and abreast of the hotel were a half dozen stone houses that seemed to have escaped direct hits during the great air raid, although their walls were punctured in shelling. Everywhere the Air Force had done a truly remarkable job of flattening Cassino.

There was a stench of death near the smoldering rubble of the Hotel Continental, but we saw only one German corpse, which lay near a steel pillbox on the western side of town.

The pillbox was embedded on the left side of the road where it curved northward along the slope of Hangman's Hill. It protruded only a foot above the curb and was so well camouflaged with rocks that it looked like a heap of crushed stones left by a road-repair gang. Its gun had been removed. Through a slit the Germans had an excellent view of the bare flats across which Allied troops must move to enter Cassino from the east.

Half a mile from the town, toward Rome, were two more German fortresses—on the left of the road, the colossal remains of an ancient amphitheater used by the Germans as a tank park, and opposite the ducal palace a square ruin of considerable dimensions with stone walls three feet thick. Here the Germans had their medical station and a storeroom filled with mortar ammunition.

Leave Little Equipment

Except for the Mark IV tanks and a portable pillbox abandoned near the Hotel Del Rosa the Germans had left very little equipment of importance. The portable pillbox, mounted on heavy wooden wheels, was designed for a mortar, being opened at the top. Its walls were steel three inches thick.

All sidestreets leading from the Via Casalina were posted with warnings of mines and boobytraps, but a British captain commanding a company of sappers told us that surprisingly few mines were found. However, a considerable part of the town was still unexplored, though by midafternoon sappers had cleared a path up the slope through the barbed wire and minefields reaching Castle Hill, a barrier that three great assaults had failed to storm.

Behind Castle Hill is a shallow vale between the ruined castle and Monastery Hill where the Japanese-American battalion had been isolated for nine days while American tank destroyers tried vainly to reduce the thick citadel built in the Hohenstauffen era.

After the Americans withdrew, bombers completed the destruction of the castle but even then its ruins continued to harbor German machine gunners. Across the vale high up the slope of Monastery Hill was the celebrated Yellow House, a large stone mansion from which enemy automatic fire took a fearful toll among the attackers trying to advance over the boulder-strewn pass below.

Neither the castle nor the Yellow House was ever stormed. When the British and the Poles closed their trap around the town and monastery two days ago, most of the defenders had vanished.

Fewer than 150 prisoners were taken in Cassino. Many came down the road from the abbey when the Poles appeared, preferring to surrender to the British.

Thus ended the bitterest battle of the Italian campaign. In today's quiet, a party of New Zealand tankers returned to Cassino and found the bodies of three comrades killed in the armored thrust following the March 15 air raid. The lead tank halted by drifted ruins was easy prey for German guns.

The New Zealanders dug three graves beside the road, while swallows came back to a town forever dead. (May 20, 1944)

Entering Rome, June 1944

Nazi Guns Put
Tragic End to
Roman Holiday

Flak Wagon Fires on Crowd
Piling on First U.S. Tank
to Reach Heart of the City

WITH THE 5TH ARMY IN ROME, June 5, 1944—The entry of Allied troops into the heart of the Eternal City at dusk last night was a moment of such wildly primitive emotion that even now, 12 hours afterward, it is impossible to write soberly of the nightmarish scene along the Via Nazionale, where jubilation gave way to frozen panic and sudden death.

The Nazis, attempting to save their retreating army from annihilation across the River Tiber, sent a flak wagon charging into the lead column of American troops. We were passing the Bank of Italy when it happened. Just ahead, around the slope of Capitoline Hill, was the

Palazzo Venezia and Mussolini's balcony. At the head of our column crawled a Sherman tank, wearing a bonnet of hysterical Romans. They fought for footholds on its turret, screaming bravos and waving Italian flags. Our jeep was next in line. Behind us, single-file on either side of the street, came infantrymen crusted with dust from a two-day march.

The Via Nazionale looked deserted and hostile as we entered it after passing the Ministry of the Interior and the Royal Opera. But suddenly house shutters flew open, and by the time we came abreast of the Exposition Palace the broad thoroughfare swarmed with cheering mobs. Troops were pummeled, kissed and pelted with roses. "Viva quinta armata" ("Long live the 5th Army") and "Viva General Clark" roared from thousands of throats when the Romans recognized the American uniforms.

Thus the stage was set for panic. The Romans scrambling aboard our jeep assured us the Germans had fled to Quirinal Hill, but they forgot the roving flak wagons by which the Nazis hoped to catch and massacre troops and partisans unguarded by tanks.

As the hour of liberation approached, these flak wagons—heavy antiaircraft guns mounted on half-tracks—raced through the winding streets, shooting explosive bullets at intersections, attempting to cover the last-minute escape of Nazi snipers and demolition crews and to ambush the American vanguard.

We were within a few hundred yards of the Forum of Trajan at the end of the Via Nazionale when a flak wagon careened around a bend in the Via 4th of November, its guns streaming red tracers into the throngs outside the Bank of Italy. I shall never forget that dreadful moment of panic.

It was like a scene from the Russian revolution. The transition from exultation to paralyzing fear was not immediate—there was that split second of astonishment when the throng merely stood agape, watching the tracers ricochet off the stone walls of the Palace of Rospigliosi.

Panic Sweeps Crowd

Then the wave of panic swept down the length of the Via Nazionale. It started as a ripple when a slight shift of the Sherman's gun turret flicked the Italian from the top of the tank to the pavement.

Our jeep was 50 yards behind the tank and directly in line of the enemy's fire. Quick thinking by the driver, Pfc. Kenneth Koplin of Huron, S.D., saved our lives. Koplin swerved the jeep over to the curbstone and we leaped over an iron guard rail into the entrance of a department store.

It was all over in a few minutes. The flak wagon, trying to dart past the tank and slaughter the infantrymen following it, was disabled by the second shell from the Sherman's 75. It lay like a helpless black beetle while the Sherman crawled to within a hundred feet and sent another shell crashing into its side. Two Nazis were killed outright and a third was dying. Three others were taken prisoner. The infantrymen had to fire their rifles into the air to save the captives from the infuriated throng.

We decided to walk the rest of the way to the Piazza Venezia. . . . We descended the stairway and stood before the huge colonaded monument of Victor Emmanuel II. Behind us was the bare brownstone facade of the Palazzo Venezia, with its little white balcony from which Mussolini spoke. Across the silent plaza came the sound of church bells and distant cheering. It was 9:15 when Americans and Canadians from the mixed force of a brilliant 37-year-old brigadier general filed past the muted balcony. In the moonlight they skirted the ghostly pillars of ancient Rome, pressing onward to the bridges of the Tiber. . . . (June 6, 1944)

On October 4, 1944, the *Herald Tribune* carried on its commentary page this reprint from *Newsweek* magazine, under the heading "From the Cannon's Mouth."

The Mediterranean area last week lost one of its best correspondents. Homer Bigart of the New York Herald Tribune *flew home after two solid years of war reporting.*

"Keep away from Homer," a correspondent once warned another. "He's always trying to build his reputation at the cannon's mouth." That jesting remark explains part of 36-year-old Bigart's effectiveness. Detailed simplicity in writing accounts for more of it. The following cable from Newsweek *correspondent Zeke Cook—who was with Bigart during part of the Italian campaign and in southern France—gives a close-up of him in the field.*

———————

Bigart is the hardest kind of worker and the fairest kind of competitor. He enjoys action, was happiest at the front and chafed when he had to spend several weeks covering the routine stories in Rome.

Although he was always up where the going was the hottest, pushing farther front than most correspondents feel is safe, probably his closest shave came on one of his infrequent days off. Bigart landed at Anzio on D-Day. A month later when things relatively slowed down and he was out rowing in a rubber boat, a German plane made a target of him. Bullets tore lines in the water around the frantically rowing Bigart but miraculously missed him. Another time a 20-mm. shell ripped through the wall of the Villa Virtue and landed in Bigart's bathtub. His comment: "Glad I don't take baths at the front."

With the 5th Army on the Cassino front, Milton Bracker, bearded correspondent of *The New York Times,* drove himself to a frazzle competing with Bigart. I remember the day Bracker came in weary from a long trip and found Bigart had been in Cassino that afternoon when it fell. Because of mines the trip was extremely dangerous (two British correspondents were killed there the next morning) but Bracker left camp at 6 that evening to match Bigart's dateline.

Another day Bigart, Bracker and Sid Feder of the Associated Press returned from a trip to the Cassino monastery ravenously hungry and too late for supper. All three prevailed on the mess sergeant to cook up some eggs and then began to write. When the sergeant set out the plates, Feder abandoned his typewriter for the mess tent. Bracker asked the busily writing Bigart if he was eating and got a "not hungry" reply. Torn between hunger, fear that Bigart's story might get out first and the thought of the profane sergeant's remarks, Bracker compromised, brought his plate to the typewriter and snatched bites between takes. Bigart didn't eat, but at midnight, after the story was in, he ended up hungrily munching a crust of dry bread.

Bigart is soft-spoken with not too pronounced a stutter and a mild solemnity that hides a wonderful sense of humor. In Rome he was waiting with other correspondents in the antechamber for a report of the first Italian Cabinet meeting. A flunky announced that the Cabinet had drafted laws to abolish Fascism, now had only to add the finishing touches, and the statement would be ready in half an hour. Bigart remarked: "All they have to do now is p-p-p-put in the l-loopholes."

––––––––––

Mr. Bigart has returned home for a temporary respite from the war. In a short time he will depart for another war assignment.

World War II, the Pacific

Leyte, a Different Kind of War, November 1944

By November, Bigart was reporting from Leyte, the Philippines. Here are excerpts from his first Pacific dispatch.

Reporter at Leyte After Europe Finds a Different Kind of War

Notes Scarcity of Japanese Artillery and Land Mines, Little Noise of Battle—But Sniper's Bullets Kill Man Just as Dead as Nazis' Railroad Rifles

WITH THE 24TH DIVISION, NORTHERN LEYTE, Nov. 14, 1944—The Ormoc road skirts the blue crescent of Caligara Bay and, quitting the last forlorn settlement of nipa huts, curves abruptly southward through a palm and bamboo wilderness matted with six-foot kogan grass. Ascending steeply, it traverses the first of five ridges damming the narrow defile through the interior mountains.

Across this pass, through which Gen. Douglas MacArthur's men must move to seize Ormoc and complete the liberation of Leyte, Gen. Tomoyuki Yamashita, the conquerer of Singapore, has flung the First Imperial Division. . . .

This correspondent, coming from the European fronts, has been impressed by the weakness of the Japanese artillery, and the failure of the enemy to employ mines with anything like the diabolical thoroughness of Field Marshal Albert Kesselring's army in Italy. . . .

Here you can drive right up to the front line in broad daylight without drawing a storm of artillery or getting blown sky high by Teller mines. And that is precisely why more correspondents have been killed here than in any comparable period in the European theater.

The newcomer gets a false sense of security. Hearing none of the usual din of battle, he comes jeeping along, admiring the scenery, when—ping—a sniper's bullet shatters his daydreams. You have only to make one excursion to the front to realize that this is a very different kind of war, and that Japanese bullets and knee mortars can kill just as surely as Col. Gen. Eberhard von Mackensen's railway guns at Anzio. . . . (Nov. 15, 1944)

Bringing Bacon Home to Leyte, December 1944

Bigart's file from Leyte also includes this piece of classic nonsense, a clear ancestor of the Bali Hai legends that found their way to Broadway.

Mess Sergeant Turns Importer, Brings Home Bacon to Leyte

WITH 32D DIVISION, NORTHERN LEYTE, Dec. 1, 1944—With some old parachutes as trading material, Mess Sergeant Edward A. Mahan, former cook at the St. Francis Hotel in San Francisco, visited one of the smaller islands of the Visayan group a few days ago and returned with 20 chickens, three dozen eggs, 100 pounds of bananas, two pigs, some parrots and stories of a lush island paradise such as forms the traditional backdrop of the middle-aged escapist's dreams.

Of course the name of the island cannot be disclosed because the Japanese might hear of it, but Mahan will be happy to give full particulars after the war. He can be reached in the kitchen of the St. Francis, where most likely he will be frying chickens in cocoanut oil according to a recipe he picked up from the women of the island.

The women, incidentally, were of a light mahogany tint, with strong white teeth, eyes like heifers' and ebony tresses cascading down over firm and deliciously rounded shoulders. Mahan, being happily married, said that was about as far as he cared to go.

Mahan learned of the island from two guerrillas who spoke lovingly of roast pork, omelets, fried bananas and fermented cocoanut sap. Mahan put it up to his colonel, a handsome old cavalryman, now dismounted, named John A. Hettinger, who promptly wished him godspeed.

Mahan, escorted by the guerrillas, reached the island without misadventure. His first vision was of green hills and distant waterfalls that were silvery columns veiled in mist like the towers of Camelot. Over the soft lapping of the wavelets against the coral shore, he heard the doleful measured croaking of tree lizards. (Tree lizards are harmless. Voyagers and Visayans need only beware of crocodiles, scorpions, and hosts of crawling insects that sting and bite. Shoes should be shaken thoroughly before each wearing.)

Nestling in the moist and verdant plain like a rare gem in a malarial setting was the village. It stopped raining, and during the brief interval of sunlight Mahan perceived a neat row of thatched huts strung along either side of the hog wallow that was the main street.

Mahan met the local guerrilla chief, who told him he was the first American to visit the island since the Japanese invasion. Apparently the Japanese left the islanders pretty much alone after a foraging party had stripped the place of pigs and poultry early in the war, departing after bayoneting two natives.

There being no church in the village, Mahan assumed that the natives were pagans. None spoke English, but the escorting guerrillas acted as interpreters.

"They took me to a large hut, where there were music and beautiful girls and roast pig stuffed with rice," Mahan related. "We squatted on the floor and ate with our fingers, and then the chief lined up 18 girls against the wall and asked me to pick a dancing partner.

"Meantime women kept coming down from the hills, bringing chickens, eggs and bananas. They wouldn't take anything, so I just dumped the parachutes, fruit bars and C rations on the floor, and told them they were gifts from the Great White Father. It was the first time they had eaten candy. They made even more fuss over the parachutes—they wanted the stuff for dresses."

That night 30 natives guarded Mahan while he slept. "I wasn't sure I could trust them," said Mahan, "so I stayed awake most of the night. The next morning we loaded the stuff aboard a sampan and headed back for Leyte.

"Half an hour after I had left, the shore defenses had been ordered to fire on all strange craft. We were about eight miles from port and only a few hundred yards from Leyte when some 105's opened up. They thought we were Japs."

Mahan ordered all hands overboard. They swam ashore, abandoning pigs, chickens and eggs. Finally the guns ceased fire after one shell tore off the sampan's bow. Mahan took some guerrillas out in small boats and salvaged the cargo.

The regiment ate well, consuming the last of the eggs today.

During Mahan's absence, Pvt. Harold Affeldt of Waterloo, Iowa, ran the kitchen. A former life insurance salesman, Affeldt knew nothing about cooking, but managed to bake a cake. "I saw my mother bake a cake once in 1936," he said. "I remembered her putting flour and sugar and eggs into a pan, measuring it by the cup. It was simple." (Dec. 3, 1944)

Landing on Corregidor, February 1945

Corregidor Invaders Battle Way Ashore in Hail of Enemy Bullets

Reporter With Them Tells How Machine Guns Raked Landing Craft and Men Fought Up Beaches to Make Contact With Paratroops

CORREGIDOR, Feb. 16, 1945—For the first 280 yards, as we made our way in a landing craft toward Corregidor, everything went well. Emboldened, we began sticking our heads up over the side. Lieut. Col. Edward M. Postlethwaite of Chicago, commanding the Third Battalion of the 34th Infantry Regiment of the 24th Division, was sitting calmly on top of a truckload of ammunition.

Ahead, in the narrow gap between "topside," the rocky plateau on which American paratroopers had landed earlier, and Malinta Hill we could see how dreadfully complete was the destruction effected by naval guns. A little village where Philippines Scouts officers and their wives once resided was completely obliterated. Nothing remained of depots and warehouses but a twisted rubble of steel. The place was ghostly.

On the right was the gaunt framework of the dock from which Gen. Douglas MacArthur escaped on the night of March 10, 1942, in a PT boat operated by Lieut. (now lieutenant commander) John D. Bulkeley, 58 days before Lieut. Gen. Jonathan M. Wainwright, who remained in command at Corregidor, surrendered.

We were beginning to think this was another Marivales. Yesterday the tip of Bataan Peninsula had fallen without a shot. But this was to be different.

The toughness of any landing should be gauged by the casualty reports. Here at Corregidor, where mopping up continues, our casualties were certainly not excessive considering the risk involved. But when men are killed or wounded directly beside you then the thing becomes very personal and hard to write about with any degree of dispassionate appraisal.

Somewhere along Breakwater Point cliff the Japanese had trundled a 40-caliber machine gun to the mouth of a small cave, and they opened fire on the craft directly below. Our boat was nearest shore and we caught the first fusillade.

Bullets bit into the armor. We groveled in the slimy bottom near the ramp, keeping as much distance as possible between ourselves and the ammunition truck. There we lay in a close huddle during the long minute the Japanese gunners gave us exclusive attention.

On my right, a doughboy suddenly raised the bloody stump of his right hand. An instant later, a soldier squatting next to him toppled dead. A bullet had gone through his back and out through his chest. The horrible tearing power of machine-gun bullets was brought home to us for the first time.

The craft came to a jolting halt. Down came the ramp and we scampered ashore, diving for cover behind a knocked-out tank.

Bullets sang against its blackened hulk, ricocheting with a vicious twang. For one frantic second we couldn't tell the direction of the fire—there is nothing more futile than lying on the wrong side of protective cover.

We knew about the gun on Breakwater Point, but this stuff seemed to be coming from a nest of pillboxes midway up Malinta Hill.

Richard G. Harris of the United Press and I decided to stay put. I managed to gouge a shallow foxhole in the rubble and Harris pressed himself against the shattered tread of the tank.

There was a quick slamming blast. Chunks of concrete pelted us, and instantly the tank and the group surrounding it melted in a cloud of dust. When the dust cleared I looked around. A mortar shell had burst 20 feet to my left and a jagged fragment sailing over my foxhole instantly killed a soldier lying immediately to the right.

That was enough. I loped to a big shell crater and stayed there until things quieted.

Postlethwaite's men were scattered from hell to breakfast. That was natural. The beach was too hot for any attempt at organization. The doughboys raced for cover wherever they could find it.

Rocket ships had churned the beach but failed to explode the mines. We saw two tanks and a duck (amphibious truck) disabled by mines. Then two jeeps with trailers loaded with mortar ammunition were hit by an antitank gun. Through the rest of the morning exploding ammunition was an added menace.

During a lull, I crept along a stone wall to Postlethwaite's shellhole command post (field headquarters). The radio operator, Joe Princiotta of 905 Avenue St. John, the Bronx, was in contact with the paratroopers. They had just staved off a "banzai charge" in sanguinary fighting and were now advancing down "topside."

The two forces met midway up the slope shortly before noon. [The paratroopers of the 503d Parachute Regiment had landed about 8 A.M. and the ground troops about two hours later.] Meanwhile Postlethwaite's K and L Companies under Lieut. Lewis F. Stearns and Capt. Frank D. Centanni stormed Malinta Hill, clearing a few snipers from the crest. The tunnels in the hill had been completely sealed by landslides during the prelanding bombardment.

The whole island, particularly "topside," was desolated. The great barracks, three stories high and 1,300 feet long, seemed intact at a distance, but drawing near we could see it pitted and gutted, a mere shell, like Cassino Abbey in Italy. We saw no trace of the batteries of disappearing guns of 1899 vintage that had formed the chief armament of Corregidor. (Feb. 19, 1945)

Freeing Luzon Prisoners,
February 1945

Air-Sea Raiders Swoop on Camp,
Free 2,100 Internees on Luzon

Amphibious Force, Paratroops Arrive at Rollcall,
Kill 243 Japanese Guards, Pack Ex-Captives
Aboard Sea Tractors and Sail Them to Safety

LOS BANOS, LUZON, Feb. 23, 1945 (Delayed)—In a brilliant combined paratroop and amphibious raid, Americans struck 25 miles behind the Japanese lines today, rescuing 2,100 internees and removing them to safety before the Japanese recaptured the camp. The entire camp garrison of 243 Japanese were killed.

Lieutenant Konishi, the Japanese overseer, had rung the bell for the dawn rollcall, and the internees were lining up outside their huts when the paratroopers dropped. Several C-47 transports flew low over the area, disgorging their chutes above a field a mile east of the camp.

Simultaneously, 23 men under Lieutenant George E. Skau of 63-17 34th Avenue, Jackson Heights, New York, who had landed Wednesday night on a wooded point of Laguna de Bay, a large lake southeast of Manila, secured the landing area and, reinforced by 200 Filipino guerrillas, advanced on the six sentry posts and two pillboxes guarding the camp.

The internees scampered back into their nipa barracks as the shooting began. Machine guns kept the paratroopers down behind stone walls on the eastern edge of the camp for several minutes and then they slipped through barbed wire and hurled a thermite bomb into two wooden guardhouses, which instantly burst into flames.

One hundred and twenty-three paratroopers, under First Lieutenant John M. Ringler of 679 Niagara Street, Tonowanda, N.Y., of B Company, 511th Paratroop Regiment, which had silenced the machine guns, met only slight sniper fire as they began rounding up the internees. . . .

They found in the crowded barracks 1,589 Americans, 329 British, 22 Poles, 89 Dutch, 15 Italians, 10 Norwegians and a handful of other nationals. Women and children made up more than half of the camp population. . . .

Immediate evacuation was essential but in their moment of liberation the internees were too hysterically happy to appreciate the peril of delay. They began picking up rags, rusty pans and blankets accumulated during three years' imprisonment. In one of the barracks First Lieutenant Benjamin Rooth of 375 Park Avenue, New York, encountered a frail middle-aged woman who refused to leave without her Persian cat. "She's been gone since Tuesday," she wailed. "I'm afraid they've eaten her."

Things were still pretty disorganized an hour later when 53 amphibious tractors (amtracs) bearing the rest of the First Battalion of the 511th rolled into camp.

Tanks Land in Bay

The straggling line of internees was just beginning to move into the evacuation center on the baseball grounds as the amtracs landed in a bay two miles to the northeast. There were no Japanese there and the natives had raised the American flag.

We crept down a narrow road across a densely wooded lowland. The country was ideal for ambush, yet no Japanese were encountered and we passed unchallenged through the deserted main street of Los Banos and pushed on toward the Agricultural College, where the camp was located, a mile to the southeast of town.

The tractor force reached the campus from the far eastern end. We heard occasional rifle fire. Major Harry Burgess of Sheridan, Wyo., led the battalion to the first objective—the camp hospital. The sick had first priority; others would have to walk. Escaping internees had brought information that there were at least 50 bedridden patients. Actually, there were fewer than 40, the majority of whom were victims of cardiac beriberi brought on by a hunger diet, and two obstetrical cases.

They were Mrs. Louise Francisco of Wichita, Kan., and her 9-day-old baby, Elizabeth, and Mrs. Oscar McCoy of Manila, whose daughter, Kathleen, was born three days ago. They were both loaded in litters on a jeep. Both women were married in the camp. Their applications for licenses had to be approved in Tokyo—a process requiring nearly three months—then a camp committee issued the licenses and one of the camp's 500 clergymen performed the ceremonies.

The other patients were mostly old men pitifully wasted by beriberi. Four had died from tuberculosis directly induced by a hunger diet. Wood for coffins became so scarce that old buildings were torn down to provide coffins against the rising tide of disease. Dr. Dana Nance and his staff of 12 Navy nurses had worked heroically. They had no X-ray, no lights and only the most primitive equipment. Under these conditions, Dr. Nance had performed 300 major operations. Finally, even his supply of sutures failed; then only the most urgent emergency operations were handled.

The hospital was evacuated quickly but up on a hill the internees wasted valuable minutes cramming bags with stuff they would never use again. Aged internees hated to leave their beds and beach chairs behind. There were frantic last-minute hunts for cats and dogs that somehow escaped being eaten during the last weeks of acute hunger.

Barracks Cleared After Delay

More than an hour passed before the barracks were cleared. Meanwhile, a thin line of riflemen kept the Japanese from re-entering the swarming campus. Occasional bullets whined overhead while officers tried vainly to stir the slowly moving line.

While the march through Los Banos was known to the enemy,

breaking an escape route through to an evacuation point was a more serious task. Along the road long columns of internees began to move, men, women and children loaded down with baggage.

Amtracs carrying sick and wounded went on ahead while long files of walking internees had no protection excepting that provided by a handful of guerrillas with rifles salvaged from Bataan.

Two Japanese started across the road directly in the path of the route being followed by a group of women internees.

Hampered by Babies

Private Bernard Coon of Oswego, N.Y., guarding the column, said: "Some of the women who had taken their babies with them thrust them into my arms and I couldn't do a thing."

Miraculously, the marchers reached Bayeo without casualties. There followed a two-hour wait while the slow-moving tractors retraced the 10-mile stretch to a point on the shallow, muddy Laguna de Bay. Before they returned for a fresh load, the internees loaded the mortars and machine guns on them.

One of the vehicles received five holes in its steel hide nearing the beach. The last boatload of internees had to make a wider arc to pass the enemy shore lines. Again the Japanese tried to reach the amtracs but their shells fell several hundred yards short.

It was nearly 2 P.M. before the last of the internees boarded the amphibious vehicles for the 10-mile ride by water to the American lines. By that time the beachhead was getting warm.

Tractor Riddled With Bullets

The Japanese placed heavy and light machine guns on the shore half a mile above the thinly held embarkation beach. One tractor was riddled with bullets. Another parked alongside and rescued the passengers before it sank.

The paratroopers' jump was one of the most successful on record. In one-two-three order the men disengaged from their ships and were completely organized within 12 minutes. There was only one jump casualty—a sprained ankle.

The internees bore the last hour of tension with remarkable calm. Not even the hot, dusty march made them irritable. During the long ride up to the lake to the American lines, they devoured every scrap of food the troops had saved from their rations.

Split-Second Timing Used

The rescue of the Los Banos internees was achieved by following intricate plans that required all the finesse and split-second timing of a Pop Warner double reverse. In the first place, exact intelligence was needed on the strength of the Japanese garrison and what its guard would be doing at the zero hour—7 A.M.

Escaping prisoners brought information that 7 o'clock in the morning was rollcall time. At that moment half the garrison would be out in a field during calisthenics, while others would be checking up on the internees.

The estimate of the garrison strength was 50 to 100. There were six sentry posts and two pillboxes, which often were left unmanned.

Twenty-two men, reinforced by guerrillas, were to take care of the guards. If possible, they were to avoid shooting, using knives wherever possible. No hand-to-hand fighting developed.

Paratroopers blossoming down set the garrison in commotion. Twenty Japanese doing squatting exercises began running around frantically. The men killed most of them and then used the thermite grenades, first as guides, and then threw them into the guardhouse where the rest of the Japanese were grabbing their arms.

Conditions Are Described

Rescued internees said that conditions at the Los Banos camp did not begin to get tough until last summer. Up to then the food was ample and treatment, by Japanese standards, was surprisingly good under the expert administration of Dr. Nance, who was former head of the Notre Dame Hospital at Baguio. Health conditions were much better than at Santo Tomas.

"Then in July we were kicked out of permanent concrete and wooden barracks and thrown into nipa barracks," said Peter

Newsome, one of the 400 Britons at Los Banos. "Some 400 clergymen, both Catholic and Protestant, and a number of nuns were crowded in with us. The Japanese did not need the building; they did it out of sheer meanness."

"In August there came from Manila a certain grim character named Lieutenant Konishi. He put the screws on and cut our rations to 200 grams of rice and corn.

"Previously we had three meals daily, including not only corn and rice but carabao [water buffalo] meat, quite a few beans and vegetables. We even had a canteen where we could buy Japanese cigarettes and candy made in the camp from sugar peanuts." (Feb. 25, 1945)

The Cost of Iwo Jima, March 1945

After Leyte and Corregidor and the liberation of the internees in Los Banos, Bigart went on to the final phase of the battle for Iwo Jima, a "desolate heap of volcanic cinders" that was crucial to the Allies. His assessment, mercifully free of military-analyst pontification, displays the development of what Kluger's *The Paper* calls a "sinewy, evocative style recognizably his own."

Reporter on Iwo Jima Learns Why the Cost Was High and Why Victory Will Be Worth It

IWO JIMA, March 8, 1945—Marine tanks squatting on the bleak crest of Mt. Yama are firing pointblank into the pillboxes and caves at the extreme northeast tip of Iwo, where survivors of the Japanese garrison are clinging to a crescent-shaped position three miles long but narrowing to only 450 yards at its center.

Organized resistance has not yet ceased, and not until enemy remnants have been hopelessly broken will Vice Admiral Richmond Kelly Turner consider the island "secure."

The Japanese are clearly unable to launch a counter-offensive. They have lost direct observation of airport No. 1 and appear to have only a few heavy guns still operating. Fighters and transport planes are now landing in complete safety. We watched fighters strafe the last enemy segments, drawing only a dozen bursts of ack-ack fire in return.

Already the southern portion of Iwo is being transformed into a great air base only 750 miles from Tokyo. The main runway on No. 1 Airport has already been lengthened. A B-29 has made a forced landing on the field. Admiral Turner, touring the island, predicted today that Iwo would become "an even better base than we anticipated."

For this desolate heap of volcanic cinders the marines have paid in blood, and more casualties will be counted before the island is secured. But the toll was certainly not exorbitant. Any one visiting this macabre piece of real estate, as treeless and bleak as slagpiles in Pennsylvania coal fields, may well wonder how the marines were able to land at all.

Two weeks ago this correspondent landed with assault troops on Corregidor. Our casualties there were heavy—one out of every five doughboys was killed or injured. Iwo was even nearer impregnable, its garrison, estimated at 20,000 men, being three times greater than that of Corregidor and having far superior fire power. Moreover, Corregidor was manned by Japanese service troops. The Iwo defenders were combat troops under skilled commanders who made very few mistakes.

"The defenses were tremendously better organized than on Saipan," Admiral Turner observed. "They were built over a longer period of time and made excellent use of the terrain."

With Major General Graves B. Erskine, commanding the Third Marine Division, this correspondent covered the terrain won by the marines in 18 days of desperate fighting. From the airport to the shattered Japanese village of Moto Yama, a distance of slightly more than two miles, Erskine's engineers counted 1,200 enemy emplacements on a narrow front.

Emplacements Masked

These emplacements were as cleverly masked as German defenses around Cassino. There were immovable conical pillboxes sunk into the crests of the hills and topped by heavy timber under sheets of concrete. Over this the Japanese heaped stone and dirt and planted grass, so that the marines often could not see the emplacements until they were directly in front of the gun slits.

Commanding the air field were at least five 47-mm. anti-tank guns, so cleverly camouflaged that some marine tanks were knocked out before the guns were even sighted.

In hundreds of holes and caverns the Japanese had stored ammunition and food secure from bombardment. Even surface emplacements could often withstand direct hits, and frequently the Japanese brought their own artillery down on the defenders when pillboxes were in danger of being overrun.

While bombs, naval shells, mortars and rockets were descending on every square yard of Iwo, the Japanese survived by staying underground. They emerged whenever the barrage lifted.

Casualties Unavoidable

The inescapable conclusion is that casualties on Iwo were unavoidable. Surprise was impossible. Here was the crucial key to the inner defenses of the Japanese. With Americans on Saipan, the Japanese could anticipate and nearly time an assault on Iwo.

So 20,000 Japanese were crowded on the tiny island. Defenses begun during the early months of the first World War were improved and strengthened. Guns were trained on every beach. Headquarters and supplies were kept underground.

There was no room for maneuver—no possibility of "end runs" to positions left undefended. Iwo's northern plateau could be taken only by frontal assault across barren lowlands exposed to murderous fire.

We had to have Iwo, and we will have to pay for it. (March 9, 1945)

Japanese Air Strike on Okinawa, April 1945

Japanese Fail in Air Attack on Okinawa Fleet

Lose at Least 150 Planes in Fiasco, Despite the Ideal Target Offered Foe

ARMY CORPS, 24TH HEADQUARTERS, OKINAWA, April 6, 1945—The Japanese launched their heaviest air strike against the 10th Army beachhead today.

In a desperate face-saving effort undoubtedly prompted by the humiliation of their failure to contest seriously the Okinawa landing, the Japanese air force sent dive-bombers toward the island. The heaviest action began at 4 P.M. and raged for three and a half hours.

[The Japanese lost 150 or more planes in the attack, Admiral Chester W. Nimitz reported in his Saturday communiqué, and press-association dispatches said that the tally was up to late Friday afternoon, when it was believed that the battle was continuing. Some American ships were hit but "all remained fully operational," Nimitz said.]

This correspondent, returning from the front, witnessed the start of the battle from a duck [amphibious truck] en route to the flagship of the amphibious force. All unit-command ships flew raid warning signals, but since the beachhead force had been under almost constant alert since early morning we could get aboard and below decks before the attack began.

It was just the sort of day the Japanese choose for raiding. The sky was completely overcast with low dark clouds. Probably the ceiling was under 1,500 feet.

Along the coral reef, landing craft were lined up as tightly as freighters at the docks on the Hudson. Offshore, heavier craft lay at anchor waiting their turn to unload.

For six days the Japanese had watched this great fleet lying unmolested within two hours' bombing time from airports on the Japanese mainland. Many times since Easter morning they had tried to penetrate the screen of Navy fighters, but never with more than a handful of planes at a time—perhaps a dozen at the most. These piddling tactics had cost them 65 planes.

Our duck was jolting across the coral shallows when black smudges of ack-ack bursts appeared on the seaward horizon. Through the murk overhead we heard the faint hum of airplane motors. On the long flat deck of an L.S.T. tied up on our right we saw the gun crews standing ready. All eyes stared upward at the cloud curtain.

It was lanced through so quickly that the machine-gunners barely had time to let loose a burst. In one instance a Zeke [Zero fighter] seemed to slow down as though the pilot was undecided which of the wealth of targets he should choose.

He must have been dazzled by what he saw. At any rate, his momentary indecision was fatal. He crashed into the water 50 yards astern of an infantry landing craft.

End of Another One

His splash had hardly subsided when another Zero dipped from the clouds half a mile down the beach. Leveling off at barely 500 feet above the reef, he approached so slowly that we thought he was a friendly plane. Then at 800 yards the guns on the L.S.T. sent a stream of red tracers into his nose. Instantly dozens of other craft and shore batteries opened fire.

The Zeke was hopelessly trapped. He was now so close that we could see the tracers pierce the flimsy cowling and fuselage. His engine caught fire. For another instant he kept a horizontal course.

Then he veered inland, trying to escape the searing hail of tracers. Flames engulfed the cockpit, the right wing dipped, and the Zeke crashed near a highway a quarter mile inland.

Now Zekes and Vals [dive-bombers] were approaching at intervals from several directions. Some flew low over the Okinawa hills hoping to avoid detection by ship spotters until the pilots were set for the pay-off.

Is Compared With Anzio

But the fleet was ready. The fighter screen tightened on the approaching enemy planes at sea. At brief intervals we could hear dogfights above the clouds, as the Navy Hellcats fought a battle of interception. The powerful shore ack-ack batteries joined the naval guns in spinning cones of flak.

At such a time, however, one feels very naked. This correspondent passed the last two hours of the raid in the wardroom with two steel decks overhead. Five Zeros were brought down uncomfortably near this ship.

This was action more prolonged than the battle off Ormoc Bay last December, when two destroyer-transports were lost and 40 enemy planes were shot down. It compared with the German raids on Anzio shipping during General Eberhard von Mackensen's first counter-offensive.

There is one important difference. The German pilots knew what they were doing. Even the Japanese on Ormoc were more skillful in singling out targets, and attacking four and five at once.

Full reports are not yet available, but from what this correspondent saw, today's action may set a new record in Japanese futility. Here was a tightly massed target of ships right in Japan's backyard. It is 350 miles to Japanese mainland bases and 400 miles to the enemy airdromes on the China coast. Yet today's challenge failed even to disperse the fleet. . . . (April 7, 1945)

Bombing Aomori, July 1945

Center of Aomori Mass of Fire
After B-29's Strike Unopposed

Reporter on 3,700-Mile Flight From the Marianas, Refueling at Iwo; No Ack-ack or Fighter Planes Met With in 425 Miles Over Honshu

GUAM, (Sunday) July 29, 1945—Aomori, the northernmost city of Honshu and the most distant target raided by B-29's from the Marianas, was in the throes of a gigantic fire early this morning when I flew over the city in the last group of raiders.

It was a terrifying sight. Not quite an hour had passed since the first Superfortress dumped its load of fire bombs on Aomori, but already one square mile in the heart of the city was solidly aflame and the main conflagration, spurred on by a 12-mile ground wind, was sweeping east and south to join countless smaller fires on the fringes of town.

We met no opposition on the record 3,700-mile flight. Although we flew 425 miles over Japanese soil not one burst of ack-ack was observed. During the one hour and 43-minute passage of northern Honshu no night fighters arose to molest us. The amazing weakness of the defense set at rest the nervous doubts of the airmen regarding the decision of Maj. Gen. Curtis E. LeMay, 20th Air Force Commander, to give advance warning to enemy cities scheduled for fire treatment. Leaflets had been dropped on Japan listing 11 cities which the bomber command had elected to destroy. Aomori was at the top of the list.

Another innovation in this attack was the employment for the first time of Iwo Jima as a staging base for incendiary raids. The refueling of the raiders during the pause on the way from the Marianas to Aomori proceeded without a hitch. The gasoline consumed by each B-29 on the flight from the Marianas was replenished. Each took off with full tanks for the 3,050-mile flight to the north tip on Honshu and then back to the Marianas.

The Iwo way station also enabled the Superforts to carry their full load of incendiaries. Moreover, it gave the crews a chance to break up a desperately tedious voyage with a few hours' rest.

Now they could reach the remotest parts of the Japanese homeland. Hokkaido with its coal and oil fields was within reach. But for their first target the raiders chose Aomori.

Aomori is a city of 90,000. It is the northern terminus of Honshu's main coastal railways and southern terminus of the rail ferry to Hokkaido. Through important marshaling yards at the southern edge of the city move two million tons of Hokkaido coal each year.

One of the great lumber centers of Japan, Aomori is sprinkled with sawmills and lumber yards. These plus three shipyards building wooden barges and small wooden freighters that carry the bulk of empire shipping have made Aomori the most inflammable city in Japan.

For the Tokyo underwriters Aomori has always been a notoriously bad risk. At least once a generation this sawdust city has been ravaged by conflagration. It has the highest insurance rates in the empire.

Until a few months ago these visitations were accepted as inevitable. Then the government razed hundreds of wooden frame buildings and used the cleared ground as fire breaks. There were three of these running from the bayfront south through the congested business district to the railroad yards, but they were doing precious little good early today.

Our aiming point was the heart of the city—the junction of the main street with the central fire break. Nearly all the built-up area was compressed in a rectangle of slightly more than two square miles. . . . But when we reached Aomori, our pilot, Capt. Wyatt J. Gay of

Milton, West Va., saw quickly that the heart of the city was an unbroken mass of flame. Instantly he altered the course. We skirted the ragged southern fringe of the fire belt and the bombardier, First Lieut. Maurice E. Lescroat of 15 Lefferts Avenue, Brooklyn, salvoed the bomb load on a row of buildings on the edge of the marshaling yard.

Directly ahead towered an enormous pillar of smoke. It rose from the inferno in a turbulent column at least a mile wide, and flattening at the top like a gigantic thunderhead 20,000 feet above Aomori.

. . . It is no use pretending that B-29 raids on smaller empire cities are exceptionally thrilling. Apart from the slight uneasiness that always comes with the landfall on an enemy shore, and another moment of tension when the ship goes into her bomb run, there is seldom anything to alter the brutal monotony of those 1,500-mile missions over water.

A conflagration seen from 14,000 feet has the same fascination as a pile of burning leaves to a small boy. It is of course different for the Japanese. The 500-pound bombs we dropped this morning are designed to break into clusters and fall in a path one-third of a mile long and 150 feet wide. You turn and flee from one swath of fire but a minute later another bomber places his string of incendiaries parallel to the fire and soon there is no escape. . . .

But now there were clouds below us, cutting off all view of land. Then six miles from the target the clouds broke and directly ahead we could see dozens of small fires in the western outskirts of Aomori, and a boiling mass of flame in the center of town.

No ack-ack came from the town but far across Mutsu Bay toward the naval base of Ominato came flashes that might have been gunfire.

Then we headed home. We crossed the mountain lake of Towada and headed for Sendai and the coast. Sixty-five miles away Sergeant Clarke at his tail gun could still see the glow of burning Aomori. It was a beautifully clear night. We picked up the Moscow radio perfectly. (July 29, 1945)

Last U.S. Air Raid, August 1945

This story, widely recognized as the last combat dispatch of World War II, displays the geographic clarity that Bigart brought to all his work.

900 Superforts Deal Japanese a Final Blow

Doolittle's B-29's Based on Okinawa
Barely Squeeze In on the War

Flyers Are Racked by Horrible Anxiety

Reporter on Raid Tells How They Awaited News
That Would Stop Flight

IN A B-29 OVER JAPAN, Wednesday, Aug. 15, 1945—The radio tells us that the war is over, but from where I sit it looks suspiciously like a rumor. A few minutes ago—at 1:32 A.M.—we fire-bombed Kumagaya, a small industrial city behind Tokyo near the northern edge of the Kanto Plain. Peace was not official for the Japanese either, for they shot right back at us.

[This was one of at least 400 B-29's that attacked three targets in

Japan in a raid early Wednesday morning, and part of some 1,000 planes that had attacked the enemy homeland in the 24 hours preceding the cessation of hostilities.]

Isesaki Burning

Other fires are raging at Isesaki, another city on the plain, and as we skirt the eastern base of Fujiyama, Lieut. Col. James Doolittle's B-29's, flying their first mission from the Eighth Air Force base on Okinawa, arrive to put the finishing touches on Kumagaya.

I rode in the City of Saco (Maine), piloted by First Lieut. Theodore J. Lamb, 28, of 103-21 Lefferts Boulevard, Richmond Hill, Queens. Like all the rest, Lamb's crew showed the strain of the last five days of the uneasy "truce" that kept the Superforts grounded.

They had thought the war was over. They had passed most of the time around radios, hoping the President would make it official. They did not see that it made much difference whether Emperor Hirohito stayed in power. Had our propaganda not portrayed him as a puppet? Well then, we could use him just as the war lords had done.

Wing Alerted in Morning

The 314th Bombardment Wing was alerted yesterday morning. At 2:20 P.M. pilots, bombardiers, navigators, radio men and gunners trooped into the briefing shack to learn that the war was still on. Their target was to be a pathetically small city of little obvious importance, and their commanding officer, Col. Carl R. Storrie of Denton, Tex., was at pains to convince them why Kumagaya, with a population of 49,000, had to be burned to the ground.

There were component parts factories of the Nakajima aircraft industry in the town, he said. Moreover, it was an important railway center.

No one wants to die in the closing moments of a war. The wing chaplain, Capt. Benjamin Schmidke of Springfield, Mo., asked the men to pray, and then a group commander jumped on the platform and cried: "This is the last mission. Make it the best we ever ran."

Colonel Storrie was to ride in one of the lead planes, dropping four 1,000-pound high explosives in the hope that the defenders of the town would take cover in buildings or underground and then be trapped by a box pattern of fire bombs to be dumped by 80 planes directly behind.

"We've got 'em on the one-yard line. Let's push the ball over," the colonel exhorted his men. "This should be the final knockout blow of the war. Put your bombs on target so that tomorrow the world will have peace."

Even after they were briefed, most of the crewmen hoped and expected that an official armistice would come before the scheduled 5:50 takeoff. They looked at their watches. Two and a half hours to go.

Morale Stays High

You might expect that the men would be in a sullen, almost mutinous, frame of mind. But morale was surprisingly high.

"Look at the sweat pour off me," cried Maj. William Marchesi of 458 Baltic Street, Brooklyn. "I've never sweated out a mission like this one."

A few minutes earlier the Guam radio had interrupted its program with a flash and quoted the Japanese Domei agency announcement that Emperor Hirohito had accepted the peace terms.

Instantly the whole camp was in an uproar. But then a voice snapped angrily over the "squawk-box": "What are you trying to do? Smash morale? It's only a rumor."

So the crews drew their equipment—parachutes, Mae Wests and flak suits—and got on trucks to go out to the line. We reached the City of Saco at about 4:30 P.M. and there was still nearly an hour to go before our plane, which was to serve as a pathfinder for the raiders, would depart.

We were all very jittery. Radios were blaring in the camp area, but they were half a mile from us and all we could catch were the words "Hirohito" and "Truman." For all we knew, the war was over.

Then a headquarters officer came by and told Lieutenant Lamb that the takeoff had been postponed 30 minutes in expectation of some announcement from Washington.

By that time none of us expected to reach Japan, but we knew that unless confirmation came soon the mission would have to take off, and then very likely salvo its bombs and come home when the signal "Utah, Utah, Utah" came through. That was the code for calling off operations in the event of an announcement of peace by President Truman.

Lamb's crew began turning the plane's props at 5:45 and we got aboard.

"Boy, we're going to kill a lot of fish today," said Sgt. Karl L. Braley of Saco, Maine.

We got San Francisco on the radio. "I hope all you boys out there are as happy as we are at this moment," an announcer was saying. "People are yelling and screaming, and whistles are blowing."

"Yeah," said one of the crewmen disgustedly. "They're screaming and we're flying."

We took off at 6:07.

We saw no white flags when we reached Japanese territory. Back of the cockpit, Radioman Staff Sgt. Rosendo D. del Valle Jr. of El Paso, Tex., strained his ears for the message "Utah, Utah, Utah." If it came in time, it might save a crew or two and perhaps thousands of civilians at Kumagaya.

The message never came. Each hour brought us nearer the enemy coast. We caught every news broadcast, listening to hours of intolerable rot in the hope that the announcer would break in with the news that would send us home.

The empire coast was as dark and repellent as ever. Japan was still at war, and not one light showed in the thickly populated Tokyo Plain.

Lamb's course was due north to the Kasumiga Lake, then a right angle, turning west for little Kumagaya.

It was too late now. There would be bombs on Kumagaya in a few minutes.

Kumagaya is on featureless flats five miles south of the Tone River. It is terribly hard to pick up by radar. There were only two cues to

Kumagaya. Directly north of the town was a wide span across the Tone, and a quarter of a mile south of it was a long bridge across the Ara River.

The radar observer, Lieut. Harold W. Zeisler of Kankakee, Ill., picked up both bridges in good time and we started the bomb run.

An undercast hid the city almost completely, but through occasional rifts I could see a few small fires catching on from the bombs dropped by the two preceding pathfinders.

The Japanese were alert. Searchlights hit the clouds beneath us and two ack-ack guns sent up weak sporadic fire.

Thirty miles to the north we saw Japanese searchlights and ack-ack groping for the bombers of another wing attacking Isesaki.

Leaving our target to the mercy of the 80 Superforts following us, we swerved sharply southward along the eastern base of Fujiyama and reached the sea. At one point we were within 10 miles of Tokyo. The capital was dark.

Everyone relaxed. We tried to pick up San Francisco on the radio, but couldn't. The gunners took out photos of their wives and girl friends and said: "Hope this was the last, baby."

This postscript is written on Guam. It was the last raid of the war. We did not know it until we landed at North Field.

The results of the raid we learned from the pilots who followed us over the target. General conflagrations were devouring both Kumagaya and Isesaki. Japan's tardiness in replying to the peace terms cost her two cities. (Aug. 15, 1945)

Over Nagasaki, August 1945

Air View of What Was Nagasaki: People Plod Across a Vast Ruin

Reporters Make First Unarmed Flight Across Japan Since Fighting Stopped; Rations Dropped to U.S. Prisoners of War, Lined Up in V Formation

IN A B-17 OVER JAPAN, Aug. 27, 1945—Two stripped-down Flying Fortresses filled with correspondents took off from Okinawa at dawn today in the first unarmed flight over Japan since the cessation of hostilities. Following is a running account of the flight, which we hope will carry us over Nagasaki and Hiroshima, the two cities struck by atomic bombs.

We also hope that our plane will develop some slight engine trouble or perhaps run low on fuel so that Capt. Mark Magnan of Wauwatosa, Wis., the pilot, will have to put down on empire soil and give us the first dateline from Japan. For although pilots have already landed in Kyushu, reporters are forbidden to join the reconnaissance party that will set out for Atsugi airfield soon, and it was not until today that the press had permission to fly over the home islands. Since no planes may fly over Tokyo, we decided on Nagasaki and Hiroshima.

We took off in perfect weather, Captain Magnan setting his course due north for Kyushu. We passed the last friendly island of Ihiya at 7 A.M. and then skirted the west coast of Amani, which is held by a strong Japanese garrison.

We have just passed Amani and are running into mucky weather. That worries us, for we hoped that the typhoon which has been battering western Japan for the last few days would have cleared Kyushu by now.

Still it's not soupy enough to turn us back, providing Magnan will take us in below the clouds. Right now we are flying at 400 feet with about two miles of visibility during squalls.

Our landfall is Cape Nomo. Its mountains glide into view through a gray mist. Below, the East China Sea is riotous with the dying gasps of the typhoon. We are bucking strong headwinds. Then suddenly the sea is becalmed and we are now in the leeward of the Goto Islands, which are hidden by mist.

Now we seem to be entering Nagasaki Harbor. The narrowing roadstead is dotted with fishing boats. We see people on their decks. They are waving but they aren't throwing any ack-ack.

A crewman comes back and tells us it isn't Nagasaki Harbor, but one of the innumerable indentations along the west coast. Quite frankly, we are lost.

Anyhow, it's Japan—there can be no doubt about it. The country-side is green and lovely, and the lower slopes of the forested hills crowding the coast are cleared and terraced for rice paddies.

[*Tribune* editor's note: A section of Mr. Bigart's dispatch is missing at this point.]

Nagasaki a Ghastly Ruin

So far there has been no evidence of the scars of war, but as we approach Nagasaki, a city once a great steel and shipbuilding center, we see a ghastly ruin.

At the industrial north end of the city was a congested district surrounding the sprawling Mitsubishi steel and armor works, stretching for a half a mile along a river bank. Little remained but twisted frames of foundries, and ships.

The tremendous heat of the blast had scorched trees and blackened buildings for at least a mile from what appeared to be the center of impact. In the heart of the blasted area everything appears pulverized—there is no trace of walls or rubble.

A broad thoroughfare has been cleared through the devastation, and along it we see crowds moving afoot. Although we make more than a score of runs over Nagasaki, we do not see a single motor vehicle. Streetcars are running, however, in the main part of town.

You would think that with the frightening bombing of three weeks ago still fresh in their minds the Japanese would fall into panic when a bomber buzzed their town. But the crowds don't even look up. . . .

To this correspondent the devastation appears even more appalling than the reconnaissance photographs indicated. The complete and utter erasure of a city cannot be easily grasped by studying a picture. The gigantic force of the atomic bomb can hardly be described because it is so much more fearful than familiar agents of destruction such as floods, cyclones and fires.

At first glance the site of Nagasaki looked as though it had been swept clean by a great flood that deposited red clay silt in its wake. But there is no debris except on the fringe of the ruined area, where the force of the blast was weaker. In the impact zone the ground is picked clean.

Drop Rations for Prisoners

As we turn to leave Nagasaki we see near the harbor mouth a prisoner-of-war camp. We are flying down the bay at a few hundred feet, scaring harbor craft, when someone yells and points to an ugly stone barracks surrounded by a high wire fence. In the yard, lined up in a symbolic V formation, are several hundred prisoners. And on the ground in front of them lies an American flag.

They are waving wildly at us as Captain Magnan brings his plane sharply about and we go back to drop rations. The first box falls into the bay, and when we come back again we see the prisoners swimming out for it.

The second and third boxes fall outside the prison gates, but on the fourth try Technical Sgt. Jack K. Goetz of Fayetteville, Pa., and Staff Sgt. George A. Kilazer of Richardton, N.D., find the range.

Two boxes fall right into the yard. We make a final pass over the prison, and, after waving at the crowd now gathered along the quay, head back to Okinawa. We saw no Japanese guards around the prison and at last glance the prisoners had procured a boat and were fishing for the missing package. (Aug. 28, 1945)

Surrender, September 1945

Japan Signs,
Second World
War Is Ended

Shigemitsu and Umezu
Represent Hirohito at
Tokyo Bay Ceremonies

MacArthur Hopes
For 'Better World'

He Uses Five Pens, Gives
Wainright One, and
Percival, Briton, One

ABOARD *U.S.S. MISSOURI*, TOKYO BAY, Sunday, Sept. 2, 1945—Japan, paying for her desperate throw of the dice at Pearl Harbor, passed from the ranks of the major powers at 9:05 A.M. today when Foreign Minister Mamoru Shigemitsu signed the documents of unconditional surrender.

If memories of the bestialities of the Japanese prison camps were not so fresh in mind, one might have felt sorry for Shigemitsu as he hobbled on his wooden leg toward the green baize-covered table where the papers lay waiting.

He leaned heavily on his cane and had difficulty seating himself. The cane, which rested against the table, dropped to the deck of the battleship as he signed.

No word passed between him and Gen. Douglas MacArthur, who motioned curtly to the table when he had finished his opening remarks.

Lieut. Gen. Jonathan M. Wainwright, who surrendered Corregidor, haggard from his long imprisonment, and Lieut. Gen. A.E. Percival, who surrendered Singapore on another black day of the war, stood at MacArthur's side as the Allied Supreme Commander signed for all the powers warring against Japan.

Their presence was a sobering reminder of how desperately close to defeat our nation had fallen during the early months of 1942.

The Japanese delegation of 11 looked appropriately trim and sad. Shigemitsu was wearing morning clothes—frock coat, striped pants, silk hat and yellow gloves. None of the party exchanged a single word or salute while on board, except for the foreign minister's aide, who had to be shown where to place the Japanese texts of the surrender documents.

Shigemitsu, however, doffed his silk hat as he reached the top of the starboard gangway and stepped aboard the broad deck of the *Missouri*. (Sept. 2, 1945)

In Hiroshima, September 1945

A Month After the Atom Bomb: Hiroshima Still Can't Believe It

The City Didn't Even Know It Was Being Raided; 100 a Day Dying, Figures Hint 100,000 Total; Correspondent Tours Ruins, Describes Scene

HIROSHIMA, JAPAN, Sept. 3, 1945—We walked today through Hiroshima, where survivors of the first atomic-bomb explosion four weeks ago are still dying at the rate of about 100 daily from burns and infections which the Japanese doctors seem unable to cure.

The toll from the most terrible weapon ever devised now stands at 53,000 counted dead, 30,000 missing and presumed dead, 13,960 severely wounded and likely to die, and 43,000 wounded. The figures come from Hirokuni Dadai, who, as "chief of thought control" of the Hiroshima Prefecture, is supposed to police subversive thinking.

On the morning of Aug. 6, the 340,000 inhabitants of Hiroshima were awakened by the familiar howl of air-raid sirens. The city had never been bombed—it had little industrial importance. The Kure naval base lay only 12 miles to the southeast and American bombers had often gone there to blast the remnants of the imperial navy, or had flown mine-laying or strafing missions over Shimonoseki Strait to the west. Almost daily enemy planes had flown over Hiroshima, but so far the city had been spared.

At 8 A.M. the "all clear" sounded. Crowds emerged from the shallow raid shelters in Military Park and hurried to their jobs in the score of tall, modern, earthquake-proof buildings along Hattchobori, the main business street of the city. Breakfast fires still smoldered, in thousands of ovens—presently they were to help to kindle a conflagration.

Very few persons saw the Superfortress when it first appeared more than five miles above the city. Some thought they saw a black object swinging down on a parachute from the plane, but for the most part Hiroshima never knew what hit it.

A Japanese naval officer, Vice Adm. Masao Kanazawa, at the Kure base, said the concussion from the blast 12 miles away was "like the great wind that made the trees sway." His aide, a senior lieutenant who was to accompany us into the city, volunteered that the flash was so bright even in Kure that he was awakened from his sleep. So loud was the explosion that many thought the bomb had landed within Kure.

When Lieut. Taira Ake, a naval surgeon, reached the city at 2:30 P.M., he found hundreds of wounded still dying unattended in the wrecks and fields on the northern edge of the city. "They didn't look like human beings," he said. "The flesh was burned from their faces and hands, and many were blinded and deaf."

Dadai was standing in the doorway of his house nearly two miles from the center of impact. He had just returned from Tokyo.

"The first thing I saw was brilliant flash," he said. "Then after a second or two came a shock like an earthquake. I knew immediately it was a new type of bomb. The house capsized on top of us and I was hit with falling timbers."

Many Buried in Debris

"I found my wife lying unconscious in the debris, and I dragged her to safety. My two children suffered cuts, and for the next hour or so I was too busy to think of what was happening in the city."

Doctors rushed from the Kure naval base—including Lieutenant Ake—were prevented from entering the city until six hours after the blast because of the searing heat of the explosion. City officials said that many indoors who were buried under collapsing walls and roofs subsequently were burned to death in the fires that broke out within a few minutes after the blast.

The first impression in the minds of the survivors was that a great fleet of Superfortresses flying at great height had somehow sneaked past the defenses and dropped thousands of fire bombs. Even today there are many who refuse to believe that a single bomb wiped out the city.

A party of newspaper men led by Col. John McCrary was the first group of Americans to reach Hiroshima. We flew in today in a B-17, our pilot, Capt. Mark Magnan, finding a hole in the clouds over Kure and setting the plane down on the tiny runway of the naval air base there with about 70 feet to spare.

The admiral in charge of the base, after telling us what he had seen and knew of the bombing, gave us two sedans and a truck and we drove down a mountain through ruined Kure and past the navy yard. A tall fence set up along the road to block the view of the yard had been removed, and we could see 10 destroyers, two submarines and some gunboats anchored in the harbor.

Haruna Seen Beached

Across the bay, beached on an island and listing to port so that the waves broke over her deck, was the battleship *Haruna*. Farther on we passed close to another beached warship, an old three-stacker that flaunted the silhouettes of 10 American planes on her mid-stack. A four-engine bomber was among the planes the destroyer claimed to have shot down. . . .

Three miles outside Hiroshima we saw the first signs of blast damage—loose tiles torn from roofs and an occasional broken window. At the edge of town there were houses with roofs blown off, while the walls facing the center of the city had caved inward.

Finally we came to the river and saw the Island of Hiro, which holds, or rather held, the main districts of Hiroshima, which means "Hiro Island."

In the part of town east of the river, the destruction looked no different from a typical bomb-torn city in Europe. Many buildings were only partly demolished, and the streets were still choked with debris.

Reporters Tour Ruins

But across the river there was only flat, appalling desolation, the starkness accentuated by bare, blackened tree trunks and the occasional shell of a reinforced concrete building.

We drove to Military Park and made a walking tour of the ruins.

By all accounts the bomb seemed to have exploded directly over Military Park. We saw no crater there. Apparently the full force of the explosion was expended laterally.

Aerial photographs had shown no evidence of rubble, leading to the belief that everything in the immediate area had been literally pulverized into dust. But on the ground we saw this was not true. There was rubble everywhere, but much smaller in size than normal.

Approaching the Hattchobori, we passed what had been a block of small shops. We could tell that only because of office safes that lay at regular intervals on sites that retained little else except small bits of iron and tin. Sometimes the safes were blown in.

The steel door of a huge vault in the four-story Geibi Bank was flung open and the management had installed a temporary padlocked door. All three banking houses—Geibi, Mitsubishi and the Bank of Japan—were conducting business in the sturdy concrete building of the Bank of Japan, which was less damaged than the rest.

Since the bank and the police station were the only buildings open for business, we asked our naval lieutenant guide if we could enter. He disappeared and was gone for several minutes.

Populace Is Curious

We stood uneasily at the corner of the bank building, feeling very much like a youth walking down Main Street in his first long pants. There weren't many people abroad—a thin trickle of shabbily dressed men and women—but all of them stared at us.

There was hatred in some glances, but generally more curiosity than hatred. We were representatives of an enemy power that had employed a weapon far more terrible and deadly than poison gas, yet in the four hours we spent in Hiroshima none so much as spat at us, nor threw a stone.

We later asked the naval lieutenant, who once lived in Sacramento, to halt some pedestrians and obtain eyewitness accounts of the blast. He was very reluctant to do so.

"They may not want to talk to you," he said. But finally he stopped an old man, who bared his gold teeth in an apparent gesture of friendship.

"I am a Christian," said the old man, making the sign of the cross. He pointed to his ears, indicating deafness, and the lieutenant, after futile attempts to make him hear, told us that the old man, like many others, apparently had suffered permanent loss of his hearing when the crashing blast of the atomic bomb shattered his eardrums.

The lieutenant stopped a few more middle-aged civilians, but they backed off, bowing and grinning. They said they were not in Hiroshima on Aug. 6.

Boys Help Clean Up

Two boys walking barefoot through the rubble displayed no fear of infection, although no doctor could say positively that the danger had ended. The boys said they had been brought in from the countryside to help clean up the city.

The cloying stench of death was still very noticeable in the street, and we were glad when the lieutenant finally motioned us inside the bank.

Except for broken windows and chipped cornices, the Bank of Japan presented an intact facade outside. Inside, however, we saw that the concussion had smashed the frail stalls and reduced the furnishings to matchwood. Under the lofty vaulted roof spaces had been roped off, and skeleton staffs of the three banking institutions sat behind crude wooden tables handing the government's new yen currency to waiting lines.

Several persons showed bad burns about their necks and faces, and nearly half the population seemed to be wearing gauze bandages over noses and mouths to protect them from germs.

Those who entered Hiroshima and stayed only a few hours appeared to suffer no ill effects, doctors said, but many who attempted to live in the ruins developed infections that reacted on the blood cells as destructively as leukemia, except that the white blood corpuscles and not the red were consumed. Victims became completely bald; they lost all appetite, they vomited blood.

A few of the main streets of Hiroshima have been cleared. Trolleys ran through the blighted areas down to the waterfront. But the public is forbidden to drink from wells, and water has to be brought in from the countryside.

Records All Destroyed

Down one street was the ruined wall of a Christian church, and near it the site of the Japanese Second Army headquarters. Hiroshima was an embarkation point for the invasion which threatened Kyushu, and the city had been filled with soldiers when the bomb fell. How many of them perished no one yet knows, for all records were destroyed by the fire. Among the army staff members killed was the chief of military police.

The city and the prefectural (provincial) government had moved to a motorcycle plant in the outskirts of town and there we met Dadai. He was introduced at first as "a high government official," but later admitted he was Chief of Thought Control.

Dadai's appearance fitted his role. He looked like a man who could not only suppress a thought but could torture it. He wore a white bandage across his brow, tied in back of his head, and the face beneath it was sallow and repressive. His tight, grim mouth hardly opened as he answered questions put to him through the naval interpreter.

He told us that the wounded were doomed by the disintegrating effects of the uranium on the white blood corpuscles. This statement, however, was not substantiated by doctors, who said they knew so little about the strange disorders that it was useless to speculate on how high the death toll would run. They cited the case of the woman who suffered only a slight cut in the explosion, yet died 18 days later.

Neither Dadai nor local correspondents seemed to believe that the atomic bomb would end war. One of the first questions asked by Japanese newspaper men was: "What effect will the bomb have on future wars?" They also asked whether Hiroshima "would be dangerous for 70 years." We told them we didn't know. (Sept. 5, 1945)

Cold War, Hot War

Mistrust in Warsaw, June 1946

After Japan, the *Trib* gave Bigart a roving assignment in Europe: Germany in early 1946, Czechoslovakia, and then Poland, where he filed this often-quoted dispatch.

U.S. Reporters in Poland Face
Rising Distrust of Red Regime

WARSAW, June 16, 1946—Jacob Berman, Communist Under Secretary in the office of the Polish Premier and an official whose influence far overshadows that of Premier Edward Osubka-Morawski, a Socialist, believes that the present impasse in relations between Poland and America—arising from the State Department's recent suspension of a credit for Poland—was caused primarily by "excitable dispatches" sent by foreign correspondents at Warsaw.

The dispatches, he says, were two-thirds fantasy and never would have been sent had the correspondents taken the trouble to consult government spokesmen.

Meanwhile, the government-controlled press faithfully follows orders to "furiously attack" American and British correspondents whose reports are objectionable to the government, and there has been no moderation of the strongly anti-American tone recently adopted by Communist and Socialist newspapers in this country.

Berman says he wants "objective" reporting. It is too easy to retort that the Communist newspaper *Glos Ludu* and Socialist *Robotnik* scarcely can be considered models of fairness. Anyhow, it is futile to talk of objectivity in a country where nerves are frayed and tempers exacerbated by political controversy verging closely on civil war.

A reporter cannot stay two weeks in the poisoned atmosphere of Warsaw without developing a bias which, perhaps unconsciously, is bound to color his reports, and there is no correspondent in Poland today who hasn't in his heart aligned himself with either the communist-dominated government or the now open opposition of Vice-Premier Stanislaw Mikolajczyk's Polish Peasant party.

It is important that the reader remember this, for although the reporter is obliged to "give both sides"—few newspapers would keep him very long if he didn't—his bias creeps in. Sometimes it's in the clever stressing of one side's arguments over the arguments of the other. Or perhaps in the sly omission of a damaging fact. Anyhow it's there, and it's to the credit of Berman's intelligence that when he speaks of objectivity he grins.

Most correspondents who go to Warsaw are, like the present writer, somewhere left of center. They are willing to concede that Poland lies well within the security sphere of Russia and that Moscow has every right to demand of Warsaw a government it can trust. If Poland wants Communism, that is no business of ours.

You would think, therefore, that we would be embraced by government propagandists with glad cries of "Comrade, you're our meat!" Instead we encounter distrust and suspicion at every turn. The slightest deviation from the government line draws a stream of abuse in which "liar" is the mildest epithet. And any correspondent who hopes to wangle a room in government-managed hotels had better shun Mikolajczyk.

The correspondent's initiation came when he presented his passport to General Grosz, director of press information at the Foreign Ministry. "Ah, yes," said the general grimly, "your paper is very unfriendly to us." He produced a clipping and began reading aloud. "But that's an editorial from *The Washington Star*," I interrupted. "Makes no difference," said Grosz. "I know you've said bad things about us."

For the first week or two a correspondent somehow manages to write nothing bad about anybody except Ukrainian bandits, which is quite safe, since none of the Poles likes them anyway. You can also do a piece about the United Nations Relief and Rehabilitation Administration and the Polish famine—provided you shut your eyes to the government's inequitable system of food distribution. But from there on you run into trouble because everything else is political.

You cannot lift a story from the Warsaw newspapers, because not one of them can be trusted. You cannot completely trust your sources, because no matter how well informed they may be you can be sure they are telling you what they think the Western world should hear.

It takes days to confirm anything and, meanwhile, there is the dreadful temptation to send it off and the hell with it. Apparently anything can happen in Poland and even the most lurid tales have a plausible ring. Moreover, if the story is anti-government, it will be blandly denied by the government, no matter how true it is.

You find yourself running back and forth between government and opposition, accumulating all the while a great stack of accusations and denials. There is no middle ground, no impartial witness. Battle lines are drawn and everyone has chosen his side. It is a war over the definition of democracy—East versus West—and because you are conditioned to Western concepts you find yourself drawn irrevocably toward Mikolajczyk.

You do it with misgivings, fully aware that into Mikolajczyk's ranks have crept counter-revolutionary forces that undoubtedly include anti-Semites and Fascists—the kind that sing, "One more atomic bomb and Lwow will again be ours," in the cafes of Krakow. They are, happily, a small minority of no more importance than the lunatic fringes in the Republican and Democratic parties back home.

Mikolajczyk knows that a crusade against Soviet Russia will bring nothing but final ruin to Poland. He believes that a firm alliance with Russia must be the basis of Poland's policy. What he wants is a broadly based government in which his party, now completely shorn of power by the small but powerful Communist-Socialist coalition, shall have a voice. He wants a free election as promised by the Allied powers at Yalta. He believes he can form a government acceptable to Stalin which is still not a police government and no more repressive than the government of Czechoslovakia.

Having gotten this off his chest, the present writer will now go on with the Berman interview. . . . (June 17, 1946)

British Take Jews off Schooner, February 1947

––––––

At the beginning of 1947, the *Tribune* foreign desk set up a plan to train foreign correspondents as specialists in "ideas rather than areas." Under this scheme, Bigart, who knew no foreign languages and never learned any, was the "trouble" specialist. This quickly got Bigart to Palestine, still governed by the British under a mandate given by the League of Nations in 1920. Immigration of Jews was limited by the British to two thousand a month; others were being turned back or shipped to Cyprus. The establishment of the State of Israel was still more than a year off, but war was already under way.

650 Jews Taken
From Schooner
In Haifa Harbor

––––––

Immigrants Resist British
Troops, Then Are Held
for Deportation to Cyprus

HAIFA, Feb. 9, 1947—Six hundred and fifty Jewish immigrants from eastern Europe reached Palestine tonight aboard a tiny two-masted Italian schooner, rechristened *Negev* (a semidesert in the south country of Palestine), and were hustled immediately aboard a British troop ship for internment in Cyprus. Some disembarked peacefully but others fought, screamed and clung to railings until they were beaten and dragged down the gangplank.

The schooner, sighted last night, was trailed by three British gunboats until, well outside the three-mile limit, she was boarded by 100 sailors. The decks showed signs of fighting when she crept into Haifa harbor at 8 o'clock tonight. Windows were smashed, a Jew with a broken neck was lying on a stretcher on the deck, and other immigrants showed cracked heads and bruises.

The boarding of the Italian-registered vessel outside the three-mile limit was not a violation of international law, since Great Britain has not yet signed a peace treaty with Italy. On the stern of the *Negev* was visible the name Merica, Naples.

The schooner tied up at the end of a long quay raked by searchlights and with two light tanks standing by. The sailors apparently had the immigrants in hand, for all were herded below the deck and two gangplanks from the deck were placed in position without opposition.

Two parties of Red Devils, husky troopers from the British Sixth Airborne Division, rushed aboard simultaneously, each trooper armed with a pick handle. The commander of the Sixth Division Artillery called to the immigrants through a loudspeaker: "We have a strong military force ready. We don't want to use it."

Extraordinary security precautions had been taken. The port area was hermetically sealed. A sundown curfew closed on Kingsway and the main commercial districts. Atop Mount Carmel, Jewish groups were holding protest meetings. Troops guarding the perimeter at the base of the mountain were told in case of attack to fire first over the heads of the demonstrators before aiming.

A spraying shed was erected near the end of the pier between the illegal ship and transport and immigrants walked or were dragged between lines of troops shoulder to shoulder.

The first batch of immigrants debarked peacefully. Then shrieks of hysterical women touched off violence. Suddenly the immigrants began resisting. They clung to cables and rails until the troopers lost patience.

White-faced, haggard, hysterical, bruised, the immigrants emerged from the hold. Some were cowed; others defiantly sang the Jewish national anthem. A thin red-headed youth in shorts was bleeding copiously from a scalp wound. Floodlights caught him as he came into view in the narrow companionway behind the deckhouse. He hesitated, blinking in the strong light like a backstage intruder who suddenly finds himself in front of the curtain. "Get on with you," yelled a trooper standing on the hatch above. He reached down and gave the youth a whack with a pick handle.

Next came a sturdy, broad-figured young woman who spat in the face of a trooper. "Give her a kick, lad," roared his captain.

After each was sprayed with D.D.T. powder, the immigrants boarded the transport *Empire Heywood* for deportation to Cyprus.

To most of the troopers the job tonight was a sickening one. But it should be emphasized that this was no army atrocity. The troops simply carried out orders from the London government. (Feb. 10, 1947)

Jewish Underground Recruits, May 1947

The Jewish Underground: Reporter Sees 50 Sworn In

Homer Bigart Taken Blindfolded to Hide-Out of Haganah in Jerusalem Cellar, Is First Foreign Correspondent to View Organization's Ritual

JERUSALEM, May 16, 1947—In a deep, thick-walled cellar in Jerusalem I watched last night the clandestine induction of 50 Jewish youths into the Haganah, the Jewish defense force which is the democratic militia of the coming Jewish state. For the first time this secret ritual, wherein Jews pledge lifetime loyalty to the struggle for the freedom of Zion, was revealed to a foreign correspondent.

By prearrangement, I met two members of the Haganah at a busy intersection near Zion Circle during an hour when the neighborhood was thronged with theater crowds, so that the rendezvous would pass unnoticed by British patrols. We walked to an automobile parked in a side street. Another Haganah youth joined us. I was placed in a rear seat between two escorts and was handed a pair of sunglasses, taped on the inside and equipped with earpieces wide enough to shut out side vision. A voice said, "Keep them on till we get there."

The Blind Ride

We drove about 20 minutes, halting once for traffic and again to pick up a fourth Haganah member. I know Jerusalem pretty well, but we turned so many corners I quickly lost all sense of direction. "You may take notes of the ceremony," said one escort, "but you must not speak to any inductees or officers."

I had a feeling we were still in Jerusalem when the automobile stopped and I was led, still blind, across a few yards of uneven pavement. I heard a door open, and we stepped across the threshold. "You may take the glasses off now," a voice said.

We were standing in a hallway so dark the escort was forced to pause a few moments until eyes became adjusted to the gloom. "Let's go," said a voice, "steps going down." With groping feet, we descended a curving stairway. At the bottom was a long corridor, equally black. At the far end a door opened suddenly, emitting a faint light. We hurried toward it and, brushing past two sentries, entered the ritual room.

A Girl Officer

It was a little disappointing. I know enough about Haganah not to expect a lot of nationalistic trappings and flummery, but I was not quite prepared for a stark, whitewashed hall that seemed at first glance to have nothing in it except a long table covered with a black cloth. As we entered two noncommissioned officers, one a girl of about 18, snapped to attention and took up positions at either end of the table.

The room was faintly illuminated by a spotlight dimmed with heavy paper. Two candles flickered through an aperture in the canvas partition that screened the rear end of the hall. It was a lofty room. High on the far end were three windows, darkened to prevent light escaping, and a small door, heavily barred and reached by steep wooden steps. In a whispered explanation, the escort said the door was designed for a quick getaway of the arms used in the ceremony.

Pinned to a canvas screen at each end was a map of Eretz Israel (Land of Israel) showing both Palestine and Trans-Jordan. Behind the screen, midway up the rear wall, was the slogan, "One hand on the plow, and the other on the sword."

The room was deathly still. From the hall outside came the muffled sound of footsteps. The door opened to admit a color guard, holding aloft the flag of Zion, blue and white with the Star of David. Then the commander entered. He was tall, dark, gray-featured and wore no insignia of rank, being clad like the rest in a khaki shirt and shorts, with a black leather pistol belt and black shoes. He was described to me as the leader of about 400 youths, equivalent to a battalion, and about 28 years old, of German-Jewish descent.

The color guard took a position behind the table, while the commander stood reserved and unsmiling to the left of it. He was a member of the Orthodox community and wore on his head a black yarmulke, or skullcap.

Groups of 10 Inducted

There were 50 youths to be sworn in—all of them Orthodox lads of 16. They were inducted in groups of 10. In tense silence the first group entered in single file, executed a smart right face and stood at attention, facing the table four paces in front of them, their eyes fixed on objects bulging beneath the black cloth.

At a command the cloth was whipped back, disclosing the table. It was spread with a silk flag of Zion, and in the center was a large open Bible with a Mauser lying beside it. At the edge of the table were 10 small Bibles, and to the left of each a revolver. On either side of the big Bible were two pictures—one of Theodor Herzl, founder of political Zionism, and the other of Joseph Trumpeldor, an early Haganah hero, killed defending the Upper Galilee settlement of Tel Hai in the Arab uprising of 1921.

An N.C.O. marched up to the commander and read the names of the new group and the names of the cadets. At command the cadets, one by one, marched four paces to the table and stood stiffly in front of the Bibles and revolvers, their eyes watching the two candles.

Reads from Deuteronomy

From behind the screen a deep voice intoned in Hebrew passages from the "war chapter" of Deuteronomy. Later I learned he read Verses 1 to 5 and 8 to 10, Chapter xx, the passages referring to courage.

"When thou goest out to battle against thine enemies," the voice said, "and seest horses, and chariots, and a people more than thou, be not afraid of them: for the Lord thy God is with thee, which brought thee up out of the land of Egypt."

The reading ended and the commander spoke: "He who is afraid should return to his home now."

None of the cadets moved.

For American readers, who might be shocked at the youth of these recruits, it should be explained that Palestine is a country where the art of squeezing a trigger must be learned early. Without possession of illegal arms—and the knowledge of how to use them—many hundreds of additional Jews would have perished in remote settlements during the prewar Arab uprisings.

Repeat the Oath

At another command the cadets placed their right hands on the Bible and pistol and repeated, sentence by sentence, the words of the Haganah oath read by the commander:

"I hereby declare," they chorused, "that of my own personal will and free conscience I enter the Jewish defense organization of Eretz

Israel. I hereby solemnly swear to be faithful throughout my life to the defense organization and its laws and its commanders, as defined in its code by highest command.

"I swear to be throughout my life at the disposal of the defense organization, to accept without condition and without exception all commands and at its call to enlist in active service any time, at any place, and to fulfill all its orders and instructions.

"I swear to dedicate all my strength and also give my life for defense and for war on behalf of my people and my country, in order to achieve freedom of Israel and freedom of Zion."

Haganah Declaration

There was a moment of silence. Then the noncommissioned officers, who had held their pistols at ready position during the oath, returned their weapons to their belts. From behind the screen the voice spoke again, reading the Haganah declaration:

"On this day of oath, when you are joining the great family of members of the defense organization, lift your eyes and gaze; from behind all screens of daily secrecy, innocence and bravery, lift your eyes and see.

"Wherever Jewish courage was needed from the very beginnings of Zionism, there stood and fell the men of Hashomer—fathers of Haganah—and defenders in the disturbances of 1921, '29, '36, members of Palmach and other units of the organization in the struggle of 1946 for immigration and in war.

"You will see them, standing on guard everywhere and ceaselessly, throughout the country and on its frontiers and abroad, for they are brothers in the family of Haganah. You will find them in endless peril on the seas. They are bringing home the remnants (of European Jewry) without a backward step. Through suffering and death they labor, for they are brothers in the family of Haganah.

"On all fronts do they fight—the fight of a nation for the return of remnants, their resettlement and their freedom. In the uniforms of soldiers and sailors, with or without uniforms, and in the uniform of Haganah, do they fight. For their hearts know only one command—the command of the defense organization.

"It is they that you are joining—fighters and prisoners and those who are falling bravely—for the whole of your life. Your compensation is the hope of freedom and the brotherhood of Haganah."

That was all. The cadets, wide-eyed and rigid during the 15-minute ritual, relaxed. They had taken an irrevocable step, one that might lead to their death in the Galilean hills or on the beaches of Sharon. But they felt a wave of relief now that the decision was beyond recall. They trooped from the room behind the color guard and their new commander.

Return to Hotel

I was ordered to put on the blinkers again, and was led down the corridor and up the curving stairs into the cool night air. Twenty minutes later the escort dropped me at the Eden Hotel.

During the ride back I was told that the cadets already had had six months of drills, marches and indoctrination. Tonight was the first time they had seen a gun displayed, and tomorrow their training would begin in earnest, with basic armed training followed by fight maneuvers.

At the end of a year or 18 months, they may be assigned to Palmach (Haganah's striking force, reportedly 5,000 strong) for two years' active duty, or with medical or signal units.

It is no secret that Haganah is well armed and numbers tens of thousands. It has been in existence in one form or another for half a century. It had its origin in the defense groups that protected Jewish lives and property in the late 1870's and in the Hashomer (Jewish watchmen), founded in 1907.

Haganah, of course, has no artillery, no field pieces, no antiaircraft weapons, no planes, no tanks and it would be hard-pressed if the Arab states were to carry out their threat and launch a war against their coming state.

That is why Jews hear with such uneasiness current rumor that Syria and Iraq, the two most fanatic anti-Jewish states of the Middle East, are seeking arms from the United States. (May 17, 1947)

Britons Hanged by Jewish Terrorists, July 1947

---

2 Britons Found Hanged; Troops Kill 5 Jews in a Fury

Armored Cars Fire on Bus; Booby-Trapping of Bodies Shocks Palestine

NATHANYA, PALESTINE, July 31, 1947—The blackened bodies of two British sergeants, Clifford Martin and Mervin Paice, kidnaped by the Irgun Zvai Leumi, were found today hanging from twin eucalyptus trees here, and tonight groups of British troops and police, inflamed by the news, killed several Jews and injured others in anti-Jewish demonstrations.

Five Jews were killed and 16 injured when British armored cars opened fire on a crowded bus in the heart of Tel Aviv.

The bus, jammed with about 40 persons, was moving along Levinsky Street in the commercial center of Tel Aviv when witnesses saw four armored cars approaching. A burst of machine-gun fire raked the bus.

One of the bodies of the sergeants had been booby-trapped by the Irgun, and when it fell to the ground it set off a mine which destroyed most of the body and slightly injured a British captain, D.H. Galatti, who cut the body down. The captain suffered face and shoulder wounds, described as not serious.

The booby-trapping of the body evoked in all onlookers—British and Jewish—an emotion of cold fury.

From the decomposed condition of the bodies it was apparent that the Irgun had carried out its threat Tuesday evening and hanged the two sergeants in reprisal for the executing the same day of three Irgunists condemned by a British military court for participating in the attack on Acra Prison May 4.

A police statement on the anti-Jewish demonstrations, issued at Tel Aviv, mentioned two dead in the bus which was machine-gunned but said three persons were killed in a cafe in the Hatikva quarter when an armored patrol allegedly opened fire on a cafe and threw a bomb into it.

A woman and a 14-year-old boy were killed in the bus, and an 8-year-old boy and several women were among the seriously injured. . . .

When news of the hangings reached Nathanya, panic seized the Yemenite quarter, Bnai Zion, where Oriental Jews feared an outbreak of violence by troops in near-by camps. Hastily gathering their belongings, families fled to the center of the town, where they tried to board buses and taxis for interior settlements. Many took off across fields. Finally, Mayor Ovid Ben Ami issued a proclamation urging public calm.

The discovery of the two sergeants was made at 6:30 A.M. by a Jewish settlement policeman named Friedman, who with a party of Haganah youths had resumed at dawn a search of the woods where Irgun had said the bodies would be found. The same wood had been searched yesterday with no result by a party of Grenadier Guards, but Mayor Ben Ami, unconvinced, asked the settlement police and Haganah, the Jewish defense force, to continue searching the vicinity.

Arabs Tell of Jeeps

The wood lies about a mile off the main road to Tel Aviv in rolling sand-dune country. It has been planted with eucalyptus saplings by the government reforestation project. It is reached by a sandy track, over which at 9 A.M. yesterday Arab squatters said they saw a white jeep and a taxi emerge.

Searchers, led by Major Moshe Arkin and the town clerk, sloshed through ankle-deep sand and covered all but the extreme western edge of the wood yesterday before darkness overtook them. Back in Nathanya, Mayor Ben Ami received an anonymous telephone message: "The place where the bodies are kept is mined. Warn civilians not to search." He relayed this warning immediately to Major Arkin's party and then notified the military.

The searchers withdrew but returned at dawn to probe the western strip of the forest. They deployed and moved seaward through the eucalyptus grove.

Mr. Friedman, near the center of the line, came upon a small clearing, in the middle of which stood two fully grown trees. He glimpsed two pair of legs, each tied together, swinging slowly in the breeze. He ran wildly through the sand track, screaming, "There they are!"

Mr. Friedman was so unnerved that when the police and military reached the forest more than an hour later he was unable to find the clearing. So the party spread out and moved cautiously through the woods.

At the edge of the clearing a police inspector warned that the area might be mined and ordered everyone back to the sand track while sappers examined the ground. After several minutes, correspondents and photographers were allowed to approach.

Sergeants Paice and Martin wore flannel shirts and white undershirts. Their heads were sheathed in their own shirts, which were tied about their necks. The breeze moved them gently. They were about two feet from the ground.

On their trousers was pinned a "communiqué" from the Irgun's "tribunal." It said that two "British spies, Martin and Paice, held in underground captivity since July 12" had been executed, not as hostages for the three Irgunists hanged Tuesday, but for five listed "crimes."

The crimes were: "First, illegal entry into the Hebrew homeland; second, membership in the British criminal terrorist organization known as the British occupation army of Palestine, which is responsible for depriving the Hebrew people of the right to live, brutal acts of oppression, torture, murder of prisoners of war, murder of captives and wounded, deportation of Hebrew citizens from their homeland;

third, illegal possession of arms, with the aim of enforcing oppression and tyranny; fourth, anti-Jewish spying while in civilian disguise; fifth, premeditated hostile designs against the Hebrew underground, its soldiers, its bases and its arms—the arms of freedom."

The communiqué continued: "The tribunal finds the accused guilty on all the charges and sentences them to be hanged by the neck until they are dead.

"The appeal of the condemned men for clemency was rejected.

"The sentence has been carried out.

"The execution of the two British spies is not in reprisal for the murder of the Hebrew prisoners of war. It is a routine judicial act of the tribunal of the underground, which has tried and will try the criminal members of the Nazi-British army of occupation.

"The blood of the murdered prisoners of war will be avenged by military operations, by the blows we shall bring down on the head of the enemy."

Before the order was given to cut the men down the area was searched for mines and boobytraps. Nothing was found.

A captain of the Royal Engineers proceeded to saw the rope from which Sergeant Martin hung. As the rope parted the captain threw himself clear. There was a large explosion as Sergeant Martin fell to the ground.

His body was blown to pieces and the neighboring tree, from which Sergeant Paice was suspended, was uprooted. Miraculously, the captain sustained only slight head cuts. Sergeant Paice's body and the remains of Sergeant Martin's body, which had been scattered over a radius of 50 yards, were taken to a nearby hospital pending official identification. (Aug. 1, 1947)

Bigart left Jerusalem in the fall of 1947 and, according to Clifton Daniel, who was there as a *Times* correspondent, the occasion was marked September 3 by a party at the British Public Information Office. This brought forth a better-than-average reporter's effort to the tune of "Lili Marlene" twitting Bigart as pro-Zionist. In 1967, an Israeli press attaché at the United Nations told me about the song and gave me seven verses. Daniel claimed authorship of three, saying the rest were added later. The

"Jewish Jaffa and Arab Tel Aviv" is a reversal of a reporter's cliché about the neighboring cities. Rehavia is the quarter where reporters lived and worked. Here is the portion Daniel claims:

> Far from Jewish Jaffa and Arab Tel Aviv
> Rabbi Homer Bigart prepares to take his leave,
> Leaving behind him the Jewish state
> He helped create, by working late.
> Farewell to thee, Rehavia!
> Farewell, Jerusalem.
>
> Rabbi Homer Bigart takes his leave of Zion,
> And gives a final twist to the tail of the Lion:
> "You British should be kind to those naughty boys
> Who play with toys that make a noise."
> Illegal immigration,
> The pride of Haganah.
>
> Gabriel Zifroni telephones the news
> Of how the dirty British are beating up the Jews.
> Homer sits down to earn his wage,
> And writes a page of righteous rage,
> And then 10 pages more,
> And then 10 pages more.

Bigart did not like the song much, the author said, but it endured. Bigart admirers, gathered for a memorial, were warned "prenez garde!" and then Daniel sang these verses. The host, David Halberstam, was equal to the moment. "I once told Homer," he said, "that one day *Clifton Daniel* would come to my house and sing for my guests!"

Finding Markos, June–July 1948

In 1948, Bigart was in Greece, covering what he characterized in a dispatch as "the weirdest assignment ever handed on by the War Department" to American officers. They were to persuade the Greek Army to go into the mountains and fight rebel forces led by Markos Vafiades, a guerrilla using the nom de guerre General Markos. The task was weird, Bigart wrote, because the Americans were to use "supreme sweetness, tact and diplomatic indirection." The project seemed bootless; Bigart reported traveling one hundred miles in Thessaly without hearing a "shot fired either tentatively or in anger."

Few correspondents were covering this offshoot of the cold war. One, George Polk of CBS, was found shot on the shore of Salonika Bay on May 16, 1948; he had been trying to get an interview with Markos. I. F. Stone called him the first casualty of the cold war, and a journalism prize was named in his honor. Bigart won the first of these, for "courage, integrity and enterprise" beyond the call of duty on the Greek assignment.

Covering Greece, Bigart got into one of his epic clashes with the authorities, this time with Dwight Griswold, chief of the American aid mission in Athens, who accused Bigart of not telling the truth, likening him to the Soviet propagandist Ilya Ehrenburg. Bigart asked the *Trib* for a transfer to Yugoslavia, saying he would return to Greece later. He did, but not in any way he could have expected. For a long time, the *Trib* sat on the story of Bigart's journey, fearing it was too leftist. But eventually, at the end of July, the *Trib* carried four long dispatches, which are here combined and condensed.

Homer Bigart's Perilous Trip to See Markos

Reporter, Approached in Belgrade by Agents of Greek Rebel Leader, Finds Much Secrecy Necessary to Get Out of Yugoslavia

WITH GENERAL MARKOS IN THE GRAMMOS MOUNTAINS, July 1, 1948—The story of my search for General Markos, leader of the Greek rebel forces, begins in the Hotel Moskva, Belgrade, on the evening of June 13. Returning from dinner, I was told by the night clerk that a stranger had called and left word that he would return at 11 P.M. with a package for me.

I gave little thought to it. Earlier I had asked the commercial attaché for letters of introduction to friends of his in Istanbul, which I hoped to visit this summer. This must be the Embassy messenger with the letters.

Promptly at 11, there was a knock at the door. A young man of perhaps 20, who looked neither Slavic nor British, pushed past me. Without a word he walked quickly across the room, fell into a chair and beckoned me to an opposite seat.

"Comrade," he began (my exchange of letters with Dwight Griswold, chief of the American aid mission to Greece, had given me a local reputation as a "progressive journalist"). "Comrade, you had planned to return to Athens via Rome. Instead you will go via Free Greece and interview General Markos. Is that agreeable?"

Very tentatively, I said yes. Any Balkan correspondent would give his right arm to see Markos.

I told the visitor to go on, but his English was so limited I could grasp little of what he said. After fruitless consultation with a pocket dictionary, he gave up, promised to return next morning with a comrade who knew English better. Meanwhile I must employ the strictest "konspiratsia"—that favorite Balkan term for secrecy. "Speak not this to Yugoslavs," said the "comrade," emphatically pressing a finger to his lips.

Anywhere else, this behavior would have been comic, but in the Balkans "konspiratsia" is commonplace. However, I did find it hard to swallow his injunction against mentioning the matter to Yugoslav acquaintances. For, although the practical support Yugoslavia gave Markos has been exaggerated by the West, nevertheless I failed to understand why agents of Markos in Belgrade could not escort me across the frontier with a wink at the security police.

Next morning he returned, bringing with him a tall, stocky, studious looking youth who wore glasses and whose plump face was beaded with nervous sweat. His name was John and he was going to accompany me on the long journey to Markos. His English was not appreciably better . . . but apart from the language difficulty, he was to prove an excellent guide, patient, tireless and unfailingly good-humored. He neither swore nor drank and was so devastatingly moral that after a week of him our friendship at times wore a trifle thin. . . .

Next day he was back again and konspiratsia thickened. Since my exit visa read via rail to Trieste he told me I would have to buy a ticket to Rome on the *Simplon Express* and obtain an Italian visa—just to make my departure look legitimate. When this was done we could take off immediately.

I hate to throw away good office money, so when I went to Putnik, the government travel agency, I bought only a second-class ticket for Trieste, saying I would pay for the wagon-lits (sleeper) on the train. John was to phone the Moskva early next morning and it was arranged that I was to say simply "I am ready" if things were in order. . . .

As the hour approached I became increasingly nervous. I knew next to nothing of the agents who were arranging this adventure. When I questioned their identity, they replied: "We could show you all kinds of papers and they would mean nothing to you. You just have to take your chances with us."

At 10 minutes to 11, I slipped through the lobby, having the good fortune not to encounter anyone, and walked to the appointed corner. John hurried to meet me and, whispering "Don't talk," led me down the hill through back alleys to the central station. We avoided the station, passing instead through the gloom of a freight yard and scrambling across tracks to the platform where a darkened train was waiting. I saw from the destination sign on the coach that it was the midnight express for Skoplje, capital of Macedonia. Already it was crowded with tired soldiers and peasants, but John took me to an empty compartment marked "reserved for invalids." It stank of garlic and soiled plush. He told me to lie on the seat. I was to play the invalid. . . .

Reaching Skoplje next afternoon we eluded ticket takers by passing through a side door and hurried to an adjacent parking space, where a battered United Nations Relief and Rehabilitation Administration truck covered with a tarpaulin was waiting. Two men in the cab motioned me to climb in the back, the tarpaulin was lowered and securely tied, and I sat in steamy darkness on a pile of cushions while we jolted down the rough road toward Greece.

I had hoped they would take me via Monastir so we could cross the border near Lake Prespa. That would bring us at least a week closer to the Grammos area, where I supposed Markos was now located. But my spirits sank when, through a slit in the canvas, I saw we were headed southeastward down the Vardar Valley. That meant we would enter Greece near Djevdjelia, behind Salonika, a long piece from the Grammos area.

At dusk the truck halted. We waited for darkness, then dismounted. . . . We crossed a field. From the shadow of the bushes stepped three men, their silhouettes bulky with slung rifles, blankets and overcoats. I wondered at all this paraphernalia, for the night was warm. Later I was to learn through extreme discomfort how essential it is to carry heavy clothing in the Greek mountains. I was deplorably equipped with a business suit and two pairs of low shoes. . . . Off we set single file up a valley that slanted southwestward toward the nearest hills. I was warned that we still were in Yugoslavia—would be for three hours. No talking or smoking.

For a while we followed the silver ribbon of a stream. The trail, now rising sharply, showed evidence of considerable horse traffic. In a few moments we found it was heavily patrolled by mounted Yugoslav frontier guards. Twice we had to duck behind bushes on hearing horses approach. The second time we were nearly caught.

The woods had thinned out and we had emerged breathless on a scrubby plateau. The patrol was upon us so quickly there was no time to select cover. I fell behind the nearest rock and heard the soft scuffing of gravel as the others hid themselves. Four soldiers rode up. We had a sickening sensation as they paused, looked around and talked quietly among themselves. They had not seen us—there was no tension in their voices. Finally, after interminable minutes in which sharp pieces of rock gouged my stomach, they rode on.

With the moon almost perpendicularly above us, we crossed the plateau. The trail zigzagged up the rocky flank of a mountain, dropped several hundred feet, then rose dizzily up again. I looked at my watch—it was only midnight and already I was so tired I could hardly see. It was a combination of fear and exhaustion such as I had not experienced since the amphibious landings during the war.

We climbed for another hour. Suddenly we left the trail and crossing an upland meadow dotted with dwarf pine, entered an oak forest on the other side. There we found another trail and, in a little while, a spring where we drank and rested. Thus, at 2 o'clock in the morning of June 17, we entered rebel Greece. (July 25, 1948)

Homer Bigart in Rebel Greece Finds Route to Markos Arduous

Reporter Visits Ill-Equipped Partisan Hospital, Learns Guerrillas Feel Their Cause Is Just, and Crosses 'Enemy' Area to Reach Rebel Leader

July 2—My first few days with the partisans involved some mental readjustment. It was startling to find that they were quite ordinary flesh and blood who shaved and bathed regularly and were kind to their horses. I found them wholly convinced that their cause was right, that the regime in Athens was completely subservient to American interests and that the only way of achieving a better life for the Greek people was through a "peoples' democracy" such as in Yugoslavia.

The great majority were Communists, for the region in which I traveled is held by the hard core of Elas veterans who had fled to the mountains when Markos called for renewed resistance. Consequently, I encountered a good deal of evangelistic spirit and frequent singing of a partisan melody that ran:

> The Anglo-American imperialists
> Come to our country as conquerors
> They will be beaten by the democratic army
> As happened to the Germans.

We are not scared of Truman's guns
Nor by Griswold's inglorious sabers.
We have written deep in our hearts
Peoples' democracy and an end to occupation.

For a week we traveled westward along the razor's edge of territory the partisans hold below the Yugoslav frontier. Markos had directed that I be given full security, and extraordinary measures were taken for my protection. There were never less than a dozen picked guards—self-confident lads of 18 and 19 who could travel great distances and were able to climb a 7,000-foot mountain hardly pausing for a rest. Generally I was given a horse or mule, although there was a shortage of animals. All the others, including John, who, I guessed, was a sort of minor political commissar, were obliged to walk.

I did not ride happily. I am over 40 and gone soft and suffered an intolerable aching from a wooden saddle that seemed designed as an instrument of torture. There was some consolation in the view. Few mountain ranges are more magnificent than the chaotic landscape of the frontier region and now, in mid-June, the country was at its loveliest, the pine forests freshly green and the upland meadows glorious with flowers. . . . The temperature dropped 40 degrees by nightfall, and huddling in sheepskin blankets, I stayed close to a fire that was kept alive all night by the partisans.

Looking at a map, the distances do not seem so great. But the terrain is so fantastically rugged that a journey must be measured in hours, not miles. Often it required seven or eight hours to traverse an airline distance of 10 miles. Hoof after hoof, the mule plodded the rocky trail up vast slopes, through forests of virgin beech and evergreen. . . . Then the descent, and more often than not, a descent so steep I had to dismount and lead the mule. . . .

One night we stayed at a partisan hospital. It was a memorable night—we slept in a real bed instead of on hard boards and feasted on lamb and rice. Here I met a remarkable woman. She was Capt. Sofia Grigoriadu of Athens, commandant of the hospital, who said that in 18 months with the partisans she had performed more than a thousand operations. Her equipment was so primitive that often amputations had to be done without anesthetic, and with a kitchen knife. Now she had a few scalpels and a small quantity of morphia.

. . . There were perhaps 80 patients, most of them recovering from bullet wounds, and in one ward there were no beds—the men lay on blankets on the floor.

"They have great moral powers of resistance," said Captain Grigoriadu. Her patients stared at us with that docile trust of the wounded.

She was certainly a heroic and competent figure but I confess that the fear which haunted me during most of the following days arose from the possibility of illness or an accident that might require the attention of Markos's medical corps. I will never forget one horrible moment when, descending the steep pitch of the Aliakmon Valley, my mule stepped on a stone covered with slime and fell heavily, pinning my right leg in the mud. There was a sharp pain and for a moment I had a vision of Captain Grigoriadu standing over me with a butcher knife, saying, "I guess we'll have to amputate just above the knee while you, Rulea, will read selected passages from Comrade Stalin's 'Principles of Leninism' to keep our patient calm." (Rulea was the hospital political commissar.)

The vision was more painful than the humiliation I felt when, after the mule was removed, I rolled up the pants leg with a martyred air and found a stone bruise no bigger than a quarter.

Most of the time we traveled by daylight without the slightest fear of ambush by the Greek Army. For 12 days the only gunfire I heard was the remote booming of a Greek Army gun that partisans said was shelling a village near Ardea. . . . Generally we stayed in peasant's hovels in half-deserted villages, eating bitter unsalted bread and goat's cheese, with sometimes a bowl of yogurt for dessert. When I ran out of cigarettes, the partisans found ripe tobacco leaves in villages, cut them with a pocket knife and rolled cigarettes with whatever paper was available. I was deprived of the consolation of liquor until, after 10 days of intolerable thirst, a village commissar produced a bottle of ouzo. . . .

Operating in support of partisan infantry along the northern frontier is a cavalry troop under Maj. Jorgas Nestorus of Siatista. It was his troops who escorted me across the only sector held by Athens troops—the 15-mile-wide valley of Phlorina that forms the southern projection of the Monastir Gap, a main route of the Nazi invasion in 1941.

Our crossing was at night under full moon. We had come down from the snow-pocked Voras mountains and waited for dusk at a cavalry rendezvous in the foothills. Major Nestorus, a bluff, bony-faced man, wondered if I had seen any Bulgarians. This was a standard joke at my expense. Athens always talked of Bulgarians and Yugoslavs fighting with Markos and it seemed that every second partisan asked how many I had counted. Then everyone would laugh.

The major gave me his own horse and selected another mount. . . . It was a lovely night and the plain was fragrant with new-mown hay. Across the flat basin were the lights of Phlorina with the dark silhouette of Mount Vermion rising behind. We rode single file through the fields of ripening wheat, crossed the railroad and forded the shallow Eleska River. Under the moon the plain was starkly naked.

At midnight we crossed the road, and, dismounting for greater security, led our horses past the hostile villages. Dogs raised a furious outcry yet no one challenged us. To the north a flare was lofted, but the village guards peering nervously into the night were apparently determined to see nothing.

The western mountains gradually took shape. We entered the deep shadows of a pass. A steep ascent brought us to the ghostly ruins of a burned village. Upward we rode through high meadows and into the forest again. At dawn we quartered our horses in a clearing and fell exhausted into the grass. (July 26, 1948)

Homer Bigart, at Greek Front, Finally Reaches Gen. Markos

Reporter, Before Meeting Rebel Leader, Finds People in Partisan Area Believe U.S. Planes Bomb Them and Blame Truman for It

July 2—With the Phlorina plain behind us, we could relax a bit. On a mountain summit near Lake Prespa, Major Nestorus lifted his arm to the southwest in a gesture embracing a vast jumble of mountains and said, "All partisan."

In this corner of Greece, the population was largely Slav. We passed villages where only the old and infirm remained. Every youth who could fight was with the partisans. The old people still cherished the dream of an autonomous Macedonia; their dislike of Athens, always intense, had been aggravated by recent bombings.

They had been told by their political commissars that Truman and Marshall alone were responsible for the American bombs and rockets that fell on their homes and that the big majority of American people, being democratic, might presently throw out Truman in favor of Wallace. . . .

In every village there were a few old men who had lived in the United States and could still speak English. I could talk with them freely and alone. Thus I was able to obtain what I believe is the true story of the so-called mass "abductions" of Greek children by partisans to Slav countries. The abduction story has become one of the main pillars of Greek propaganda and virtually all the American officers and correspondents in Athens (including myself) reported it last March. . . .

In the village of Vatokhorton, a Greek Orthodox priest, the Rev. George Erakle, formerly of St. George's Church, Brooklyn, told me: "Three months ago, planes came every day. We put the children in those pillboxes on the hill (pre-war pillboxes against the Italian invasion through Albania) but it was too cold for them. We had to send them across the frontier—there was nothing else to be done. So about 140 left." No word had been received of the children and the priest was unable to say whether they were in Yugoslavia, Bulgaria, Romania or Czechoslovakia.

Further down the road was the village of Kroustalopiyi. There, Tom Nestor, who once had a candy store in St. Louis, told me there had been six raids, the last on March 9. On Jan. 15, a woman was killed and a girl wounded. Those were the only casualties, but most of the villagers decided to send their children north. Escorted by five young women of the village, 150 children departed in three groups. Nestor's five children went with them. . . .

John, my escort, had talked by phone with the general staff. Markos couldn't see me tomorrow—he was off in the Konitsa sector—and left word that I be shown partisan positions near Nestorion. So the interview was set for the following day and it was arranged that I was to meet the general somewhere along the trail he was taking back from the west. . . .

The next day we rode over the backbone of the Pindus. . . . I was aroused at dawn and taken to a guarded house. After a moment I was led upstairs to a bare room where the only furniture was a plain wooden table and two chairs. Markos was sitting at the table and opposite him was a rather cadaverous looking man I recognized as Roussos, his foreign affairs minister.

A typical snafu nearly cost me the interview after two weeks of painful and exhausting travel. Neither Markos nor Roussos speaks English and John was clearly incapable of accurate translation. Markos was impatient to reach the battle. The only solution was to ride back eastward with him to the next village where there was a woman who spoke English well.

We found her with no difficulty and at Markos's suggestion rode a little beyond town as a precaution against air attack and paused in a shady churchyard. I had no camera but Roussos produced one and took a roll of film which he gave to me. . . . (July 27, 1948)

Markos Still Open to Peace Bid,
Says Only U.S. Aid Props Athens

Homer Bigart Gets First American Interview With Rebel Leader Who Says He Can Hold Out Indefinitely in Northwest Greece

June 29*—My interview with General Markos was his first with the American press. He expressed complete confidence in the ability of his Andartes to hold indefinitely their strong positions in the Grammos and Upper Pindus ranges of northwestern Greece. He claimed defensive victory as the first two weeks of the Greek Army offensive ended with no appreciable dent in the rebels' lines.

The partisan leader said heavy casualties had been inflicted on the Athens forces in their futile battering of his mountain fortress. He estimated enemy losses at 4,500. From a slip of paper he read his own casualties up to June 27—65 dead, 390 injured and "perhaps a few captured."

"Athens rejected our peace overtures," he said. "They thought they saw in it evidence of weakness. Well, they wanted a fight and now they are getting it."

We talked in the churchyard of a mountain village. . . . The day was beautifully clear with a breeze so sharp that Markos wore a leather jacket over his British battle dress. As a precaution against spying aircraft, we sat beneath trees, the general with his maps spread on the ground around him. From the distant Nestorion front came the heavy rumble of Greek Army artillery.

Markos looks so unlike the published photographs of him that at

*The *Tribune* printed the date of the actual interview on the third dispatch, despite the inconsistency of having July datelines precede it.

our first meeting I had failed to recognize him. The spreading mustache which he affected two years ago has been closely cropped. He is not as lean as photos had indicated but solidly built and of medium height. Were it not for the rough life of a partisan chief he would have a tendency to stoutness. His eyes are closely set and deeply lined from squinting into the wind and sun. The brown hair under his partisan cap was long and bushy; rebellious strands kept sliding down his forehead as he talked. His mouth is broad and expressive. He has the gift of a quick and charming smile that can alter instantly a face which, in repose, seems hard, impatient, pitiless. . . .

Markos filled in a few facts of his little-known personal history. Born 41 years ago in Asia Minor, he migrated to Greece in 1922, held a variety of small jobs in Salonika, then helped to organize the tobacco workers union as one of the main props of Communist strength. He was arrested six times, serving a total of nearly five years in jail. The German invasion found him in exile on the Island of Gavdos, whence he escaped and joined the Elas resistance movement. Asked how he became leader of the partisans, he replied smiling, "By fighting." . . .

He apologized for my long and devious journey and insisted that great precautions be taken for my personal safety in passing through his lines. He asked where I wanted to leave partisan territory and I said the outskirts of Ioannina would be fine since there would be American officers stationed there who would see that I got on the plane for Athens. . . .

I was to have a strong patrol which I could use at my own discretion, traveling as many hours as I liked and resting whenever I chose. I was glad he gave this order, for my disappearance must now be causing some concern at the *New York Herald Tribune*. I knew I could stay away a week or 10 days without worrying the office because my plan had been to spend several days in Rome buying clothes before returning to Athens. But now two weeks had passed and I was still at least 50 travel hours from Ioannina. We would have to travel much faster. (July 28, 1948)

Kati Marton, in *The Polk Conspiracy*, quotes an undated letter Bigart sent to William Polk, George's younger brother, before leaving Belgrade. "I am leaving tomorrow for Greece," Bigart wrote, "hoping to get the story your brother went after and to find out if the guerrillas can shed any light on the murder. If I have any luck, I hope that the stories I send will be regarded as a sort of personal memorial to George, who never forgot there were two sides to every story and who gave his life trying to get 'the other side.'"

In the National Archives, Marton found a message from Secretary of State George C. Marshall putting Bigart under twenty-four-hour guard while he remained in Athens.

As for Markos, he faded from the scene in 1949 and was thereafter variously reported dead, insane in Tashkent, or, later, a suicide. In 1983, at the age of seventy-seven, he re-emerged in Greece after thirty-four years of exile in the Soviet Union, where he had learned clockmaking, married and become a father. He died in Athens on February 23, 1992, at the age of eighty-six.

The New York Times on October 19, 1986, carried an interview with him by its correspondent David Binder. Binder said that Markos recalled his interview with "Homeros," and this was included in the Binder dispatch. When the mention was edited out, Binder sent his carbon copy to the retired Bigart, who wrote back that he was not surprised. If you saw what the *Herald Tribune*, in its great phase of anti-Communism, did to my Markos interview, he wrote, you would hardly feel bruised.

Korean War

From a Foxhole, July 1950

On June 25, 1950, North Korean forces attacked South Korea, bringing a swift response and the arrival of United States ground forces on June 30. Bigart, who had been working in the *Tribune* Washington bureau, was soon at the front.

From a Foxhole in Korea

WITH AMERICAN FORCES IN KOREA, July 10, 1950—American troops in forward positions narrowly escaped another enveloping thrust by North Korean Communists today, and were able to avoid annihilation by great luck in withdrawal. The unit suffered severe casualties and was forced to leave all its heavy equipment behind.

This correspondent was one of three reporters who saw the action, and was the only newsman to get out alive. The others, Ray Richards of International News Service and Corp. Ernie Peeler of *Stars and Stripes,* were killed by enemy fire.

A particularly grisly feature of the action was the shooting in cold blood of seven Americans who were captured by the Communists. The men, four of whom were driving jeeploads of ammunition forward in a last-gasp effort to keep the force supplied, surrendered to the hordes of North Koreans who were overrunning the roads. The Reds dragged them from their jeeps, tied their hands behind them and shot them in the face, ignoring their cries for mercy.

The small American force, commanded by Capt. Charles Alkire of Missoula, Mont., had the task of defending a low ridgeline overlooking Chonui. It was another in a series of desperate holding actions by which the Americans hoped to buy time. It was not an encounter anyone will remember except those who were there, and the outcome will have no bearing on the ultimate results. It is worth telling only as an example of what happens when men are thrown into action without adequate preparation. Important lessons can be learned from this seemingly trivial engagement.

We reached the hill late Sunday afternoon, in time to see a series of air strikes against withered ground behind a shadowy, filthy cluster of huts immediately below us. The Red spearhead of two divisions was putting heavy reliance on the main road from Seoul for supplies, and the highway northward for a distance of 10 miles was crawling with enemy vehicles. All we could see, however, was a naked ribbon of clay running northward from the town about a mile to where the road dipped behind a screen of hills.

High columns of black smoke rising behind the hills proved that our jet planes had found victims. It was a cheering sight for the infantry, all of whom hoped the enemy would be too disorganized to jump off at night.

This was the set-up: Captain Alkire's men were spread out thinly along the ridge. A lone American tank, lying back of the hill, was to challenge any Communist armor that poked its nose around a bend in the road that was nestling against the western base of the hill. It was too lightly armored to risk a duel with the 60-ton Russian-made monsters of the enemy. Only by delivering a lucky blow at close range could our tank hope to knock out the intruder.

Across the road, on the opposite bank of a shallow stream, were two score men under Lieut. Raymond Bixler of Lebanon, Mo.

Bixler's men, whose job was to hold the left flank, did not have too good a position. High wooded hills lay immediately to their left, and it was from this direction that the enemy launched his main attack.

Bixler's men were destined to be overrun and many of them slaughtered in their foxholes. The brave lieutenant, gathering as many survivors as he could, withdrew to safety in the nick of time.

We passed an uneasy night on the hill. At intervals our artillery banged away at possible enemy assembly points in the flats of Chonui. "Outgoing mail" screeched close overhead, but the hullabaloo failed to disperse swarms of mosquitos that made things miserable until the horrors of the morning caused us to forget our lesser woes.

Whether by accident or design, deserted Chonui was set afire at dusk and burned fitfully throughout the night. That was a break for us. The flames prevented any enemy attempt to assemble in the town, and silhouetted for our gunners any Communist attack to storm our positions frontally.

Colonel Joins G.I.'s

The colonel himself came up to the hill at dusk and announced he was going to stay for the show. (Security prevents naming of field officers, those above the rank of captain and below that of brigadier general.) His presence relieved some of the tension and there was a noticeable boost in morale. Somehow troops always feel less expendable when the Old Man is around, sticking his neck out just like any G.I.

As darkness closed in, Lieut. Robert "Soupy" Campbell of Syracuse, N.Y., who was responsible for hill positions, briefed his squad leaders. Campbell was worried about the right flank, and with apparent good reason. There a ridge trailed off into a series of lesser heights with gullies between them.

"They can slip behind those knolls and cut us off," the officer warned his men. "We've got to get mortar fire on that flank."

"Don't shoot unless you can spot a sniper," he cautioned. "Unnecessary shooting will only give our positions away.

"We're going to stay here. But I'm not kidding anybody. It's going to be tough."

The fatal element in our defeat was a ground fog that rose thickly at dawn. It billowed upward from the plain, and under its protective screen the North Koreans moved swiftly and decisively. Not until 8 o'clock was the curtain lifted and by that time the enemy was in position to deal the death blow.

Reporter's Log of Attack

I found a foxhole within hearing distance of the colonel's, and made this log of the attack.

5:55 A.M.—We hear the enemy jabbering over on the left, but can't see 50 feet through the fog. The show starts any minute now.

6:10 A.M.—There goes a whistle. Lots of shooting on the left. Some shooting out front. Quiet on the right.

6:35 A.M.—The line is holding and everyone feels better. But the Old Man is irked by trigger-happy people just below us. He asks what the hell they think they are shooting at. "Don't waste ammo!" he roars. "Wait until you get infantry to shoot at, and then lower the boom."

7 A.M.—Very quiet now. The Reds have taken a breather. Oops, incoming mail. It's going mortars. This ain't good. And trying to knock out our heavy mortars, back near the road. No tanks yet.

7:30 A.M.—Much yelling over on the left, then rapid small-arms fire. They're going after Bixler again. Wish this fog would lift so we could see what it's all about.

Enemy Tank Comes Up

8 A.M.—We can see the village now, still burning and smoking. Someone hollers: "Here comes a tank from the road." It's a big fellow with a long gun, maybe an 88. He crawls up to the south edge of the village, gropes for concealment in a cluster of buildings, and looks us over at 500 yards. Our machine gunners open up, but the Old Man puts a stop to that. "You can't bend those babies with 50-caliber stuff."

8:05 A.M.—Hey, that wasn't the first bogie. One of them must have come in under the fog, and he's back in the rear, shooting at our mortars. This ain't good. And here come three more into town. We'll catch hell for sure.

8:10 A.M.—The Old Man called for air support. The three new bogies have joined the comrades out in front of us, bunched up in a fat target. Flames are licking at the buildings but the tanks stay put.

Bixler Is Cut Off

8:30 A.M.—The enemy has bypassed us with another tank and a small body of infantry. Bixler is cut off but his men are holding. Our artillery is giving us close support—some of it too close for comfort.

8:45 A.M.—Not much hope of bringing up ammunition, with Red tanks and infantry sitting on the road. But the Old Man says there's still enough ammunition, if the boys keep their discipline.

9 A.M.—Things aren't too bad out front. Machine-gun fire from the

hill is keeping the tanks in the village buttoned up. The enemy infantry has just made a half-hearted attempt to climb the hill, but they had to take cover from a storm of mortar and artillery fire. When the artillery got too hot the Reds started running, and our machine guns knocked them over as they ran.

9:20 A.M.—The Old Man phones the outpost: "We are holding here. Everyone hold."

Air Support Requested

9:30 A.M.—Less firing now. A flight of bombers overhead, but they are strategic stuff, no hope for us. The Old Man repeats his request for air support.

10 A.M.—The tanks below have unlimbered their machine guns and are spraying the hillside. They are concentrating their fire on our right flank, probably to cover the long-expected infantry attack in that direction.

10:30 A.M.—Somebody on the phone nervously is asking what the score is. "Are you thinking of running to the rear?" asked the Old Man sarcastically. "Well, get that damn thought out of your mind. You've got a hole to sit in, a carbine and some good people around you."

11 A.M.—There is intense fire on the left and it's getting rough again for poor Bixler. Everyone is wondering what's happened to the counterattack. Relief must be getting close, because supporting fire is dropping in our immediate rear. Some survivors from the rear are straggling up the hill. The squad from the 75-mm. recoilless rifle gets a warm welcome because each brought two bandoliers of ammunition. Our supply is running low.

11:15 A.M.—Hoping to pinch off some enemy infantry when they fall back from our frontal attack, the Old Man alerts everyone in the rear.

Bixler Ordered to Stay

11:25 A.M.—We can see enemy troops moving in on Bixler's position. Bixler reports: "Need more men. Quite a few casualties," and he asked permission to withdraw. The Old Man makes a tough decision. "You will not take off," he ordered. "Relief is on the way."

11:30 A.M.—"Where the hell is the Air Force?" asked the Old Man. Two American jet fighters pass along the brilliant sky, circle the village a few times, then skim down in rocket runs on the tanks. The enemy bogies are partly hidden in smoke and, although some of the rocket shells zip into the burning village, there is no visible evidence of a hit. When their rockets are exhausted the jets hang around for a while, strafing tanks and enemy infantry positions. If they do nothing else, the jets keep the enemy infantry under cover and give Bixler badly needed respite.

11:32 A.M.—Suddenly things take a bad turn. Our own artillery apparently thinks we have abandoned the hill. Shell patterns are falling smack on the ridge line. We crouch low in our foxholes, getting showered with dust and pebbles from near misses. In the midst of this uproar, Bixler messages that he is surrounded and very depleted.

11:35 A.M.—"Everybody on the right flank is taking off," someone shouts. The Old Man looks around and sees groups of men running to the rear. "Get those high-priced soldiers back into position," he yelled. "That's what they're paid for."

11:40 A.M.—A young Nisei from Hawaii, Corp. Richard Okada, is trying to halt the panic on the right, exposing himself to the artillery fire. Corporal Okada rounds up enough soldiers to man a greatly reduced perimeter. Pvts. Clyde Stapleton of Nennington Gap, Va., and Otis Solo of Mallory, W. Va., helped him.

11:50 A.M.—The Old Man is still in communication with the regiment and tries to get the artillery to lift from our hill, but it's coming in harder than ever. This can't go on. While we are pinned down by Americans, the enemy is closing in.

12 noon—The Old Man is debating whether to stick here or run for it.

12:05 P.M.—He shouts an order that no small arms will be thrown away: "It's a long walk back, and we will probably meet Reds on the way."

On signal from the Old Man, we leaped from our holes and ran, crouching and dodging, across open ground to an orchard sloping down to rice paddies.

Walking a Tightrope

Crossing these paddies when you are very scared and in a hurry is like walking a tightrope for the first time. The little earthen levees holding back the water are not very wide at the top, and you keep slipping knee-deep into the mud.

At this precise moment two jet planes, looking for enemy infantry, came over and started what looked like a strafing run at us. We had no casualties, but some of the boys acquired a lifelong aversion to rice.

Reaching a no-man's-land of wooded hills, we split into two columns, one taking a higher trail to the southeast while the rest, with the walking wounded, struck out for the nearest contact with our troops. Fortunately we were recognized and crossed our lines without incident.

Lost Ground Is Regained

The counterattack was pressing forward, and, although the rescue party reached our abandoned position too late, it succeeded in regaining and holding all lost ground. This was important, for it recovered much abandoned materiel and secured a valuable prize.

It developed that our light tank had managed to slap a surprise shot at an advancing bogie at pointblank range. Late today the light tank was proudly towing its victim to the rear for study by the headquarters intelligence section. It was the first enemy medium tank captured by the Americans.

The rescue force also ran into the gruesome atrocity which the North Koreans had perpetrated. Official pictures were taken of the seven unfortunates who had been bound and shot.

Not until late today was it established that Richards and Peeler were dead. I saw them last night down the road. They told me they intended to spend the night there, hoping to get a jeep ride back to headquarters to file their stories of the coming battle. (July 12, 1950)

Landing at Pohang, July 1950

This story, although it has no more action than Bigart's report of his placid voyage to England in World War II, created a storm. In a time of fierce press rivalries, it became a world exclusive, with the Army saying it made an error and let the dispatch through despite an embargo. But Henry Lieberman of *The Times*, who competed against Bigart in the Far East, once said that Bigart was "helpless like a cobra" when it came to getting dispatches filed. Read the Associated Press post-mortem and cast a vote.

G.I. Landing
On East Coast
Is Unopposed

Soviet Submarines
Are Reported Near

1st Cavalry Division Is
Put Ashore After Only
10 Days of Preparation

A KOREAN BEACHHEAD, July 18, 1950—In the first amphibious assault landing since World War II, reinforcements came safely ashore this morning at Pohang, a port in southeast Korea, to bring relief to hard-pressed American forces.

It was the first cheering news since the Americans began their long retreat down the Korean peninsula two weeks ago.

The troops landed today were of the First Cavalry Division, liberators of Manila, now under the command of Maj. Gen. Hobart R. Gay.

The landing was unopposed. This was fortunate, for the scratch team hastily assembled by Rear Adm. James H. Doyle was clearly in no condition for a sharply contested beachhead.

It was a shoestring operation, unlike anything since Guadalcanal. Normally such an operation would require three months' planning. This show was thrown together in 10 days.

Plans were necessarily haphazard. Only two of the ships assembled by Admiral Doyle were adequately prepared for amphibious landings.

Plenty of air cover and gun power was available from the fleet. Intelligence reports indicated, however, that the North Korean Communists had not yet reached the beachhead area in their sweep down the peninsula. In fact, Gen. Douglas MacArthur's headquarters reported that a small American unit operating on the east coast had pulled a successful counterattack, dislodging Communists from a town 20 miles to the north.

Far more worrisome to Admiral Doyle was the immediate threat of an approaching typhoon. . . . This harbor, exposed to the northeast, offers no shelter, except possibly to smaller craft. Thus Admiral Doyle may be obliged to put his big ships out to sea, leaving his LST's to ride out the storm in harbor.

Under pressure of this threat, a secondary peril was almost forgotten. Soviet submarines have been on the prowl in the Sea of Japan and there were possibilities of a nasty incident.

An American antisubmarine patrol had reported the presence of unidentified submarines. Since North Korea has no submarines, the prowlers must be Russian. If they should attack, World War III might begin here with a naval action.

This operation got under way Saturday afternoon under circumstances that were fully as dreamy and unreal as the nightmarish events on the Korean peninsula to date.

For a change, this was a pleasant fantasy. Our sailing resembled a departure for a Korean cruise. Wives and children waved goodby from the shore. A brass band tooted "Anchors Aweigh." There was a clay-pigeon shoot from the fantail of the flagship. No shuffleboard, however.

Ships Battened Down

At sunset the journey became hot and uncomfortable. Admiral Doyle, determined not to take any chances, ordered all ships battened down during darkness. No open portholes. No smoking on deck. Below deck the troops and passengers suffered in the steamy heat.

The passage through the narrow Shimoneseki Strait was made in daylight, with the help of Japanese pilots. Occasional groups of Japanese fishermen and school children cheered from shore. There could be no concealment of our intentions. We were clearly bound for Korea, but we hoped the spectators could not guess our precise destination on the peninsula.

The journey was uneventful. There was a submarine alert the first day out, but nothing materialized. Once a destroyer steamed close by to deliver a sailor with appendicitis. The flagship carried a mobile medical unit with doctors and nurses to be landed in Korea.

The beachhead area was so placid that most of the landing craft came right into the dock, bringing their soldiers in dry. Natives said there were no Communist troops short of 30 miles, but that scattered guerrilla groups occasionally harassed the road.

. . . By midmorning this dusty flea-bitten village was intolerably hot. There was no air, and the harbor was mirror-calm. Back of town lay a semicircle of barren leprous hills. The brilliant sky held no threat of the approaching typhoon. (July 19, 1950)

Army's Error
Led to Leak on
Korea Landing

Officer Released Bigart's
Story to *Herald Tribune*
Before Security Deadline

TOKYO, July 19, 1950 (AP)—The United States Army's Public Information Office made a hurried investigation today to discover why the news of Tuesday's amphibious landing in South Korea was disclosed prematurely.

It gave Homer Bigart of the *New York Herald Tribune,* one of 22 news and radio correspondents on the operation, an unexpected beat.

All correspondents sent stories of the landing back to Tokyo by Navy courier. They were to be held for a minimum of 48 hours or until the landing had been announced officially.

As an apparent afterthought the veteran Mr. Bigart gave a carbon copy of his story to a returning correspondent with instructions that it be turned over to the P.I.O. for filing. This is done frequently by field correspondents who do not maintain Tokyo offices.

Mr. Bigart's duplicate and his original, which was in a manila envelope, both reached Maj. Buel A. Williamson, P.I.O. executive officer. The original was turned over to the A.P. for relay to the *Herald Tribune,* pursuant to instructions, and was held for the embargo period.

Major Williamson said he assumed the copy handed him did not cover the embargoed landing, so he sent it to the nearby telegraph office to be filed.

"We never read these stories, just pass them on as a courtesy," Major Williamson said. "There was nothing on this one to indicate that it was to be held for release."

All of this was discovered after an investigation—by Major Williamson.

For a while there was considerable confusion in Radio Tokyo, the press headquarters.

Other Reporters File Story

Word that Mr. Bigart's story was in print got back here fast in inquiries from home offices. Under voluntary censorship, each correspondent then had to decide for himself whether to use the story that all had, but were withholding.

Most followed the age-old journalistic code, that news in print no longer is secret. They rushed out their own stories.

The official announcement was made several hours later that the First Cavalry was in South Korea. It did not mention the amphibious landing.

[At the request of Mr. Bigart, whose dispatch reached New York at 7:30 P.M. Tuesday, the *Herald Tribune* asked for clearance on details of the landing from the security division at the Pentagon in Washington. Military officials replied that it was permissible to say that American troops of the First Cavalry had landed on the east coast of Korea, but that Pohang should not be identified as the beachhead until announcement was received from Tokyo. The *Herald Tribune* followed this advice in the exclusive story which it published in its *City* (first) *Edition.* Subsequent press association dispatches from Tokyo mentioned Pohang, so the name of this port was restored to Mr. Bigart's original story.]

The purpose of the embargo was to insure that the beachhead was secure and to make sure the Navy task force would not be imperiled by advertising its location. Against an enemy with a sizable air force this could be serious.

This incident caused some correspondents to make another request for formal censorship. Their idea is that they cannot be protected against a competitor's release of a story like this without Army scrutiny of all copy. (July 20, 1950)

Walker's Stand-or-Die Order, July 1950

Stand-or-Die Order to Troops Came as Shock to U.S. Officers

WITH AMERICAN FORCES IN KOREA, Monday, July 31, 1950—Gen. Walton H. Walker's order Saturday to the American forces to stand or die on the present battle lines in Korea came as a profound shock to most of the officers of the United States Eighth Army.

They had known, of course, that the situation was dangerous. But the prospect of staging a Dunkerque or a Gallipoli withdrawal had never really occurred to them before General Walker told them to put any idea of an evacuation from Korea out of their minds.

The worst that could happen, they felt, was a retreat to beachhead positions. There, at least, they could have flanks anchored on the sea, and there would be enough American soldiers to man the shortened line. Withdrawn inside a tough beachhead shell, they could gather strength until the hour arrived for a general offensive.

The Walker order against yielding another inch would make little sense if taken literally. The American units are still badly spread out with wide and vulnerable gaps between them. To make a final stand in the present haphazard positions would invite continued piecemeal destruction of the American forces.

What General Walker meant was that there must be no more of the withdrawals in which some American units have run like rabbits, without inflicting much damage on the enemy. He told the officers that the conduct of some American squads and platoons under fire has left much to be desired.

The main trouble, most observers agree, is that this is a peacetime Army, composed mainly of youths who had no thought of fighting when they signed up. They are not combat-minded, and it will take some time to make soldiers of them. They went into the fight as if it were a picnic and promptly lost heart when it proved to be a tough and nasty assignment.

For the human deficiencies, there is no one to blame. Americans like to go soft in peacetime. But there is no excuse for deficiencies in basic field materials. For example, Americans have always prided themselves on their knowledge of radio and telephone communications at the front. Some of the communications material is obsolete and some of the radios and much of the telephone wiring were discovered to be rotted by fungus after lying in storage for five years on the island of Okinawa.

There have been a number of tactical mistakes, many of them resulting from a basic original miscalculation—the underestimation of enemy strength. If nothing else is gained from the Korean experience, it should at least produce a drastic re-examination of the work of American intelligence agencies. (July 31, 1950)

Firing on Reds, August 1950

Americans Atop 1,000-Ft. Peak
Direct Fire on Reds' Taegu Line

'Bowling Alley' Below Strewn With Wrecked
Red Tanks and Trucks After a Week's Fighting

WITH AMERICAN FORCES IN KOREA, Aug. 25, 1950—For the last eight days, Charley Company of the 27th Regimental Combat Team has been perched on the scrub-covered summit of a mountain almost a thousand feet above the main road leading into Taegu from the north.

From this strategic height, Capt. Alfred S. Burnett of Knoxville, Tenn., and his hawk-eyed artillery observer, Lieut. Glen Record of Solomon, Kan., have been calling for strikes on North Korean Communist armor trying to storm the mountain pass that is the real key to Taegu.

Last night, Charley Company (C Company) had to beat off another attack by Red infantry who assaulted the height "screaming like a bunch of girls at a basketball game," as Capt. Burnett described it.

This morning when I reached the summit, the valley road and narrow plain seemed lifeless. Directly below, for a distance of a mile, the road was strewn with the accumulated debris of a week's fighting.

There were the huge corpses of 10 Russian-made tanks, one burned and blackened and another with its whole turret blown off by an internal explosion caused by a direct hit from a white phosporous shell. Among these dead beetles lay one American tank which by a sinister stroke of fortune had run upon one of our own mines.

Tilted crazily in ditches were six Russian-made light armored vehicles, most of them mounting high-velocity guns. Two smashed anti-tank guns and seven wrecked motor trucks completed the junkyard.

It was one of those ideal observation posts that usually are acquired only by the enemy. Directly below in the line of vision was a road junction vital to the Reds and usually within their jurisdiction. But by now scores of American guns are "zeroed in" on the junction and the enemy no longer attempts to run his vehicles past this intersection and down the mile-long straightaway which the Americans call "the bowling alley."

The observation post was also a window on a large expanse of territory behind the enemy lines. We could observe his lateral supply routes—winding trails branching from the valleys along the ascending staircases of rice paddies.

Guns Trained on Reds

Once we saw six Korean women hauling ammunition along a trail to Red positions in the hills. Occasionally small groups of the enemy, never more than four men in a group, would scurry across the naked, shell-pocked floor of the valley.

We had a moment of exhilaration when two Red soldiers tarried beneath a tree long enough for Lieut. Record to lay in a few shells. It was a properly savage thrill to see the Reds pause in the shade and light cigarettes, and to know that death-dealing shells would descend on them momentarily.

But the Red soldiers were to live. The shells fell a little short and splattered harmlessly in a ricefield.

Just after noon we had some excitement at close range. Three hundred yards to our left and across a deep ravine was a razorback ridge somewhat higher than the observation post. During the attack in the night the enemy had succeeded in mounting a machine gun on the spiny crest, but the nest was knocked out quickly and the gun was abandoned.

Suddenly, as we sat watching the valley, Sgt. Corbin H. Bridges of Fort Smith, Ark., who had been sweeping the ridge with his field glasses, gave a yell. Five or six North Korean soldiers were tumbling over the skyline in an attempt to salvage the machine gun.

Capt. Burnett's men reacted swiftly with fire from rifles and machine guns. But the telling blow was struck by the mortar section. Sgt. Dennis Baker of Chambersburg, Pa., placed a mortar shell smack in the center of the enemy group. When the smoke cleared, one of the Reds lay lifeless on the forward slope, two others, obviously wounded, were crawling over the skyline and the rest disappeared. The machine gun had not been moved.

At another juncture, we had a grandstand seat for an attack launched by a small force of Americans and South Koreans down the Bowling Alley below us. Two American platoons, one led by Lt. James R. Wilson of Aguilar, Colo., and the other by Lieut. John B. Hammond of Manchester, N.H., were to secure the village of Chongpyong, on our right and slightly to the rear, and allow a South Korean force to pass through them and occupy a hill mass immediately in front of us.

Americans Reach Village

Supported by tanks, the Americans reached the village without incident. But the South Koreans, moving in closed-up single file on either side of the road, offered too attractive a target. The enemy waited until the South Koreans had bunched together in a dried-up stream bed and then let loose with mortars and a high-velocity gun.

The effect was terrific. In a few minutes the South Koreans were thoroughly disorganized and running rearward. Later we learned that their commander and their second-ranking officer had been killed by one shell burst.

The Americans were also obliged to fall back. The attack had failed and again Capt. Burnett's men were stuck far out ahead of the Allied force.

"The attack was well planned but the South Koreans were 30 minutes to an hour late in coming up," commented Capt. Martin L. V. Merchant of Ilion, N.Y., whose Fox Company (F company) had contributed Lieut. Hammond's platoon to the attacking forces. (Aug. 26, 1950)

Jeep Ambushed, September 1950

Two Reporters
Are Wounded in
Korea Ambush

3 Others Escape Unhurt
After Guerrillas Fire on
Jeep Bound From Front

WITH AMERICAN FORCES IN KOREA, Monday, Sept. 4, 1950—Philip Potter of the *Baltimore Sun* and Jean de Premonville of the French news agency Agence France Presse were wounded late last night when a jeepload of five correspondents was ambushed while returning from the front.

Potter suffered a bullet wound in the calf of the left leg. De Premonville was shot in the left thigh. Neither man was in serious condition. The others in the party, Alex Valentine of the British news agency Reuters, Henri de Turenne of Agence France Presse and this correspondent, were unhurt.

We had left the battlefield east of Yongsan at 6 P.M. after witnessing the attempt by the First Marine Division to reduce the Communist beachhead east of the Naktong River in that sector. A torrential rain, the first in many weeks, had drenched us, and we faced the dismal prospect of a night-long ride over a mountain road to Pusan.

None of us had the slightest fear of an ambush once we had left the immediate front. There have been some instances of North Korean Communist guerrilla bands penetrating to a depth of 10 miles or so behind the American lines and causing mischief. But we reached Miryang before nightfall, and felt reasonably confident that we were out of danger.

Ambushes Nightly

It developed that we knew very little of the conditions in the unfamiliar country that we were to traverse, for our route took us through the heart of a region where the Communists have many sympathizers. Unknown to us, there had been a series of nightly ambushes on the narrow, twisting road between Samnangjin and Wondong. On Friday night, three South Korean soldiers were killed and seven wounded in an ambush on this lonely 10-mile stretch. On Saturday night, five American soldiers had to shoot their way out of a roadblock.

East of Samnangjin, the road curves away from the Naktong River and climbs a high ridge. We reached the summit without trouble and began the steep descent into Wondong. It was still raining very heavily and the night was so pitchy black that we were obliged to keep our headlights blazing. None of us knew the road and as there was the added hazard of washouts, our driver, a South Korean, held the speed down to 10 miles an hour.

Spot Ideal for Ambush

Halfway down the slope was a hairpin turn and just beyond this curve a spot where the road was cluttered with boulders. It was ideal for an ambush. A driver yielding to panic would probably wreck his vehicle against the steep incline on the left or plunge into the ravine at the right.

We had rounded the curve and were approaching the rough spot when the guerrillas opened fire. One bullet penetrated the windshield and passed between Valentine and myself. It had been fired from some type of automatic small-arms weapon and the gunner was somewhere ahead of us. Another gun opened fire from our rear and scored at least two hits on the jeep. The firing continued until we stopped the jeep and turned off the lights.

This was a terrible moment of decision. There was a single carbine in the jeep but it was solely for morale purposes. It wouldn't shoot. We had our choice of abandoning the jeep and lying down in a ditch or proceeding down the road with headlights ablaze—an easy target for the sniper ahead.

We chose the latter course. Without arms our chances of survival had we stayed were more risky than going ahead.

Fortunately the Reds had ceased firing. They had temporarily lost the target because of the sudden cutting off of our lights. Perhaps it was just as well that the carbine wouldn't shoot. They would have picked up the flash and resumed fire.

Jeep Slides Into Ditch

But we couldn't stay there forever. We yelled some confused and contradictory instructions to the driver, who knew perhaps a dozen words of English. After some agonizing moments, he caught the idea that we wanted to get out of there. We tried it first without lights, but we slid into a ditch and the rear wheels spun sickeningly without taking hold. The two French correspondents leaped from the back seats and started pushing while Valentine threw the jeep into four-wheel drive. A good lurch put us back on the road.

But we needed lights and Valentine had to snap them on. As soon as he did the sub-machine guns chattered again. In our haste to start we nearly left de Turenne behind. We heard him shouting, "Don't leave me!" Potter reached out and helped him into the jeep.

Valentine's expert driving took us around a bend in the road and we breathed easier. Neither Potter nor de Premonville realized at first that they had been hit and it was not until we reached Wondong that Potter discovered his leg wound.

At Wondong we found six American soldiers who said they had had almost nightly brushes with guerrillas in hiding around Wondong station, which they were guarding with the help of South Korean police.

Capt. William Cudworth of St. Paul, Minn., and Lieut. Donald Morrison of Cleveland gave first aid to the two wounded correspondents and later put them on a train for Pusan. (Sept. 4, 1950)

Marines at Inchon, September 1950

The following page-one dispatch was run alongside one from Marguerite Higgins dated two days earlier giving details of the landing in the port of Inchon.

The Marines Push On

Crush Counter-Attack, Drive on Seoul, But Run Into Trouble at Hill 650

WITH THE UNITED STATES MARINES NEAR SEOUL, KOREA, Sept. 17, 1950—Elements of the First Marine Division accomplished today a seven-mile advance that brought them to within 15 miles of Seoul, the

South Korean capital. The most rapid progress came in the afternoon, after the marines had crushed a morning counter-attack by the North Korean Communists, during which six Red tanks were destroyed in five minutes.

The advance was highlighted by the capture of the Kimpo airfield, the only major airfield in the Seoul area and the largest field in Korea. This was one of the most important objectives of the Inchon campaign.

A second major objective of the operation, capture of high ground dominating the main road and railroad running from Seoul to the Pusan beachhead, where the bulk of the Red forces are engaged, was proving a more difficult task. The marines encountered their first stiff opposition from an estimated battalion of Communists holding strong positions on Hill 650. A battle for the summit of the hill was still going on at nightfall.

The marine advance on Kimpo was so rapid that the small Red force defending the field apparently had not had time to mine the 6,000-foot asphalt runway. But the runways and other facilities of the field had been damaged extensively by American air raids.

After stopping the Red counter-attack, the marines broke through a ring of low hills that lie just beyond Inchon, and moved into flat terrain. They met only sporadic resistance from an estimated platoon of badly frightened Communists who would fire a few volleys from prepared positions and then retreat. The Kimpo field was held by about 500 Red troops but they had no mortars or artillery support.

The marines were being slowed not so much by the enemy as by logistical problems. The landing of reinforcements and equipment has been delayed by the poor port facilities at Inchon.

In the Red counter-attack this morning, six Russian-made T-34 tanks crawled at first light to a point within six miles of Inchon, in an area where the road from Seoul threaded a shallow pass between a range of low, grassy knolls. Marine outposts atop the knolls allowed the tanks to enter the pass unmolested. The tanks descended into an open plain. Two of them stayed on the road. The rest debouched into a cornfield.

It was a trap. Marine tanks on high ground a half-mile to the west picked them off as they came into view. High velocity 90-mm. shells made blazing wrecks of all six of the Red tanks within five minutes. Meanwhile, the marines opened up with machine guns on the Red infantry walking beside the tanks. The pass and the fields below soon were littered with enemy dead.

MacArthur Sees Carnage

This mangle of bodies was seen by General of the Army Douglas MacArthur when he visited the front line later in the morning. One of the Red tanks was still ablaze. On the turret of another were strewn the torn bodies of Red tankmen who had been machine-gunned as they emerged from the escape hatch.

Only one marine casualty was suffered in the repulse of the counter-attack. Since the start of the invasion, marine casualties have been phenomenally light.

The way the marines flushed small coveys of Reds from gullies and cornfields was a model of deadly efficiency. Seizing the advantage of high ground, the marines moved along the crests of ridges and knolls, quickly spotting enemy groups which were striving frantically to set up roadblocks in the valleys below. (Sept. 18, 1950)

The Great Retreat, December 1950

Bigart Surveys Situation as Eighth Army Continues Its 'Great Retreat'; Criticizes Strategic Decisions

SEOUL, Dec. 5, 1950—The full impact of defeat—the worst licking American arms have suffered since Bataan—has not yet been felt by the great bulk of American troops in Korea. The retreating soldiers are too weary and too preoccupied to think of the consequences.

Those who participated in the great retreat, those who are moving southward tonight on dusty crowded roads to new positions in a series of desperate rear-guard actions, have no time to brood over the grim prospect for tomorrow. In this situation a man asks only to stay alive. He becomes a hoarder of days, and each sunrise is lovelier than the last.

Later, when the drug of fatigue has worn off and the fear of imminent death has subsided, there will be bitterness. Already some of the thoughtful officers are beginning to question the sanity of recent military decisions which may not have caused, but certainly accelerated, this crisis. The most questionable decision of the last few weeks was General of the Army Douglas MacArthur's abortive offensive, which the enemy quickly turned into defeat.

Before the offensive was launched it was noted by observers that any attempt to push beyond the neck of the Korean Peninsula would be unsound, even if the Chinese Communists withdrew. To fan out a small force along the rugged fastness of a 700-mile frontier with Red China and the Soviet Union simply made no sense. It was an invitation to disaster. Any frontier with a Communist power is exceedingly difficult to seal. That was learned by the American military mission to Greece.

Adequate vigilance of the lengthy frontier would have required a force many times that which the United Nations threw into the Korean campaign. Had our commands all reached the border, we would have been obliged to disperse our forces in small garrisons at isolated points. There would necessarily be unguarded gaps through which "volunteers" from China could cross and recross the frontier at will, exposing the garrisons to the constant threat of annihilation.

Yet, despite the certainty of border incidents that would compel the U.N. troops to remain in Korea indefinitely, General MacArthur's headquarters did nothing to discourage the belief that practically everyone would be home by Christmas.

General MacArthur's chief of intelligence, Maj. Gen. Charles A. Willoughby, said last Friday that he knew there were 10 Chinese Communist corps either in Korea or on the Manchurian side of the Yalu River when the "home by Christmas" offensive was launched on Nov. 24. Presumably General Willoughby passed this intelligence on to General MacArthur.

If Supreme Command, Allied Powers, knew all this, why was Maj. Gen. Edward M. Almond's 10th Corps given the green light to go traipsing up into the far reaches of northeastern Korea, leaving behind an attractive vacuum between it and Lieut. Gen. Walton H. Walker's Eighth Army on the other side of the peninsula? Instead of buttoning up with General Walker, General Almond seems to have been fighting an independent war of his own.

It did not require any deep thinking by the Chinese Communist commanders to strike their heaviest blow down the center of the peninsula. The right flank of the Eighth Army was open and inviting. It was the sort of situation that the Chinese Reds, skilled in the Soviet technique of wide-sweeping envelopment, knew how to exploit. The Chinese counteroffensive quickly accomplished the dual result of caving in the Eighth Army's flank and isolating General Almond's corps. To escape envelopment, the Eighth Army was forced to fall back rapidly, with its flank still ragged and sloppy.

Meanwhile, the 10th Corps faces the imminent prospect of a Dunkerque. Nor is the situation much better with the Eighth Army. For although General Walker's troops escaped entrapment north of Pyongyang, thanks mainly to the skillfully conducted withdrawal by the First Corps under Maj. Gen. Frank W. Milburn, they are no longer capable of regaining the initiative from the overwhelming Chinese Communist forces, and they may be obliged to pull back into a defensive beachhead perimeter.

The overall strategic picture is even more depressing. Two-thirds of the existing trained professional troops of the United States Army are pinned down a in a part of the world where little damage can be inflicted on the archenemy, the Soviet Union. This is not a place where the West can achieve a victory.

A unit commander, noting that the Chinese Communists had won with virtually no artillery, no armor and no air power, said: "We've got to choose our own battleground, where superior weapons can be effective. We should avoid fighting in this sort of terrain against an enemy that has a great reserve of manpower. We can't hurt Russia here." (Dec. 6, 1950)

Bigart Accused of Undermining MacArthur, November 1951

Bigart's work in Korea brought him a 1950 Pulitzer Prize for foreign correspondence, his second, a point of pride with him ever after. It also won familiar denunciations from the military. After General MacArthur was dismissed from his command in April 1951, his supporters pressed the attack. This appeared in *The New York Times* of November 28, 1951.

Willoughby Hits
Korea News 'Bias'

MacArthur's Aide Says Stories
Caused Chief's Dismissal—
Reporters Deny Charges

Maj. Gen. Charles A. Willoughby charged yesterday that "biased, prejudiced and inaccurate" news coverage of the Korean war had contributed to the dismissal of General of the Army Douglas MacArthur from his Far Eastern command. . . .

General Willoughby, former chief of intelligence for General MacArthur, made specific accusations against six war correspondents and three news magazines of having "created an atmosphere of tension, uneasiness and distrust between Tokyo and Washington." The general said:

"This is believed to have been the major cause of the MacArthur-Truman split. A whispering campaign bears fruit in human relations—

even the most complaisant husband will sooner or later pick up gossip, if it is repeated often enough and loud enough."

He named as "among" writers guilty of alleged distortions, Joseph Alsop, syndicate columnist; Hanson W. Baldwin, military correspondent of *The New York Times;* Homer Bigart of the *New York Herald Tribune;* Hal Boyle of the Associated Press; Drew Pearson, syndicate columnist, and Christopher Reed, former member of the *Herald Tribune* Far East staff.

He named *Time, Newsweek* and *U.S. News & World Report* as magazines that "appeared to go out of their way to create defeatist thought patterns and to belittle the country's armed forces."

Writing in *Cosmopolitan Magazine,* General Willoughby said that the Hearst and Scripps-Howard newspapers have "invariably been reliable and well-informed." *Cosmopolitan* is a Hearst publication. . . .

General Willoughby's accusations were immediately challenged by most of those whom he accused. . . . Mr. Bigart, now in Paris, cabled: "General MacArthur and his tight little circle of advisers have never been able to stomach criticism, whether from a war correspondent or the President of the United States. In an attempt to silence criticism, they have adopted the line that anyone who questions their judgment is 'inaccurate, biased and prejudiced' and that any criticism of them involves a slur on the whole army." . . .

Mr. Alsop said, in part: "Men like Homer Bigart and Hal Boyle who were frontline correspondents right through the war knew a damn sight more of what was going on than General Willoughby, so far as I was able to observe." (Nov. 28, 1951)

The *Trib* returned Bigart twice more to Korea and also in the early fifties assigned him to assess the Indochina war, the struggle over the Chinese off-shore islands and gave him a long stint in Teheran during an oil crisis. Between crises, he was assigned to Washington, where he covered the Army-McCarthy hearings in the spring of 1954.

Guatemala

Covering a Non-War,
June 1954

In 1954, the Central Intelligence Agency, as Harrison Salisbury has amply documented in his history of *The New York Times, Without Fear or Favor,* was working in Guatemala to overthrow the leftist government of Col. Jacobo Arbenz. So concerned was the Agency about keeping its coup-making covert, Salisbury writes, that it used "duplicitous means" to keep Sydney Gruson, the *Times* man in Mexico City, off the scene. Bigart, on the scene, filed a Latin American synopsis to the tune of Evelyn Waugh's "Scoop," raising doubts about the indigenous quality of the revolution. The coup came four days later and by autumn, Col. Carlos Castillo Armas, the rebel leader, was president and the customary aid agreement was signed with the U.S.

It's Best Done From a Bar in Honduras

How to Cover a War in Guatemala

TEGUCIGALPA, HONDURAS, June 25, 1954—This former mining town, now the capital and chief city of Honduras, is at present swollen in population by a horde of "gringo" journalists attempting to cover the uprising in Guatemala from the bar of the Hotel Prado.

It is about 100 miles from the bar to the little Guatemalan village of Esquipulas, where Col. Carlos Castillo Armas, supreme chief of the movement of national liberation, has set up temporary headquarters.

Normally the gringo newspaper men would tear themselves away from the creature comforts of the Hotel Prado and attach themselves to the rebel leader. There are, however, some good reasons why they prefer to sit tight and raise a glass to the revolution.

One reason is money. You can get to the frontier only by chartering a private plane. You can rent a very small plane for $150 a day but a DC-3, familiarly known as the workhorse of World War II, costs $200 an hour.

By jamming five correspondents into a plane that normally seats three, you can cut the cost to about $30 a man. Having lined up a pilot, usually an American barnstormer, you take off at dawn from Toncontin Airport here and head for the frontier town of Nueva Ocotopeque, already known to the gringos as New Octopus.

There is no news at New Octopus. There is no sound of gunfire from across the border. The scene is distressingly tranquil.

But presently a light, single-engine plane with a propeller smaller than a double-bladed canoe paddle comes bobbing over the mountains. The young pilot is a Guatemalan rebel. With luck, he can be persuaded to lift you over to Esquipulas.

Now comes the second reason for staying back in the Prado bar. Colonel Castillo is a friend of the gringos. But he would just as lief not have them hanging around headquarters. One day, descending from the sky like locusts, these gringos appeared to outnumber his troops.

Naturally, Colonel Castillo would like to make his uprising look like an all-Guatemalan deal. The anti-Communist Guatemalans may be split into factions but all of them are staunchly nationalistic.

Just a Sleepy Town

Assuming you reach Esquipulas, there is still no sign of conflict. The little town sleeps in the shadow of a massive church which looms as white as a wedding cake on a hill at the end of a cobbled street lined with shops. Colonel Castillo may be found in a little pension, or boarding house, at the other end of the street.

There is no war story at the rebel headquarters. The insurgents are still unblooded. The slim 39-year-old colonel says he hopes to unseat President Jacobo Arbenz without bloodshed. A cynic might assume, however, that the colonel is marking time until a junta, a revolutionary committee, is organized that can deliver the army to his side without fighting.

So you return to Tegucigalpa and find that a larger amount of blood has been spilled in a student riot not far from the Prado bar.

After the discomforts of the war theater, where fleas and vicious red ants never call a truce, Tegucigalpa is a wonderful place. The climate is ideal. This is the rainy season, but the rain comes in brief, heavy downpours with long periods of sunshine between them. It is cooler than New York, for the altitude is 3,200 feet.

Apart from the air-conditioned climate, there is little to say about Tegucigalpa except that the name is an Indian word meaning Silver Hills. There are still some silver and gold mine workings near town.

Tegucigalpa is perhaps the smallest and most primitive of the Central American capital cities. It also has the distinction of being one of the few capitals in the world without a railroad. Engineers found it tough enough to build a highway across the jumbled mountains surrounding the city.

Built on a Mountain

The city proper is built on the side of a mountain, its pastel-colored stucco houses rising in tiers on a verdant slope. A muddy little river, the Choluteca, washes the bottom of the mountain and across the stream is the flat, dull suburb of Comayaguela, where the students fought the police Wednesday night.

Tourists seldom come to Tegucigalpa. There is no reason why they should. About the only amusement is the golf course at the country club, a scabrous nine-hole wasteland with virtually no greens.

One of the highlights of the week for permanent residents is the Sunday morning ride to the airport. It is a ritual in which the entire American colony indulges. The Americans go out to greet the plane from Florida, which brings Miami newspapers fat with comics. (June 26, 1954)

Middle East

In October 1955, about the time of his forty-eighth birthday, Bigart left the *Trib* for the *Times*. The anecdotes about this change are many, and he probably contributed a few himself. After his retirement, in an interview for the *Times* oral history project, he called it the easiest phone call he ever made, with the *Times* managing editor, Turner Catledge, replying, "Come on over." One cause of the shift, he said in the interview, was that his ex-wife, Alice Veit, had shifted to the *Times* and "sheepishly" he followed her. She may have played a role, but the *Trib* was surely going downhill financially and Bigart knew it.

In the *Times*'s obituary of Bigart, printed in the appendix, Clifton Daniel, a subsequent *Times* managing editor, says that Bigart was never disloyal to the *Times,* but he was never in love with it as he was with the *Trib.* The *Trib* always sent him first class, Bigart said, and he believed *Times* editors and auditors behaved like bureaucrats. In fact, he referred scathingly to one foreign editor as "the clark," giving the British inflection to the title. On another occasion, he spoke of "pallid clerks who are in charge of my destiny."

In truth, *Times* people were a little intimidated by Bigart—two-time Pulitzer winners are rare indeed—and they tiptoed around him more than was good for a working fool. In one famous Bigart tale, a *Times* city editor, perplexed by the unhappiness of his staff, many of whom had also come from the shabbier plant two blocks to the south, asked Bigart reverently how the *Times* could be made more like the *Trib*. "You could take out the air-conditioning," Bigart said.

Israelis Mop Up in Gaza, November 1956

Bigart spent most of 1956 back at the eastern end of the Mediterranean, covering Cyprus, where communal warfare and efforts to oust the British foreshadowed its independence, and in Israel, where tensions and incidents were overtures to the Sinai-Suez War. On October 30, he was in Magyarovar, Hungary, covering the uprising. But as Soviet troops maneuvered for the attack, he was returned to Israel for the end of the war there. This dispatch is enhanced by Bigart's sense of history.

Israelis Are Mopping Up

12,000 Prisoners Taken

TEL AVIV, Saturday, Nov. 3, 1956—Israel's lightning conquest of Egypt's Sinai Peninsula and the Gaza Strip is complete except for mopping-up operations. The ancient Philistine capital of Gaza was the last town to fall.

In its drive, Maj. Gen. Moshe Dayan's tough Army had killed, captured or put to flight 30,000 Egyptian troops east of the Suez Canal.

With Israel's southern flank secure after only four days of operations, the Government faced with calm confidence reports that Jordan was being reinforced by Syrian troops and that the Syrian-Jordanian-Egyptian defense pact was about to become operative.

Gaza collapsed after a three-hour fight yesterday morning. A United Nations truce aide, Lieut. Col. Robert Bayard of the United States, arranged the surrender of the Egyptian commander at 11:30 A.M. An Israeli armored column entered at noon.

An estimated total of 12,000 prisoners was taken in the 30-mile Gaza Strip, which had been occupied by Egypt since the truce in the 1948–49 Israeli-Arab war.

At dawn, before the attack began, a destroyer of the United States Sixth Fleet evacuated 30 United Nations aides from Gaza beaches. Six truce observers led by Colonel Bayard stayed behind to effect a quick surrender and save the 50,000 inhabitants of Gaza from the agony of prolonged street fighting. . . .

The surrender ended organized resistance, except for scattered pockets on Samson Hill, a sandy ridge north of Gaza named for the Biblical hero who pulled down the Philistine temple. There Egyptians, occupying some houses and entrenched in a nearby orange grove, held out for a few more hours with mortar and small-arms fire.

Egyptian Remnants Trapped

Last night continued fighting was reported only in a few unidentified places in central Sinai, where the remnants of the Egyptian force appeared hopelessly trapped. Large numbers of Egyptians were said to be fleeing along the northern coast road toward Port Said.

A considerable force had surrendered near El Arish, Israelis said, and Israeli forces were pressing westward from that main Egyptian supply base.

The deepest penetration, however, was achieved over desert trails in central Sinai leading toward the southern terminus of the Suez Canal. There, the Israelis reported, their forces were within 13 miles of the canal.

This advance of more than 100 miles across the center of the Sinai wilderness was said to have been accomplished less than 90 hours after the Chief Rabbi of the Israeli armed forces placed a Torah in the lead-off jeep and told the troops:

"You are about to enter holy soil. For in this land Moses, our teacher, received the law." . . .

Israel has never recognized the Egyptian title to Gaza and is expected to move to incorporate the strip as Israeli territory. . . .

Yesterday was a day of jubilation for a score of frontier settlements along the Gaza Strip. For eight years, Nahal Oz, a communal settlement directly opposite Gaza, has lived in fear of attack.

Yesterday settlers could look across two miles of flat fields to the sandy ridges of Gaza and observe on the western skyline long columns of Israeli troops and armor.

Crowds of settlers crossed the shallow trench marking the frontier and walked to the outskirts of Gaza. There was not much to see.

Gaza is a clutter of adobe and stucco houses set among orange groves and vineyards.

Their southern edge is Jebel Muntar, the hill where defending Turks inflicted a painful defeat on the British in World War I. The Egyptian defenders were less tough.

Among Arab inhabitants, the prevailing sentiment was one of undisguised relief that Gaza had been spared with apparently slight damage and loss of life.

A white-bearded man cried out to newsmen: "It's all finished. Thank God!"

Crowds of ragged children saluted troops. In the central square, hundreds of men sat on the ground awaiting screening.

"What will you do with them?" a soldier was asked.

"I expect they will all get a pair of shoes and the first square meal they have had in months," the soldier replied. (Nov. 3, 1956)

Yemen Opens Up in War With British, January 1957

Yemen, at the southwest corner of the Arabian peninsula, was a place virtually unseen by Western reporters. So when it suddenly popped open in 1957, it was a natural for Bigart, a veteran of the Middle East. After his coverage of Israel, Bigart was unwelcome in most of the Arab world and at one point could not even get a transit visa for Beirut, Lebanon. But war creates odd allies, and the Yemenis were willing, so he was assigned to what Lewis Jordan, the *Times* news editor, called Yemen's "little bit of war." The *Times* memorialized the event with a promotion advertisement showing its bemused correspondent standing in the Taiz marketplace.

Remote Yemen Opens Kingdom to Inspection

Small Arab Nation Bids for Support in Fight With British

TAIZ, YEMEN, Jan. 25, 1957—The isolated Kingdom of Yemen has opened its shutters to the outside world.

Engaged in sporadic fighting with Britain along her frontier with the Aden Protectorate, Yemen decided that the appropriate way to appeal to world opinion would be to invite inspection by Western newsmen.

Consequently, three British newsmen, three Americans and one Swiss suddenly found the door open to one of the least-known nations. They have been told they may go where they please and write what they please about this mountainous land at the southern end of Arabia.

There is no easy road to Yemen. To reach Taiz from Aden requires eight hours in a jeep. It is only 125 miles but the road is a rough track across the sandy desert of the western part of the Aden Protectorate, past the green oasis of the Sultanate of Lahej, then over a black desert of volcanic rock to the Yemeni frontier.

Beyond the frontier the trail winds upward through boulder-strewn wadis, or valleys. Finally, in the uplands of southern Yemen, the trail emerges from a world of emptiness into a fertile area fed by mountain streams.

Taiz, the present residence of Imam Ahmed, the Yemeni ruler, sprawls at the base of a 9,800-foot mountain. It is a city of 12,000 inhabitants, built almost entirely of stone. Towering above the narrow streets off the walled square are the twin whitewashed minarets of Al Ashrafia mosque, which stands on a terrace with the forbidding gray cliffs of Jabal Sabir in the background.

Ruined castles perched on the rocky crags of the mountain behind Taiz give the place a romantic look. Taiz, which has electric lights and one paved street, is tucked in a fold of the mountain, but the city has burst out of its ancient walls and new suburbs now cover the flanking heights.

The King's garden, an expansive plantation of coffee bushes, tomato patches and groves of oranges, limes and papayas, is spread in terraces below the city.

It was observed that the townspeople seemed healthy and energetic, much more alert than the lowland Arabs. This probably is due to Taiz' 4,500-foot altitude, which affords a dry, cool climate.

A great curiosity, but no unfriendliness, was exhibited by the crowds in the market place.

Yemeni national dress is far different from the flowing robe and white headdress of the Saudi Arab. The Yemenis wear colored turbans wound over embroidered skull caps. The robes usually reach just below the knees and are gathered at the waist by a gold and black embroidered belt that always contains an ornate curved dagger.

Only one man was seen in Western dress. He was a Foreign Ministry spokesman, a Cairo-educated young man who welcomed the newsmen on behalf of his Government and promised that they could go anywhere in Yemen and stay as long as they liked and write what they liked.

An Interview Indicated

The newsmen were escorted to a Government guest house. There the Foreign Ministry spokesman explained that the Imam, who suffers from rheumatism, was taking baths at Sokhna, on the coastal plain, but might permit an interview later.

The spokesman charged that the British had strafed the Yemeni villages of Harib, Gadaba, Al Beidha and Sheaib in the last month. The newsmen could visit these places and view the destruction, he said.

He said that the British were stirring up Aden Protectorate tribes against Yemen and that they had two motives: "They want to colonize us, and they want to prevent us from cooperating with Egypt and the other Arab states."

On the other hand, Yemen claims the protectorate of Aden as part of Yemen.

Friday being the Moslem sabbath, all Government offices were closed. The newsmen were taken on a tour of the Imam's gardens, where bearded men in dark turbans were hacking off bunches of green bananas and dropping them down deep holes in the sandy earth. The King's gardener, a stout, purple-robed man with the inevitable curved dagger hanging from his embroidered belt, said the bananas were stored underground three days to ripen.

Bordering the garden were ghat bushes. The spokesman said the Government was trying to discourage the wide addiction to chewing ghat leaves, which have a mild narcotic effect similar to that resulting from the smoking of marijuana. In town many Yemenis were seen wearing selected bunches of tender young leaves in their turbans.

More pleasant is the custom of sniffing aromatic herbs. Several varieties of these were thrust under the noses of the visiting newsmen as they sipped strong Yemeni coffee in an open cafe.

Having no paper currency—the national bank opened only a year ago—Yemen's standard money is the Maria Theresa thaler. The plump double-chinned visage of the Austrian Empress stamped on these heavy silver coins of 1780 is familiar to all Yemenis.

Cairo broadcasts boom from every radio in the market place. Pictures of President Gamal Abdel Nasser of Egypt are displayed and the city is flooded with cards showing a triumphant President Nasser in the foreground with beaten soldiers carrying the flags of Britain, France and Israel in the rear.

Never before had so many Western newsmen been admitted. For centuries the land of the Imam had been closed to all non-Arabs except for a few diplomatic and technical missions. The country's pastoral civilization has changed little since the days of the Prophet Mohammed.

Word had been passed through Yemeni commercial agents in Aden that Imam Ahmed had invited to Taiz all newsmen who wanted to undertake the journey—all, that is, except any who might have had an Israeli visa in his passport. Immediately there was a wild scramble for Maria Theresa silver coins, and for as many "wonder drugs" as Aden chemists could provide against internal disorders.

The thaler rose from 70 to 80 cents on the Aden money mart. Chemists ran out of specifics for stomach trouble and malaria.

Then, their suitcases bulging with heavy coins, the newsmen got into Yemeni jeeps festooned with bunting and papier-mâché roses that rattled in the desert wind like scrub oaks in a snowstorm.

The Yemeni drivers proved astonishingly good. They lurched across the churned-up dunes without stalling. They wheeled in and out of rock-strewn valleys without smashing a tire.

In the thinning air, the blue mountains of Yemen looked deceptively near as the jeeps neared the frontier. At the border the red and white flag of Yemen flew from a stone guardhouse where short, lean, black-bearded Yemeni carrying long rifles surrounded the vehicles to stare at the foreigners. (Jan. 28, 1957)

Yemeni Ambush, February 1957

Yemenis Ambush British Platoon

2 Cameron Highlanders Die, 6 Wounded by 'Dissident' Tribesmen in Arabia

DHALA, WESTERN ADEN PROTECTORATE, Feb. 5, 1957—With a skirling of bagpipes, a platoon of the Queen's Own Cameron Highlanders set out yesterday on a return march to Dhala from a remote outpost six miles south across the high Khuraiba Pass.

An hour later the Camerons, following a goat path up a wadi (valley) rimmed with sheer cliffs, stumbled into an ambush. Two soldiers in the leading section were killed by the first volley. Six others, including the piper and the company commander, Maj. Christopher Grant, were wounded.

The assailants were "dissident" tribesmen, probably members of the Azraqi tribe. In the Amiri country, where Dhala is the market center, most tribes are now in revolt against the youthful Amir Shaful Bin Ali Shaif, a trusted ally of the British. According to the British, these dissidents receive money and arms from Yemen.

Trapped in the Wadi, the Camerons did not panic. The column took defensive positions behind rocks and returned fire on the tribesmen, who were shooting down at them from stone parapets atop a cliff.

Shooting Lasted 30 Seconds

The wounded were dragged to cover. One soldier, fatally wounded near the heart, fired the 10 rounds in his magazine, then rolled over on his weapon and died.

It was all over in 30 seconds. The tribesmen, numbering about 15, estimated from their volume of fire, withdrew. But the Camerons were still in a tough predicament.

They were less than five miles from Dhala but the trail was so steep and rocky that the six wounded men could not possibly be carried over it. Walkie-talkie radio was useless because the messages were blocked by an impenetrable wall of mountains between the wadi and the Dhala headquarters.

Slim 19-year-old Lieut. Anthony P. Runge, the commander of the platoon, took one of his men and made a dash through the wadi and over the mountain pass to the Dhala plateau. They were not fired on.

By late afternoon reinforcements were moving south from Dhala. They came under light fire as they neared the wadi but joined up with the ambushed column before dark.

Wounded Flown to Aden

The wounded were carried a mile to a small settlement where they were sheltered in a mud house. Capt. Brian O'Dowd of Liverpool, the company's medical officer, treated their wounds.

He decided that the men would have to be evacuated by helicopter.

This morning a helicopter made three trips over the mountains, shuttling the wounded to the airstrip here. They were taken by plane to Aden.

Meanwhile another sector of the Yemen frontier was enlivened by what a British communiqué called a "heavy attack by Yemenis." This action took place today in the Manawa area of the Beihani Amirate.

The communiqué said a force of 150 Yemenis attacked across the border but were driven back by units of Aden Protectorate levies, Government guards, Beihani tribal guards and Beihani tribesmen. Three Yemenis were killed. There were no casualties among the protectorate forces, the communiqué said. (Feb. 6, 1957)

Israelis and Syrians Exchange Captives, March 1958

Israelis and Syrians Exchange Captives In Warlike Setting

BNOT YAAKOV BRIDGE, ON ISRAELI-SYRIAN BORDER, March 29, 1958—Israel and Syria exchanged prisoners today with the curt formality of nations already at war.

Across the Bnot Yaakov (Daughters of Jacob) Bridge above the rain-swollen Jordan River, 41 Syrians and five Israelis moved to freedom, some after more than a year in prison camps.

All were able to walk the short span except one Syrian soldier who was carried on a stretcher.

The Syrian group numbered 35 soldiers and 6 civilians. Most of the

Syrians were captured last Dec. 12 when Israeli Army units invaded Syrian territory near the northeast corner of the Sea of Galilee to destroy gun positions threatening Israeli fishermen.

The Israeli group consisted of four soldiers and one civilian. The soldiers were captured in Syrian territory Dec. 8, 1954. A fifth soldier taken in that action was found dead in his Syrian prison cell a little more than a month after capture. United Nations observers were told by the prison director that the youth had hanged himself.

The exchange was carried out smoothly under the direction of the United Nations truce supervisory organization.

The negotiations were delayed more than a year because both sides demanded prisoners who could not be traced.

Shortly after 11 o'clock on this dark rainy morning an Israeli convoy left the police station at Rosh Pinna for the Syrian frontier. An ambulance led the way, followed by two army trucks, with curtains drawn, containing the army prisoners, an open truck on which Israeli soldiers manned a machine gun and a police station wagon carrying the Syrian civilians. These civilians, seized as "infiltrators," included a young girl.

Before descending a steep twisting road to the Jordan channel, the convoy waited 30 minutes at an Israeli checkpoint near the ruined village of Mishmar Hayarden (Watchmen of the Jordan), which the Syrians destroyed in 1948.

The Syrians were late. Finally, a Syrian convoy was spotted creeping down the mountain on the opposite shore: two ambulances, two empty buses and a truce car painted white.

Halfway up the Syrian slope and easily visible was a long line of trenches and strong points, apparently unoccupied, but which the Syrians are threatening to use if the Israelis carry out a plan to divert Jordan River water at a point just below the Daughters of Jacob Bridge.

The convoy passed through the fortified line and paused at the Syrian checkpoint, a two-story stone building with a gaping hole in the roof caused by Israeli shells eight years ago and left unrepaired.

The truce teams met in the center of the bridge over a swift, murky stream, barely 20 feet across, which looks more like a drainage ditch than a river. There were frigid bows and handshakes. Then the convoys were motioned forward, each stopping just short of its end of the bridge.

Wearing Winter Coats

A Syrian colonel, tall and wearing sunglasses although the day was dark, strode to the rear of the Israeli trucks. The flaps were raised, exposing the Syrian soldiers wearing the winter overcoats they had on when captured last December. On the back of each garment was a large circle of blue paint with which Israeli guards had branded them prisoners.

The colonel read out a list of names. One young soldier stood up in the truck and repeated his name in a loud voice to the merriment of a few hundred young, tough Israelis who had gathered from nearby settlements.

Then the Syrians dismounted and stood in the road for several minutes, surrounded by Israelis, before they were marched across the bridge.

When the Syrians had cleared the far end of the bridge the four captive Israeli soldiers and one civilian were delivered. Flowers and bottles of wine were pressed on them. The soldiers looked pale but otherwise in fair condition. The civilian, who had disappeared Aug. 15, 1954, while spraying Huleh swamps against malaria, said he was quite sick and asked to be taken to a hospital.

The freed soldiers were driven to a police station at Safed and given new uniforms. (March 30, 1958)

Eichmann Trial

Israelis Anxious,
April 1961

―――――

Trial of Eichmann
Stirs Israeli Fears

MAAYAN ZVI, ISRAEL, April 8, 1961—Survivors of German concentration camps await with dread the opening of the trial of Adolf Eichmann. Too many ghosts and too many harrowing memories will be revived for them when the proceedings open Tuesday in Jerusalem's Beit Haam, or House of the People.

Here on Mount Carmel among a prospering kibbutz of mostly German, Austrian and Czechoslovak refugees one finds no trace of exultation over the vengeance about to be wrought against the murderer of their kin.

These survivors only hope that the trial will be brief. They would have preferred to have had Eichmann shot dead in Buenos Aires by his Israeli abductors last May instead of being brought to Israel for a show trial that will assail them with half-forgotten horrors.

"I don't like the trial," said Mrs. Margalit Masad, a survivor of the Bergen-Belsen camp. She suppressed a shudder and looked out the open door of the cottage across fields ablaze with scarlet poppies that the Israelis call "blood of the Maccabees." Children rolled in the new grass and the hillside rang with youthful laughter.

Mrs. Masad had been 16 when the Nazis found her in Rotterdam in 1942. She was separated from her parents at the first assembly camp outside Rotterdam and she never saw them again.

"Those of us who lived through that awful time don't want to relive it in our memories," Mrs. Masad explained. "Perhaps for the others the trial might hold some lessons, but I doubt it. I doubt anyone who wasn't there can ever understand what it meant."

She looked again across the fields to the sea. Here at Maayan Zvi she had found contentment, was happily married to the treasurer of the kibbutz and had three children. She would not read about the trial, she said, and she hoped her children would hear nothing of it.

"We can't revive the victims," Mrs. Masad said. "We can't get any of them back."

Next door 66-year-old Mrs. Margarete Bagainski contended that she had seen Eichmann several times at the Theresienstadt camp. She could only observe him from a distance because all Jews had to vanish from the prison camp street when a whistle signaled his arrival.

"Always when he appeared it was the signal for thousands to be taken away in transports," she said. "But we had no clear picture of what was happening. Only in the final months of the war was it known to us that the transports were taking people to the gas chambers at Auschwitz."

Mrs. Bagainski said her husband had been shot as a hostage in Berlin in 1942. Her two eldest boys were later taken to other camps and apparently killed for she heard nothing further of them. Two surviving children live with her here.

"Eichmann has to be destroyed," Mrs. Bagainski said. "I don't regard him as a human being. No human being could have accomplished what he did. But I don't see why the trial needs all this publicity. It brings back too much painful memories. He should have been executed as soon as he was caught."

But her son Joachim, 24, spoke up: "I'm not against the trial. The trial is a legal necessity. But I hope for the death penalty."

Josef Goress, the kibbutz secretary, said he had lost his parents in a concentration camp. "They can't be made to live again," he said, but he added that the trial might do some good by somehow improving relations between Israel and West Germany.

"I was never one who believed that the German people today could be held responsible for the deeds of previous generations," he declared.

"By dealing with actual perpetrators like Eichmann we can shift communal guilt from the German people."

None of the settlers found that they could blame Dr. Israel Kastner, the Government official who was accused of having made a deal with Eichmann whereby a handful of Zionists were allowed to go to Switzerland while most of the Hungarian Jews were turned over to the Gestapo.

It was "humanly understandable" that Dr. Kastner should try to salvage "the youngest and strongest" Jews rather than the "weakest and oldest," Mr. Goress said.

"If you're in a sinking boat you try to save your children, not your grandparents who may die in a few years anyhow," he added. "In Kastner's position and under the circumstances I don't believe he was guilty of any moral or legal wrong."

The trial is expected to shed new light on the Kastner-Eichmann relationship. Dr. Kastner won a libel action several years ago but was later murdered in Tel Aviv. (April 9, 1961)

Testimony on Warsaw Ghetto Uprising, May 1961

Warsaw Saga Stirs Trial of Eichmann

JERUSALEM (ISRAELI SECTOR), May 3, 1961—The story of the Warsaw ghetto uprising stirred a thronged courtroom today at the trial of Adolf Eichmann.

Israelis stiffened with pride as survivors of the ghetto revolt told of the killing of Nazi tormentors with homemade weapons in the ghetto fighting of April 1943.

After listening for days to sickening accounts of how European Jews had marched with sheeplike acquiescence into the gas chambers of Nazi death camps, spectators found welcome relief in testimony that depicted desperate heroism.

Eichmann, who is charged with the initiation, planning and execution of the Gestapo (secret police) program to annihilate six million Jews, was almost completely ignored. The three Israeli judges and most spectators gave their rapt attention to the retelling of the story of the ghetto revolt. The prisoner in the glass cage seemed to have been forgotten.

Suddenly the room went dark except for an island of light where the prisoner's cage was bathed in the glare of emergency spotlights. The power had failed.

The minds of the 800 spectators were wrenched from the drama of the Warsaw ghetto to the sallow, humdrum, clerklike figure in the dock.

Eichmann squirmed uneasily and turned his head away from the glare of the naked lights. For nearly 15 minutes he was the target of all eyes.

The glass shielding Eichmann is supposed to be bulletproof. All visitors, regardless of station, are thoroughly searched before entering the court. But even with these safeguards the Israeli police tensed in the darkness of the windowless auditorium.

Some spectators had reacted with angry murmurs to previous testimony of Nazi atrocities and only yesterday a man had been dragged raving from the balcony, shouting that he wanted to strike Eichmann.

Judges Sit in Shadows

The three judges, shadowy figures at the rear of the stage, remained seated on the high dais until it became apparent that the blackout could not be remedied quickly. Then a recess was declared.

Five minutes later the lighting was restored and the court returned to its preoccupation with events in Warsaw 18 years ago.

At the end of the session Attorney General Gideon Hausner introduced a document which he implied would connect Eichmann with the repressions that led to the Warsaw ghetto uprising.

Mr. Hausner described this as a photostat of minutes of a meeting Eichmann attended in April 1942 with representatives of the Nazi Foreign Ministry. These minutes showed, the prosecutor said, that Eichmann had asked the consent of the Foreign Ministry officials to application of all security measures necessary to the maintenance of public safety and order to "all inhabitants of the Warsaw ghetto."

Apparently Eichmann took this precaution, Mr. Hausner said, to head off any possible Foreign Ministry objections about mistreatment of non-Polish and non-German Jews trapped in the ghetto when it was sealed off.

Israel is extremely sensitive to suggestions that the Eichmann trial is just an elaborate show. It was apparent that Mr. Hausner had carefully set the stage for the day's testimony on the Warsaw revolt.

Kol Israel, the Government controlled radio, put today's session on the air. It had suspended its daily trial broadcasts after the opening days to avoid "show trial" charges.

Lesson for Israelis

The Warsaw testimony seemed clearly to have been designed for psychological and educational reasons.

Israeli officials have been disturbed by evidence that the postwar generation of Israelis cannot understand and are ashamed of the docility European Jews displayed during the Nazi terror of World War II.

Since the start of the week Mr. Hausner had asked one death-camp survivor after another why Jews faced with certain doom had not revolted. Witnesses had replied that they considered resistance futile, that they feared reprisals against their families and that they were weary and preferred death to further torture. The testimony today was different.

At the start of the morning session the tribunal announced it would ask a West German court to examine four witnesses requested by the defense. The defense had asked that the four, all former Nazi officials, be brought to Israel. But Attorney General Hausner warned that all would be subject to arrest if they set foot on Israeli soil.

The four are Eberhard Von Thadden, who was in charge of Jewish affairs for the Nazi Foreign Office; Herrman Krumey, former SS (Elite Guard) major and a subordinate of Eichmann; Dr. Frank Six, former SS superior of Eichmann in the 1930's, and Dr. Hans Merten, former military administrator in Salonika, Greece.

The presiding justice, Moshe Landau, conceded that in principle it was preferable that witnesses appear in this court. But he said that since the Attorney General had refused to grant immunity, the witnesses would have to be interrogated in West Germany under terms of the legal-aid agreement between that country and Israel.

Both defense and prosecution will submit questions to the four witnesses. Dr. Robert Servatius, Eichmann's lawyer, said that under German court rules these questions could be put to the witness only through a German judge.

The Story of Warsaw

The first witness today was Mrs. Zivia Lubetkin Zukermann, a thin woman with a sharp, embittered face. Mrs. Zukermann, a survivor of the desperate group of young men and women that sparked the Warsaw ghetto uprising began her story in a quiet, deadly earnest voice.

Even before the Nazis sealed off the Warsaw ghetto in the fall of 1940 there were ample signs, she said, of the German intention to degrade and humiliate Jews. Jews had to wear yellow badges and were prohibited from holding foreign currency and from buying tools.

"Already it could be said that Jews were outside the protection of the law and the Germans could do with us as they pleased," Mrs. Zukermann said.

She recalled how on Yom Kippur (the Day of Atonement) in 1940, there was a radio announcement that henceforth all Jews must live in ghettos.

"In this prison, this ghetto, there were no rules at all," she said.

The ghetto was guarded by Gestapo men, but there were also "simple German soldiers," Mrs. Zukermann said, who could come into the ghetto to plunder, to kill, to torture, to take people to forced labor, and to do as they pleased.

She told of growing hunger, of children begging for a piece of bread, of children with hunger-swollen bellies digging in garbage pails for potato scraps.

Despite the deepening misery, there was still no spirit of resistance, the witness said. She said there was an underground but that recruits came slowly.

"Jews simply refused to believe they would be exterminated," she declared. "We could not believe that in the 20th century a nation would pronounce a sentence of death on a whole people."

The liquidation of the ghetto began in July 1942, she said, when Jews were told that all jobless would be transported east where "conditions would be better." These "jobless" were sent to Treblinka, an extermination camp.

Meanwhile Jews trained to fight with sticks. Eventually, Mrs. Zukermann said, they accumulated a small armory of rifles, grenades, Molotov cocktails (gasoline-filled bottles with rags for wicks) and other homemade bombs.

The uprising began, she said, on April 18, 1943.

"At midnight we learned that the ghetto had been surrounded by German troops," Mrs. Zukermann said. "Morning came. I was standing by an attic window and suddenly I saw thousands of armed soldiers enter the ghetto, as though they were going to the front against Russia."

Mrs. Zukermann said she was part of a group of 20 men and women.

"It was strange to see these 20 Jewish men and women standing up against the great enemy, glad and merry because we knew that while they would conquer us, we would go down fighting," she said.

Mrs. Zukermann stuck out her chin and threw back her shoulders. Her pinched face was livid with hate.

"Many of you will not believe it," she said, "but when the Germans came up to our post and marched by and we threw those hand grenades and bombs and we saw German blood flowing on the streets of Warsaw there was rejoicing among us."

"It was wonderful, a miracle," she declared. "Those German heroes retreated leaving their dead and wounded behind. We went out and gathered arms.

"Of course the Germans came back. The fighting continued for days, but not all days were like the first.

"We suffered more casualties and killed fewer Germans. It was clear to everyone that it was almost certain we could not remain alive. But we were fighting to avenge our brothers and it was easier to die."

The other witnesses today included Mrs. Zukermann's husband, Itzhak, and Dr. Adolf Abraham Berman, an Israeli Communist and brother of Jakob Berman, a Stalinist member of the Polish Cabinet before Wladyslaw Gomulka returned to power as head of the Communist party. (May 4, 1961)

As a child, in a studio photograph.
Courtesy of Else Holmelund Minarik Bigart

With his sister Margaret in Hawley, Pennsylvania, probably the mid-1920s.
Courtesy of Else Holmelund Minarik Bigart

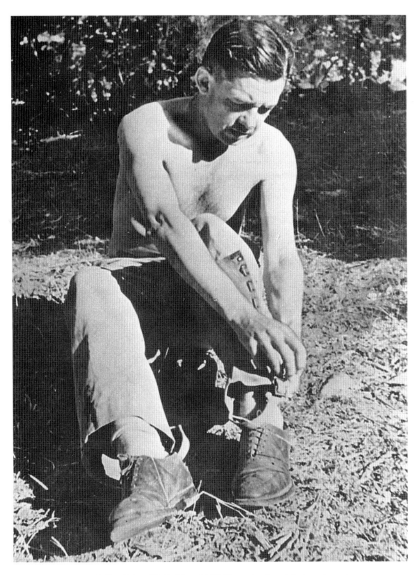

Homer Bigart of the *New York Herald Tribune* lacing his leggings in a
bivouac area in Sicily. (Caption as published August 29, 1943.)
Herald Tribune—Acme, 1943

Correspondents test flying gear as part of training to fly with bomber crews over Germany. *From left:* Gladwin Hill, the Associated Press; William Wade of New York City, International News Service; Robert Post, *The New York Times;* Walter Cronkite of Kansas City, United Press; Homer Bigart of Hawley, Pennsylvania, the *New York Herald Tribune;* and Paul Manning of Pasadena, California, Columbia Broadcasting System. The two others who trained were Denton Scott of Elmira, New York, of the Army magazine *Yank,* and Private Andrew Rooney of the Army newspaper *Stars and Stripes. Associated Press, 1943*

This photo and the caption given above ran with Bigart's dispatch of February 27, 1943, about the daylight raid on Wilhelmshaven, although Post was already dead, and the reporters knew it even if the papers did not report it for a day. The photo was taken earlier in February.

Homer Bigart, war correspondent for the *New York Herald Tribune,* just before embarking with Allied troops who landed below Rome. (Caption as published February 3, 1944.)
Herald Tribune—Acme, 1944

Reading the *Tribune* in yard in Hawley while on home leave in 1944.
Courtesy of I. Reines Skier

A page from Margaret Bigart Crowe's huge scrapbook, to give a faint idea of the impact of the big Bodoni war headlines.

5th Army Attacks, Drives Germans Back; Montgomery Nearing Salerno With Relief

Homer S. Bigart, Anna Schardt Bigart, and their son, Homer, in the yard of the family home in Hawley, Pennsylvania, in the fall of 1944. The correspondent had left the European theater and was on leave before his Pacific assignment. *Courtesy of Else Holmelund Minarik Bigart*

This is the photograph distributed in 1946, when Bigart won his first Pulitzer prize, for covering the Pacific war.
Associated Press

Three reporters on the scene in Palestine in 1946: John Donovan of NBC (*left*); Bigart (*center*); and George Polk of *Newsweek* and CBS. After Polk was murdered in Greece in 1948, Bigart was invited into the mountains by insurgents to interview their leader, the guerrilla General Markos, whom Polk had apparently been seeking when he was slain. Bigart dedicated his interview to the memory of his friend, and won the first George Polk Memorial Award for his four dispatches.

Milbry C. Polk and William Polk

Interviewing the Greek rebel leader, General Markos (*left*), in a churchyard in the Grammos Mountains in 1948. The uniformed woman in the middle is the rebel soldier who acted as interpreter. The photo was made by the foreign minister of the rebel movement, known only as Roussos, who shot a roll of film and gave it to Bigart, who had brought no camera. The *Tribune* used a photo of Markos only; the trade weekly *Editor & Publisher* carried a different picture of these three; and the *Saturday Evening Post* later used a photo of just Bigart and the interpreter, incorrectly describing it as a roadside interview with a partisan.
Courtesy of Else Holmelund Minarik Bigart

In March 1949, the Overseas Press Club in New York presented awards for 1948. Bigart (*left*) won the first George Polk Memorial Award for interviewing General Markos, the man Polk was apparently seeking when he was slain. Elmer Davis of the American Broadcasting Company (*center*) won for radio interpretation of foreign news, and James Reston of *The New York Times,* for press interpretation of foreign news. The winners got gold watches, except for Bigart, who got $500 but had to buy a tuxedo. He typically groused to his managing editor, George Cornish: "Between the tux and the taxes, I'll be in the red." Richard Crandell, picture editor of the *Trib,* told *Editor & Publisher* that this was "Homer in disguise."
The New York Times

This was taken either during the non-war in Guatemala in 1954, or in Cuba in 1958. It is one of a small group of snapshots Bigart kept.
Courtesy of Else Holmelund Minarik Bigart

Bemused in the bazaar in Yemen in 1957. This photo was used with a promotion ad that the *Times* ran in *The New Yorker*. There were not many opportunities to photograph Bigart in the Arab world, and the *Times* seized this one. *The New York Times*

In 1955, soon after joining the *Times*, Bigart was assigned to a story in Fort Knox, Kentucky, where he encountered a youthful Gay Talese, then on leave from the *Times* sports department. *Times Talk*

This engaging photo was taken in 1959 by the paratrooper and reporter Mike James, a colleague and fellow despiser of editors, auditors, and other authority figures.

A moderately baffling 1958 photo, identified as taken in a Cuban rebels' camp. This would be the assignment when Bigart interviewed Fidel Castro, and the government of Fulgencia Batista briefly jailed him. Bigart, who in his smoking years was seldom photographed without a cigarette, here sports a Cuban cigar. The caption in *Times Talk,* the house organ, refers to a pig but none is visible. *Times Talk*

Four snapshots in Vietnam in 1962.
Courtesy of Else Holmelund Minarik Bigart

Probably in Vietnam.
Courtesy of Else Holmelund Minarik Bigart

H.C. Xpywed   Mme Nhu (will l.)

Bid Bra
Tom Lambert   DR TRAN VA
Dang Duc Kho

Fritz
To old
Buddy
B'sa

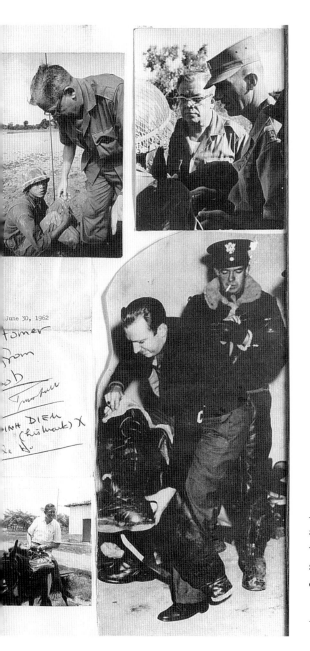

A framed group of snapshots and memorabilia, complete with phony signatures on a song written for Bigart's departure from Saigon.
Courtesy of Else Holmelund Minarik Bigart

Bigart and John Kifner, one of his many fans among the younger reporters, with guardsmen at the Newark riots of 1967. In the later Harlem riots, Bigart was in the office transcribing notes from Kifner on the scene when rioters began to rock the phone booth and Kifner became alarmed. "Don't worry," Bigart said, in a typical allusion to editors, "at least you're dealing with sane people."

The New York Times

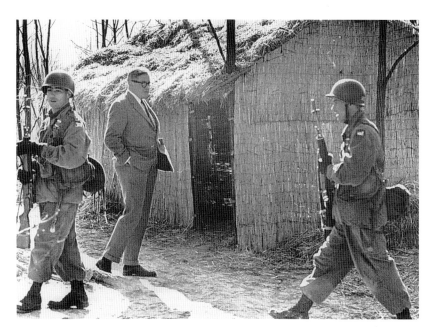

In 1968, trainees at Fort Dix, New Jersey, were working with mock-ups of Vietnamese huts. Bigart's business suit gives the scene a further air of unreality. *Photograph by Patrick Burns, The New York Times*

A typical expression of wry exasperation. This 1972 photo was used with the *Times* obituary of Bigart, and an enlargement was used at a memorial gathering on September 25, 1991. Bigart's friends, young and old, remarked on how familiar the expression was.

The New York Times

In his accessible front-row seat in the *Times* city room at the end of the day.
He is working with a galley proof, possibly the long advance obituary of
David Ben-Gurion, which Bigart wrote and kept up to date, but which was
not needed until December 2, 1973, after Bigart was retired.
The New York Times

On the farm in Nottingham, New Hampshire, in 1972, just after retirement.
Photograph by Betsy Wade

In a working posture in his room at the Mayflower Hotel in Washington on May 5, 1973, just before the ceremony for *More* magazine's A. J. Liebling Award.
Photograph by Betsy Wade

At the *More* award ceremony, in the front row. To his left is his wife, Else Holmelund Minarik; to his right is Herbert Nagourney, then publisher of *Times* Books. To Mrs. Bigart's left is Linda Amster, chief researcher for the *Times.*
Photograph by Betsy Wade

Homer and Else Bigart.
Photograph by Betsy Wade

Bigart greets Wade, who ended up sitting on the floor at the overcrowded gathering.
Photograph by Nancy Moran

J. Anthony Lukas (*left*) and David Halberstam (*right*) doing the "counter-convention" honors for Bigart's "four decades of single-minded attention to his craft, persistent skepticism toward all forms of power and tenacious pursuit of social injustice long before such reporting became fashionable."
Photograph by Betsy Wade

At the Minarik-Bigart farm in Nottingham, New Hampshire, 1985.
Photograph by Frank O'Brien, © *The Boston Globe*

Vietnam War

World War II and the Korean War were demarked by dates. Not so America's longest war, in Vietnam. The U.S. virtually took up where the French left off; President Truman sent cash aid and thirty-five advisers to anti-Communist forces in Vietnam in 1950 and from there the U.S. involvement expanded under Eisenhower, Kennedy, and Johnson, reaching a peak of 543,000 troops in April 1969 before President Nixon began a withdrawal.

The *Tribune* sent Bigart to Vietnam in September 1945, in December 1950, and again in 1953, when he wrote a gloomy three-part assessment of the stalemate in the seventh year of the French-Indochinese war. Nine years later, the *Times* sent him back in the early period of the U.S. escalation, from January to June 1962, when the U.S. was ostensibly limited by the 1954 Geneva cease-fire to 685 advisers in Vietnam although there were already almost 5,000 Americans on hand. His dispatches point out, in *Times*-like locutions, what he told the young Neil Sheehan outright: It doesn't work any more.

But he had difficulty getting to the action. On February 12, 1962, he wrote in a letter: "This is a most frustrating place to work. The Americans and Vietnamese both seem to view reporters with the deepest suspicion. There is an absurd atmosphere of conspiracy. Yesterday a c-47 transport engaged in dropping propaganda leaflets on Communist-controlled areas was apparently shot down 80 miles northeast of Saigon. There was no announcement until about 24 hours later, at noon today. There were eight Americans on board. We don't know to this minute what happened to them. Apparently the plane had Vietnamese air force markings. Why then was it piloted by Americans? Apparently we are bashful about being involved in propaganda drops. I found out too that we are jamming Radio Hanoi. But this was kept secret because we always held jamming was immoral when the Russians did it. I'm afraid all this nonsense is too hypocritical for me."

It was his classic chafing at trying to function on the basis of briefings and communiqués. But there is no front in a guerrilla war. "I've applied to get shot at," he said in his letter, "but getting the necessary security clearance from US and Vietnamese propaganda engineers takes time. I was furious in Hue when I learned that Essoyan, the AP man, had been taken on a combat mission from Saigon. The ban on reporters riding on helicopters was reimposed next day."

Two of his January dispatches thus do not report on combat, but are prescient on two issues that outlived the war: Agent Orange and DDT.

U.S. Destroys Foliage, January 1962

U.S. Spray Strips Foliage Hiding Vietnam Reds

SAIGON, VIETNAM, Jan. 18, 1962—United States planes have sprayed jungle growth along the Saigon-Saint Jacques road to remove foliage hiding Communist guerrillas.

The results are not known yet. The chemical mixture is supposed to kill all trees and brush, but withering and dropping of leaves may take five days to three weeks.

The 70-mile route connecting Saigon with a popular seaside resort had been unsafe for months and diplomats with seashore villas have had to travel by air.

A high South Vietnamese official said today that defoliant chemicals would also be sprayed on Viet Cong plantations of manioc and sweet potatoes in the highlands. The exact locations of these plantations have already been plotted by aerial surveys.

Tests have shown, he said, that manioc and sweet potatoes die four days after having been sprayed. These are the two most important food staples for the Communist bands in the mountains, especially manioc, a plant from which tapioca is made. When dried, it can be stored indefinitely.

The spraying operation along the highway was accompanied by the dropping of pamphlets assuring farmers that the chemicals were harmless to humans and animals.

Defoliants will play an important part in plans to isolate the Communists from their food sources in the highlands.

Another move, this one inspired by the British success against the Communists in Malaya, involves the creation of "white zones" in the highlands. This entails the linking of new land-development centers with nearby villages of primitive mountain tribes, which have been major targets for Communist infiltration.

Civil guard and self-defense units from the land-development centers, in which thousands of Vietnamese from the crowded coastal strip have been resettled, will undertake the defense of the tribal villages. A network of trails providing easy access to the villages is being built, and over these will go food and medical supplies and social service workers who will attempt to win the loyalty of the tribesmen. (Jan. 19, 1962)

DDT Killed the Cats That Ate the Rats, January 1962

Bigart disliked looking at his dispatches as they appeared in the paper, except when he pulled the clips for research on later stories. He said he hated to see what had been done to them. So when William Prochnau, researching his book on early correspondents in Vietnam, visited Bigart after his retirement to New Hampshire, he had to read this story to him before he could ask about it. Bigart was incredulous. "They carried *that* in the *Times*?" he asked. Yes, they did.

A DDT Tale Aids
Reds in Vietnam

Crop Loss Laid to Rats After
Spray Is Used and Cats Go

QUANGNGAI, VIETNAM, Jan. 31, 1962—American DDT spray killed the cats that ate the rats that devoured the crops that were the main props against Communist agitation in the central lowlands. The result: the hungry, embittered rural population is tending to support the Communist insurgents.

This highly oversimplified explanation of the disaster in six provinces overrun by field rats is believed by many Vietnamese.

Experts attached to the United States Operations Mission concede that the cats vanished from the villages after huts had been sprayed with antimalarial DDT. Mosquitoes succumbed but apparently so did puss.

However, the experts downgrade the cat's role as a destroyer of rats. They contend that the rodent population explosion is due less to the disappearance of the cats than to a combination of favorable factors: moisture, climate, availability of food and, chiefly, the Government's failure to insure adequate supplies of rat poison.

Lapse of Judgment

Through some glaring lapse of judgment, pesticides were removed from the commodity import list in 1959. The price of rat poison doubled. By October 1960, there were only two tons of it left, an amount insufficient to discourage the rats in one province.

Meanwhile, rats two-thirds the size of cottontail rabbits and weighing up to four pounds began devouring rice, sugar cane and vegetables in the coastal provinces. Local floods added to the misery. Then came the worst menace of all—a major invasion by the rice leaf hopper, a tiny insect that sucks plant juices.

Again the Government of President Ngo Dinh Diem found itself almost completely unprepared. There was a drastic shortage of insecticide and sprayers. The hoppers destroyed 40 percent of the rice crop in the four northernmost provinces. Large sections of the population are destitute. The Government is spending millions of piasters shipping rice to the stricken areas.

For many months Communist propaganda has been harping on the Government's failure to do anything for the farmers. This line is effective.

Now at last both the United States and the South Vietnamese Governments are awake to the peril. After months of strenuous urging by the United States the Government had agreed to reorganize and consolidate its farm services.

Agreement has been reached on an emergency plan for plant protection. The United States has just provided $800,000 for sprayers, rat poison and insecticides.

Though the program has top priority, the first shipment of 40 tons of rat poison and 7,000 sprayers will not reach Vietnam until late April. (Feb. 2, 1962)

Airlifting Pigs,
February 1962

Pig Airlift Braves
Snipers in Vietnam

POST SIX, CENTRAL VIETNAM, Feb. 4, 1962—United States Army helicopters delivered seven pigs to Post Six today under Communist sniper fire.

The frightened swine, a calf and several chickens and ducks were airlifted to relieve the hungry garrison. Ninety Vietnamese soldiers guarding this forlorn outpost on a tributary of the Cai River had eaten nothing but rice for so long that beri-beri threatened.

From surrounding heights guerrillas fired random shots into the stockade as three helicopters landed. Undeterred, the Vietnamese troops poured from dugouts and fell upon the livestock with glad cries.

It was New Year's Eve by the Chinese calendar and the troops had faced the holiday with an empty larder. Tonight, thanks to the United States Army they were living high on the hog.

The relief of Post Six was accomplished without the loss of a single pig. However, for long minutes bullets crackled through the mountain air as the first helicopter landed.

Out sprang Lieut. Col. William Dickerson of Elizabeth, N.J., who was nearly struck by a falling pig on a similar relief mission a few weeks ago. On that occasion the pigs were dropped from a C-123 transport plane by parachute and one broke from a wicker basket attached to a parachute. It just missed the colonel, who had landed by helicopter.

Today no pigs were required to jump. Colonel Dickerson supervised the speedy unloading of rock salt, cabbage and rice. Then the second helicopter landed with pigs and fowl and the third with a calf.

There was only one error during the mission—an Annamese sergeant serving as swineherd for the flight mistakenly left the plane with his wards and had to be yanked back into the cabin as his helicopter rose.

Post Six will be abandoned soon because it is too difficult to supply. It has no refrigeration facilities so pigs and poultry must be flown in and slaughtered when needed.

Low-lying clouds had shrouded the mountains for 31 consecutive days and had prevented meat deliveries until today. The day began like the preceding days with a drizzling rain falling from a somber sky. The chickens cackled despondently as they were loaded.

The helicopters took off from the I Corps Headquarters at Danang (formerly Tourane) on the South China Sea. After a flight of about 30 minutes in a generally southwestern direction over steep forested mountains they reached Post Six.

The fort sits in a deep hollow surrounded by peaks reaching as high as 4,000 feet. Enemy eyes can follow every movement in the stockade.

Through holes in the cloud cover the post could be glimpsed—a familiar star-shaped stockade with a straw-thatched watchtower, a small red brick headquarters building sprouting radio antennas, a clutter of straw huts, trenches and a mud parapet with its apron of barbed wire.

Soldiers ran to level patches of ground marked with white strips where the helicopters were to land. A rocket flare shot up through the murk as a navigational aid.

The holes in the cloud cover closed, however, making the valley bottom look like a basin of dishwater. With the stockade out of sight, the helicopter pilots had no choice but to go back with the undelivered meat.

It was decided to try again after lunch. The stock was watered and fed. A good omen was seen in the fact that the pilot, Lieut. Kenneth Henrich, came from Needham, Mass., while a crewman, Sp. 16 Richard L. Duncan, came from Hamburg, Iowa.

Together with Warrant Officer John A. Walsh of London, Ont., they succeeded in the mission in the afternoon. (Feb. 9, 1962)

Reds Elude Trap,
March 1962

About two months into his Vietnam assignment, Bigart was still having no luck in his efforts "to get shot at"—getting aboard a helicopter to accompany a raid. When he learned that the visiting Washington columnist Joseph Alsop had gone along on a raid, he blew up. William Prochnau, researching on Vietnam correspondents, reports that Bigart's cable to Emanuel R. Freedman, the foreign editor, said: "If you cannot protect me from this petty Pentagon favoritism, you will have my resignation forthwith." Two days later, Bigart was aboard an H-21 Shawnee for a raid on a "clutter of huts" named Cai Ngai that was described as a Communist stronghold.

Prochnau points out that the Bigart notation that three dead Viet Cong were found and twenty-five others were estimated to have been killed while fleeing marked the start of the body-counting that typified the coverage of combat in Vietnam.

U.S. Copters Help
In Vietnam Raid

Five Craft Hit, One Felled—
Bulk of Red Force Slips
Out of Troops' Trap

CAI NGAI, VIETNAM, March 8, 1962—United States Army helicopters carried a Vietnamese battalion in a successful raid today against this Communist stronghold near the southern tip of Vietnam.

Five helicopters were struck by Communist bullets and one was disabled. There were no American casualties.

The disabled craft, riddled by eight bullets, suffered power failure just as it cleared the last screen of palm trees before the village. It had enough forward momentum to drop safely in a communal rice paddy and unload its troops, who went into action as soon as they leaped to the ground.

Cai Ngai, a clutter of huts along a canal 20 miles southwest of Ca Mau in An Xuyen Province, fell easily after a brief fight. Three Communist guerrillas were killed in a bamboo thicket at the edge of the village. Strafing by Vietnamese fighter planes killed an estimated total of 25 more who had been seen to flee in the encirclement.

A Communist armament factory, a food supply depot and a first-aid station were captured and destroyed. About 20 suspected Viet Cong guerrillas were seized.

But as usual the main enemy force got away. It slipped through the trap even though the airborne attackers had achieved excellent surprise in their vertical envelopment of the village.

The degree of shock among the Red guerrillas was reflected in their failure to inflict a single casualty on the attacking troops. Apparently the Viet Cong felt so secure in this deeply pro-Communist zone that the village was left undefended by mines or foot traps of sharpened bamboo spikes.

In the biggest hut the Viet Cong forces had hastily abandoned preparations for a victory dinner, presumably to celebrate a success two weeks ago when they killed more than a score of Government troops in ambush and also killed a district chief.

The Government troops failed to exploit the Viet Cong state of shock. They bunched up and dawdled in drainage ditches and under the shade of coconut trees until an American adviser cried out in exasperation, "Let's move the thing forward."

The operation had been delayed three hours by poor visibility. Sixteen helicopters of the United States Army's 57th Light Helicopter Company had left Saigon before dawn in clear weather. But nearing Ca Mau the pilots encountered smoke and cloud.

In the still air the smoke lay so heavily under the low cloud cover that Maj. Milton Cherne of South Holland, Ill., ordered the mission to fly back to the Pan Tho airstrip and await improvement. It was noon when troops of the Second Battalion, 32d Regiment, were finally loaded at Ca Mau.

According to the battle plan, the attacking force split into two groups. The first group of about 250 men was to be landed south of the village to cut off escape into the swampland. The second group was to be shuttled in about an hour later and dropped north of the village, blocking flight in that direction. Communists seeking other escape routes were to be strafed by Vietnamese fighter-bombers.

Basically the action went according to plan. On the first flight from Ca Mau the helicopters flew close to the ground so that they could not be detected from any considerable distance. "This is all Viet Cong country," explained Lieut. Salvatore Formica of 77-05 88th Avenue, Woodhaven, Queens.

The pilot brought their helicopters up sharply to clear the trees of Communist-held Cai Ngai, then slowed for the drop into the rice fields across the canal. From the village came a burst of small-arms fire.

"I could hear the crack of the muzzle blast," said Chief Warrant Officer Donald E. Herman of East St. Louis, Ill., co-pilot of the craft hit by eight bullets. "We had engine failure just as we were going over the trees."

One disabled helicopter meant that a whole platoon of Vietnamese troops had to be detached for its protection.

"It is a million dollars' worth of equipment," explained Capt. Robert Bebber of Knoxville, Tenn., adviser to the 32d Regiment.

The disabled helicopter had come down about 200 yards short of its goal, as did all the following craft, and this made a larger gap on the left flank than the planners had intended.

Captain Bebber saw that the opportunity was lost for exploiting the surprise. "Things are going too slow," he kept telling the battalion commander.

There was no more firing from the village. Finally, the Vietnamese left their ditch and moved cautiously across the rice paddies to the palm grove. There one soldier accidentally shot another in the foot. This was the only Vietnamese casualty observed.

By late afternoon it was apparent that the battle was over and that most of the 200 Communists estimated to have been in the village had got away.

Captain Bebber said he was certain the area was full of Communist guerrillas. "We sure hit a nestful this time," he said, "but we just didn't move fast enough." (March 9, 1962)

The Talk of Saigon and an Expulsion Order, March 1962

———————

The following story was never published, and its survival as a piece of paper can be credited to procedures on the *Times*'s foreign desk in the days of metal type. Bigart filed the dispatch, on request, as a "Talk of Saigon," a type of article reporting on events and undercurrents not suitable for separate stories. The context gave Bigart a chance to insert a sly note showing that the U.S. was not adhering to international limits on foreign military advisers.

After it was set in type, the editors decided against it on March 30, for reasons unrecorded, but probably because it had grown stale waiting for space in the paper. The desk "late man," in all likelihood the venerable Herbert French, directed the printer to invert a handful of type slugs, to prevent accidental use of the story, and then to print a proof. The single proof, rubber-stamped "killed by editor," was as usual filed in the clipping morgue, in folder B-759,129, the Bigart bylines, where it yellowed with clippings from that period.

Unpublished or no, this dispatch was cited in a move to expel Bigart from Vietnam. An account of what he described in a letter as "the recent squalid incident" was requested by Ruth Adler, then editor of the *Times* house organ, *Times Talk,* and it is also reprinted below.

U.S.O. Plays Saigon

Bored, Troubled U.S. Troops Get
A Chance to 'Laugh With the Girls'

SAIGON, VIETNAM, March 21, 1962—A United Service Organization show hit Saigon yesterday. It was the first U.S.O. presentation in Southeast Asia. It symbolized even more than the recent arrival of a military police unit how deep is the American involvement in South Vietnam's fight with the Communists.

"Laugh With the Girls," as the show is called, is the ultimate manifestation of the American presence here. It played to capacity houses in downtown Saigon and at nearby Tan Son Nhut Airport. Some observers said the total attendance may even have exceeded the limit of 685 men set by the Geneva cease-fire agreement for foreign military personnel in South Vietnam. Fortunately, the official attendance figure was unavailable so the International Control Commission, which is in charge of policing the cease-fire, cannot complain.

Bored with their supporting and advisory roles in an apparently endless tragedy that few of them understand, the Americans responded to the 90-minute revue of songs, jokes and the inevitable striptease with whistles, yells and cheers.

"Entertainment is sadly needed in Southeast Asia," said Jack Lemaire, the show's master of ceremonies. "We feel signally honored that we were chosen as the test show for this area."

•

There has not been much fun.

Early springtime is hot and muggy in Saigon. The ceiling fans in the base theater at the airport merely stirred the sultry air. But it was just as uncomfortable in the crowded hall as in the tent city half a mile away where the 57th Light Helicopter Company of the United States Army lives.

These tents are unbearably hot in the daytime and mosquito-ridden at night. Cold-water showers and hard canvas cots, and ankle-deep mud outside accentuate the discomfort. But the main morale problem and the one that half a dozen U.S.O. shows probably could not ease is the continued uncertainty over the tour of duty.

Pilots and crewmen so far have escaped injury in the actions in which eight helicopters have been hit by Communist bullets. No one expects this luck to last. After a few casualties, there may be a proposal for a point system providing for the earlier return of men who have accumulated a certain number of hazardous missions.

The pilots say, however, that they would prefer a fixed tour—one considerably shorter than the rumored 18 months.

Apart from the helicopter men, who have the perilous job of carrying Vietnamese troops into areas controlled by Communist guerrillas, most other American units seldom are exposed to Communist fire. For these, the main problem is . . .

[16 lines of type are inverted here]

. . . reached the provinces. It was scheduled for Danang, but had to be canceled because no suitable quarters could be found for the girls.

•

Besides amusement, Saigon offers instructive glimpses into the workings of the authoritarian Vietnamese regime. Pictures of Ngo Dinh Diem are plastered everywhere. But Americans rarely see him in person for he is very aloof. Americans are more likely to encounter South Vietnam's indomitable Mme. Ngo Dinh Nhu, palace hostess for the bachelor President and the First Lady of Vietnam.

During the palace bombing Feb. 27, Mme. Ngo Dinh Nhu stepped into a bomb hole and fell from a second-floor bedroom to the basement. But the indefatigable First Lady would not stay down. Ignoring her physician's advice, she was up in a few days presiding at the first national convention of her Women's Solidarity Movement. The next day she reviewed a mammoth parade at which she made a thinly veiled denunciation of the United States for insisting on broadening the base of Ngo Dinh Diem's regime.

Mme. Ngo Dinh Nhu will be going abroad soon. However, reports that she will be absent for several months have been denounced as wishful thinking by Government sources. She is going to Mexico and Europe, but her exact schedule is a secret. She will be back in plenty of time to run for re-election to the National Assembly in August.

Some sources said she might even be back late next month to fight against drastic revision by the National Assembly of the social purification bill. The President has sent the bill back to the Assembly with suggestions for certain modifications.

The purification bill, which Mme. Ngo Dinh Nhu warmly supported, would outlaw cockfights, fishfights (between Siamese fighting fish), prizefights, beauty contests and other "vain" entertainment.

It would ban Western dances, especially the twist and the striptease. If severely enforced, it would kill U.S.O. shows. (unpublished)

Bigart Tangles With Red Tape
In Vietnam Jungle

SAIGON, SOUTH VIETNAM—At 4 P.M. on March 23 I was summoned to appear before the director general of the Department of Information, Republic of South Vietnam.

Such summons are always unpleasant. Departments of Information, of course, never handle information. They exist for the correction of mental aberrations that afflict foreign correspondents.

Wondering where my copy had been found repellent, I stopped first at the shop of Dang Duc Khoi, who is a special press adviser to the Presidency. Khoi is a Buddhist but he seems more attuned to reality than most Christians here.

"Have I been naughty?" I asked Khoi. "Will they throw me out?"

Khoi assured me that my stories were jewels of objectivity. Suspecting perhaps that my intimations of deportation were based on wishful thinking, Khoi exhorted me to banish such thoughts. Besides, the director general would never dare try to oust me. Here he was wrong.

From *Times Talk,* April 1962

The heat was terrible that day and I was sweaty and fretful when I mounted the stairs to the Office of Truth. The director general had just returned from a symposium on "The Free Press" and in consequence his mannerisms seemed more saccharine than usual.

But he came to the point quickly.

"I have to inform you," he purred, "that a decree for your expulsion has been signed by the Minister of Interior. You must leave by plane tomorrow."

"Thank you for giving me so much advance notice," I replied.

He evidently thought I would beg for time. Finally he asked whether I wanted a few extra days to pack. He said he might just be able to swing it. But there is a limit to self-degradation and I gag at asking favors from information directors. "It's up to you to say when I must leave," I told him.

I asked the reasons for my expulsion. He said he did not have the decree handy (I was never to see it) but he would call Interior and find out. He phoned someone and then said: "You have spread false information which is considered to be tendentious and against the government and people of Vietnam."

"I have been expelled from only one other country—Communist Hungary," I told the director general.

"We are in a state of national emergency," he replied.

(To be perfectly candid, I am also considered undesirable by Egypt, Syria, Lebanon, Jordan, Saudi Arabia and by the Imam of Oman.)

The interview was over. An aide, Du Phuoc Long, showed me to the door.

I took a taxi to the Embassy and told the story to my friend Robert Barbour of the political section. He called in William C. Trueheart, the chargé d'affaires, who said he would ask for an explanation from the Foreign Office. Meanwhile I informed Khoi of developments.

Back at the hotel a Government courier served a summons for me to appear immediately at the Department of Immigration and bring my passport. I fled to my room. The phone rang and it was François Sully of *Newsweek*. He was in the same fix. Then Khoi dropped by and said perhaps it would be better to answer the Immigration summons.

But at Immigration Sully came running downstairs shouting: "Don't go up there! They want you to sign an expulsion decree." He had demurred, pointing out to the authorities that it was after 6 P.M. and past closing time.

I was struck by his Gallic logic. Leaving Khoi, I went down the street to the Embassy, turned in my passport to the Marine Guard for safekeeping and informed Barbour that I was off next day by helicopter for Father Hoa's village at the southern tip of Vietnam. Trueheart, meanwhile, extracted a promise from the Foreign Office that I wouldn't be heaved out for three days. Trueheart e'er won.

Returning to Saigon last Saturday, I was informed by Khoi that it was all a mistake. I could stay. There had been an error in the translation of one of my stories. (Officially there is no censorship, but cable copy is read by information people who sometimes delay transmission or may even refuse to let some stories go through.)

Not until Monday was the offending story identified. It was a Talk of Saigon piece (never used) and the passage that caused the flap was a couple of lines about President Diem being aloof these days while his sister-in-law, Mme. Nhu, got around quite a bit. Someone, perhaps deliberately, had twisted this about in translation so as to derive a salacious inference that the President was spending time with Mme. Nhu. Khoi had insisted on seeing the original copy and the hoax was thereby exposed.

This is one explanation. Ambassador Nolting has heard another—that my stories tended to pessimism and failed to reflect much enthusiasm for the Government. The palace had marked me as anti-regime and stooges were combing my copy to seize upon some excuse for expulsion.

(Sully was never told his offense. The expulsion order against him was finally lifted several days later.)

At Sully's request, none of the correspondents here wrote about the deportation orders.

Besides, how do you write a story about yourself in *The New York Times*? In the third person? And what category would it fall in: News Analysis? Talker? Or should it detonate a Blockbuster? I've often wondered why this categorizing of news isn't carried to the ultimate limit. The readers would know that Page One stories were IMPORTANT, that split-page features were HUMOR. CRACKAJACK or KNEESLAPPER might designate local yarns that lent themselves to coy headlines. FANTASY might do for editorial page offerings. In foreign news, PYGMY POT-POURRI could alert the reader against pieces from the emergent African republics.

Anyhow I regarded my reprieve with mixed feelings. This has not been a happy assignment.

Saigon is a nice place to spend a few days in. The food and wine are good, the city is attractive, most hotels and restaurants are air-conditioned. But to work here is peculiarly depressing.

Too often correspondents seem to be regarded by the American mission as tools of our foreign policy. Those who balk are apt to find it a bit lonely, for they are likely to be distrusted and shunned by American and Vietnamese officials.

I am sick of it. Each morning I take a pen and blot off another day on the Saigon calendar. At this writing, I have 83 more days to go.

Isolating Rural Villages, March 1962

U.S. Helps Vietnam
In Test of Strategy
Against Guerrillas

BENCAT, VIETNAM, March 28, 1962—Deep in a rubber plantation four miles north of here, South Vietnamese and Americans are engaged in an important test in isolating a rural population from the Viet Cong Communist guerrillas.

This experiment is crucial to the success of Operation Sunrise, the first comprehensive plan to pacify South Vietnam. Operation Sunrise was begun modestly in this area a week ago. The operation is subsidized directly with United States money, military planning and technical aid.

In this region, 1,200 families are to be moved voluntarily or forcibly from the forests controlled by the Viet Cong and resettled in new strategic villages. The abandoned villages will be burned to deprive the Viet Cong of shelter and food.

The Communist guerrillas have been blackmailing and threatening villagers to force them to provide supplies.

The first step in Operation Sunrise involved encirclement of a half dozen settlements. Government forces failed to make the maneuver a complete surprise: a hundred men were able to flee to the forest before the ring closed. The troops met slight resistance. Two guerrillas were killed. On the government side, one civilian was killed and one soldier wounded.

70 Families Volunteer

The government was able to persuade only 70 families to volunteer for resettlement. The 135 other families in the half dozen settlements were herded forcibly from their homes.

This harsh, desperate measure was approved by the Americans because it worked so well for the British in Malaya. There, the forced resettlement of a half-million people was the turning point in the British defeat of the Communists.

The vital features of the Malayan plan are discernible in Operation Sunrise. An important difference is noted, however, in the matter of compensation.

In Malaya, the British paid compensation on the spot for anything the farmers left behind. Here, the money is withheld until the resettled families indicate they will not bolt to the woods.

So far, little of the $300,000 in local currency provided by the United States Operations Mission has reached the farmers. Some volunteers have received the first part of the 1,500 piasters, or $21, promised by the government.

By way of further compensation, the government has promised land, building materials, agricultural tools and emergency food and clothing. Until homes are built, the families are housed in long communal barracks without walls.

Pigs, chickens and dogs were underfoot today as a large group of American officers and civilians trooped through the shelters, under rubber trees.

Some families had been allowed to carry away beds, tables and benches before their homes were burned. Others had almost nothing but the clothes on their backs. A young woman stood expressionless as she recounted how the troops had burned the families' two tons of rice. She was overheard by a man in black peasant garb who had identified himself as an army psychological warfare lieutenant. He cautioned the woman's listeners that she was "very bad" and that the burned rice was probably Viet Cong stores.

Only a few old men were visible among the uprooted families. The Vietnamese officers were asked what was being done to get the husbands to emerge from the forest and rejoin their families.

Leaflets Dropped

They replied that planes had dropped 24,000 leaflets promising amnesty. Also, the women are allowed to make one trip back to the deserted settlements that have not yet been burned to retrieve household effects. It is almost certain, officials said, that during this journey the wives will seek out their husbands and give them safe-conduct passes to the temporary camp.

The families are being subjected to a barrage of government propaganda. Loudspeakers told them why they had been uprooted: first, that the old settlement had no doctor and no schools; second, the Viet Cong conscripted their rice and made them sabotage roads; third, when forced to work for the Viet Cong, they were often victims of government bombs and bullets.

The trees were plastered with cartoons; banners suspended between trees promised, "we will root out all the Viet Cong who destroy our villages."

The camp seemed well-organized. Civic Action officials distributed food and clothes. Nurses instructed mothers in infant care.

"It's no happy hollow," Maj. Marvin L. Price of New Kensington, Pa., conceded. "But at last we've got a framework for getting people in the mood for helping themselves." The major had helped to plan Operation Sunrise.

Observers said it certainly was better than former operations wherein families were roughly ordered out of their houses, often with no time to gather their possessions, and marched off to a stockade with no provision for food or water.

Last week, for example, Miss Eliza M. Corbin of University Park, Pa., a United States mission adviser on rural home improvement, found 630 tired, dirty women and children living in a stockade in adjacent Phouc Thanh Province. They were getting insufficient rice and the children were ill from impure water. Miss Corbin quickly collected three tons of relief supplies from the Mennonite Central Committee and Roman Catholic relief agencies. (March 29, 1962)

Setting Up Fortified Towns, March 1962

Vietnam Sets Up Fortified Towns

Diem's Chief Adviser Opens 'Showpiece' Village

SAIGON, VIETNAM, March 31, 1962—Strategic villages are springing up all over Vietnam. Thousands of Vietnamese farmers are moving into settlements protected from Communist guerrillas by mud walls, moats, barbed wire and bamboo hedges.

Today the most elaborate of the strategic villages and one that has already become a showpiece for visitors was opened officially by Ngo Dinh Nhu, brother and chief adviser to Ngo Dinh Diem. The village, Cu Chi, consists of four hamlets with a total population of 6,270.

It is situated on a dusty plain about 20 miles northwest of Saigon. It has an elaborate complex of defenses—miles of walls commanding an encircling ditch and dozens of watch towers protected by barbed wire and bamboo stakes.

A year ago this was very insecure territory. Today one could drive here without a military escort.

Little Spontaneous Enthusiasm

The village shows disheartening signs of over-regimentation. Almost everyone who greeted Ngo Dinh Nhu was in uniform. Most of his audience consisted of blue-uniformed young troops. There was little spontaneous enthusiasm. Security measures were tight and grim soldiers with submachine guns were seen everywhere on the route of inspection.

Americans who know Cu Chi said they had heard complaints from farmers. These farmers said they had had to work six to eight weeks without pay on fortification of the hamlets and had not even been supplied with food. They also said they had to contribute bamboo, a crop they usually sell only when they have a bad year. They were further annoyed by having been ordered to buy flags and then having to buy more flags because the first set was not the proper size.

Ngo Dinh Nhu arrived with a large group of diplomats. They inspected several elementary schools and a Buddhist temple. The officials said Cu Chi was 85 percent Buddhist.

William Z. Gardiner, director of the United States Operations Mission, was delighted to find at one school a notice acknowledging that the United States had contributed most of the required funds.

From the flag-draped stand along the main highway Ngo Dinh Nhu said that the Communists had boasted of dominance over the Cu Chi district. He said that the people here had been considered pro-Communist but that all they really wanted was peace and freedom.

Once security was assured, Ngo Dinh Nhu said, the village would have the opportunity to elect local leaders. There would be no more arbitrary arrests, he said, and laws would be applied justly.

Cu Chi's opening is not connected with Operation Sunrise, launched in another part of Binh Duong Province last week. That operation involves the transfer of rural families out of isolated areas vulnerable to Communist control.

A Vietnamese official estimated that 500,000 rural families would be moved by Operation Sunrise and subsequent operations.

The burden of defending these new strategic villages and rural resettlements will fall on the Self-Defense Corps, which numbers about 65,000, and the Civil Guard, which has about the same numerical strength.

These forces are controlled by province chiefs. This defense is considered so important that American military advisers are being stationed with each of the 39 province chiefs to help attain a greater degree of planning coordination.

Self-Defense and Civil Guard units have always been prime targets for the guerrillas. Formerly their posts were poorly defended and guerrillas often made off with government weapons after overrunning them. Now both groups are being trained by Americans. The Civil Guard gets a minimum of 12 weeks' training, the Defense Corps gets a minimum of six weeks, and both are much improved. (April 1, 1962)

Reds Still Winning,
April 1962

Reds Still Win
In South Vietnam

Guerrillas Gain Despite Aid
to Loyal Forces by U.S.

BIEN HOA, VIETNAM, April 18, 1962—The Communists are still winning most of the clashes in the arc of South Vietnam provinces from the Cambodian frontier to the South China Sea.

They are scoring victories despite better training and better arms for the government forces and despite the fact that United States military advisers attached to Military Region 31, which is the nine northern provinces, have increased from a dozen at the start of the year to 142.

The latest group of Americans is assigned to the Fifth Division, which is based here.

Others are scattered from Tay Ninh near the western frontier, the holy city of the Cao Dai sect, to a lonely hole called Gia Ray, a whistle stop in Long Khanh Province on the main railroad linking Saigon and the North.

An American captain and three enlisted men who are training Gia Ray's Self-Defense Corps seldom hear the whistle these days because the Viet Cong guerrillas keep removing the tracks and derailing the trains. The team frequently runs out of rations and must live on rice.

Gloom Not Dispelled

The gloom of situations like this is not dispelled by the modest initial success of Operation Sunrise.

Operation Sunrise, hailed as a potential military and political solution of the Communist attempts to establish a corridor across Vietnam, got off to a widely publicized start in March. Two hundred and twenty-three isolated families in Binh Duong Province were rounded up by Fifth Division troops and were herded into a new village called Ben Tuong.

The new village of Ben Tuong looks hopeful. Some men who had run away from their families on the approach of government troops have been coaxed into the fortified perimeter.

This morning, troops began surrounding other settlements in Binh Duong, rounding up inhabitants for another new village.

It is too early to say whether the plan will work. Americans here believe in it. But they warn that the general security situation has worsened in the region.

The Communists are better trained and better armed than six months ago, according to Maj. Samuel J. Merrill of Palatka, Fla., administrative officer of the American detachment.

"When I arrived last September," he recalled, "the Vietcong were rarely encountered in groups exceeding four or five. Now they are frequently met in bands of 40 to 60. They used to run away on the approach of Vietnamese troops. Now they sometimes stand and fight. That's an indication of more leadership and training and better equipment."

The Viet Cong guerrillas still find the Self-Defense Corps outposts the easiest source of guns and ammunition.

As an example of the Vietcong resurgence, three Communist battalions operating in Zone D in Phuoc Than Province merged last month as the "Main Force Liberation Regiment."

Besides the new regiment, there is a separate battalion of hard-core regulars and 29 companies of regional troops.

The regular Vietnamese troops in the area are the Fifth Division, plus 36 companies of rangers. (April 19, 1962)

Bigart left Vietnam when his six months were over in June 1962. The correspondents held a party for him on June 30. This time the tune was "Clementine," but the lyrics echoed all his wars: Bigart was a burr under the saddle of authority, including Ambassador Frederick Nolting, Jr. As signed by "R.M.S.," most surely Robert Shaplen of *The New Yorker,* here are a few of the seven verses:

Homer Bigart, you are leaving
You are leaving fair Saigon,
And with you we are pleading,
To let bygones be bygone.

We will miss your constant growling,
And your wit so sharp and bright,
As you keep on prowling,
Prowling for a juicy fight.

Helpful Homer, says Fritz Nolting,
Life will not now be the same,
Everything has been revolting,
Since the day that Homer came.

Ngo Dinh Diem has been regretting
He could not bid you farewell.
He has found it too upsetting
That you thought life here was hell.

Madame Nhu will not be twisting
When she hears you're fully packed
Her sole reason for desisting
Is the new morality act.

Passing through Tokyo on July 5, he wrote in a letter: "The foreign desk is making noises about my doing a roundup when I return so I am in no real hurry to come back. I hate writing about Vietnam, being thoroughly fed up with the subject."

But he did write the long piece, and it ran July 25, under the headline: "Vietnam Victory Remote Despite U.S. Aid to Diem."

Although Bigart had left the scene of his last war, he did not leave the subject. In the ten more years that he worked for the *Times,* along with spot stories and long series on poverty and hunger in the United States, the civil rights struggle, the American Indian movement, the Eskimos, he covered the Calley, Medina, Levy, and Kent State trials, which grew out of the war. Trials were not something he liked a lot; as one reporter said of Bigart and the Eichmann trial, it was impossible to see the defendant as an underdog, and Bigart wanted an underdog. This was surely true of these later trials.

The Calley trial, a result of what became known as the Son My or Mylai 4 massacre, on March 16, 1968, threw into sharp focus major questions about the United States involvement in Vietnam. It became the longest trial in United States military history, with forty-six days of testimony alone. Here is a dispatch from Calley's time on the stand.

The Mylai Trial,
February 1971

Calley, on Stand,
Tells of Hatred

He Says Army Taught Him
to Treat All Vietnamese
as Potential Enemies

FORT BENNING, GA., Feb. 22, 1971—First Lieut. William L. Calley Jr., accused of killing 102 men, women and children during the alleged massacre of South Vietnamese civilians at Mylai, took the witness stand today and said he had been indoctrinated by the Army to treat all Vietnamese, including children, as potential enemies.

He told how he had come to regard them all with deepening suspicion and hate.

The short, stocky 27-year-old officer, now the chief defendant in the Mylai case, said that although he had attended Army classes on the Geneva Convention, he could not recall anything he had been taught about the rules of war.

He was on the stand for 93 minutes reviewing his early background and his Army career up to the eve of the alleged massacre.

What did stick in his mind, he told the court-martial panel of six officers who will decide his guilt or innocence on four counts of premeditated murder, was the sickening horror of the conflict.

While still in Hawaii, he had read some action reports of the 25th

Division, which had been in Vietnam for a year. From these reports, he said, he drew this conclusion: "It was essential that troops in Vietnam put out of their mind the World War II and Korean concept of giving candy and chewing gum and things to the children."

The children, he told the jury, were "even more dangerous" than men and women because, although they seemed so innocent, they threw grenades and were "very good at planting mines."

His fear and hatred of the Vietnamese was heightened, he said, during the enemy's Tet offensive of early 1968.

Shortly before Mylai, his men ran into a minefield and suffered heavy casualties, he went on. He was away on a rest and recreation leave when it happened, he said, but he got back in time to see a helicopter bring back the gear and the bodies of his buddies.

"I think the thing that really hit me hard were just the heavy boots," he said. "There must have been six boots there, with the feet still in them. Brains all over the place, and everything was just saturated with blood. Rifles just blown in half. I believe there was one arm and a piece of a man's face, half a man's face, on the chopper with the gear."

Describes His Feelings

Q. (by the chief defense counsel, George W. Latimer) And what was your feeling when you saw this? A. I don't know if I can describe the feeling.

Q. Well, at least try. A. Anger, hate, fear, generally sick to your stomach, hurt.

Q. Did this have any impact on your future actions? A. I think [it] instilled an even deeper form of hatred towards the enemy, but I don't think I ever made up my mind or came to any conclusion what I'd do to the enemy.

Q. All right, now did you have any remorse or grief over anything? A. Yes sir, I did.

Q. What was that? A. Remorse for losing my men in a minefield, remorse that these men ever had to go to Vietnam, remorse for being in that sort of a situation, where you are completely helpless. I think I felt mainly remorse because I wasn't there. Although there was nothing I could do, I think there is a psychological factor of just not being there when everything is happening.

'Weren't Playing Games'

Lieutenant Calley told of the pervasive fear engendered by the Tet offensive and described an incident when it "dawned on me that we weren't playing games, that we weren't supposed to be a bunch of Boy Scouts out there playing."

He was on leave at a seashore village.

"I woke early in the morning, and there was about six mama-sans coming down the street with their choggie baskets and their wares to sell at the market. That is what I presumed. I don't know where they were going, but just trying to get a head start so they could get a good place at the market.

"And on every corner the white mice [South Vietnam police] had a machine gun set up and I'd say it was about a half an hour before full light, and they cut them [the women] down. And that is how strict the war was becoming. At that time, you weren't supposed to move or be in an area. You'd best not be there, or you'd be dead."

"Rusty" Calley proved a taut witness. Although he holds a Bronze Medal and a Purple Heart, the only decoration he wore today was a Combat Infantryman's Badge. He was freshly barbered, and from his prematurely receding hairline a long brown lock was plastered to his forehead.

In the beginning his heavy-lidded eyes, which give him a perpetually sleepy look, darted nervously from defense table to spectators, with only a few glances at the jury.

But under the gentle questioning of Mr. Latimer, the young officer relaxed slowly and turned more frequently to the somber-faced jurors, five of whom have had combat experience in Vietnam.

The small courtroom, with its patriotic decor of red carpet, white walls and blue curtains, was thronged. Mr. Latimer asked the judge to enforce the rule against any outbursts by spectators during Lieutenant Calley's testimony.

The lieutenant spoke of his early youth in Miami. He said that he came from a "stable" family, a family without friction and a reasonably prosperous family. The father ran his own heavy construction machinery business.

Was Claims Investigator

Lieutenant Calley said that he ran into some trouble in the seventh grade—"for cheating, basically, sir"—and got generally poor marks as he went on through military schools and a junior college. The family encountered hard times. Lieutenant Calley's father lost his business, and the family moved to North Carolina, where the mother died of cancer.

"Rusty," meanwhile, had a number of menial jobs—busboy, dishwasher, short-order cook—"not that I knew how to cook," he told the court with a self-effacing chuckle—and a car drier in a minute car wash.

Then he was briefly a strike-breaking freight car conductor on the Florida East Coast Railway and finally an insurance claims investigator.

He was jobless in San Francisco when the draft notices caught up with him. He started East, but his car broke down in Albuquerque, where he went to a recruiting station and enlisted.

This morning, a psychiatrist, Dr. Wilbur M. Hannan of Alexandria, Va., testified that Lieutenant Calley had told him he had no intention of "destroying" all humans at Mylai but wanted to use some of them to clear minefields.

Lieutenant Calley never used the word "kill," Dr. Hannan said. The lieutenant told him that the military avoided that word because it caused "a very negative emotional reaction" among the men, who had been taught the commandment, "Thou shalt not kill."

Instead, Lieutenant Calley employed the word "destroy" or the phrase "waste 'em," which meant something quite different from kill, the psychiatrist said.

Lieutenant Calley felt he was not killing human beings but destroying enemies, that he was carrying out legal orders, Dr. Hannan said.

The psychiatrist suggested that no American soldier—except psychopathic killers—could properly be tried for the Mylai incident or any similar action.

"It amounts to war," he said. "And if you're going to blame war on anyone, it might as well be God—you can't blame groups of individuals or nations."

He said that Lieutenant Calley had suffered no "diagnosable mental illness" but insisted that the young officer, because of personal background, training and combat stress, had been unable to commit premeditated murder at Mylai. . . . (Feb. 23, 1971)

On March 29, Calley was found guilty of killing at least 22 Vietnamese, including babies, and he was sentenced to life at hard labor. President Nixon modified this to three years, mostly under house arrest.

Bigart's legacy to future war coverage did not end with his dispatches. He taught the next generation.

Murray Kempton, in a *Newsday* column, painted a vivid picture of Bigart at the time of Korea.

"He was a great if unobtrusive teacher; but he could be demanding," Kempton wrote. "I had a friend with the misfortune to arrive in Korea just when the Chinese had broken the American advance. He was driving his jeep toward the noise when he came upon Homer Bigart walking away from it.

"'How far is the action?' he asked, and Bigart replied, 'Just over the hill.' My friend plunged forward to be carried back in too quick order with wounds no less painful for being short of mortal. Later, he recalled the encounter with a measure of bitterness, and I felt constrained gently to chide Bigart with it. 'Well,' he replied, 'he asked me a question and I answered it.'

"I henceforth understood that however alien cruelty was to his nature, Bigart was a severe instructor and that my friend had been not unusefully taught that to come upon him in a rear area was to be soundly cautioned not to proceed further toward a front that was heading your way fast enough in any case."

He had no plan to be a mentor; he told Mary Marshall Clark in an interview for the *Times* history project, in only a slight overstatement of the case: "I never offered any free information to anyone in my life." But he did teach the young correspondents in Vietnam, giving them precept and example. David Halberstam said: "To our generation in Vietnam, I don't think his importance can be overestimated. We were his lineal descendants in the sense that someone of such consuming integrity had preceded us, and in the kind of honor he represented.

"I was aware every day that he was going to read my story."

Halberstam did not directly follow Bigart to Vietnam; there were a couple of fill-ins over the summer. So Bigart left a long helpful memo, in which he said that the young U.P.I. man, Neil Sheehan, would be good.

In addition to the major lesson Sheehan learned from Bigart, that the U.S. military interventions were not working any more, an account given in Harrison E. Salisbury's foreword, the young man got a secondary indoctrination early in his assignment. Salisbury also tells this story in his history of *The Times,* "Without Fear or Favor," and Halberstam tells it too in a profile in the August 1972 issue of the journalism review *More.*

Of the Sheehan-Bigart tie, he wrote: "It was an odd friendship. Bigart, the veteran reporter at the height of his powers and shrewdness, hating the war, the assignment, sensing that everything was going to go wrong, and Sheehan, young, energetic, loving everything because it was new and fresh."

Sheehan, referring to Bigart as his professor of journalism, retold the event once more at the memorial gathering for Bigart in New York on September 25, 1991.

On Saturday, May 12, 1962, Sheehan filed a story that three hundred Viet Cong had been killed in My Tho in the Mekong Delta. Sheehan got it from a colonel who had been a good news source, but without being aware that the colonel could hold a lot of liquor without showing it, and he had been drunk. The story arrived in New York before deadline for the Sunday paper, and it was placed at the top of Bigart's story for the day, a dispatch about a train blown up by the Communists; in newspaper jargon, Bigart's story became a shirt-tail to Sheehan's: "Vietnamese Slay 300 Reds in Clash." The editors fired off a message to Bigart asking why he did not have the story of the My Tho attack.

About 8 A.M. in Saigon, Sheehan was awakened by a call. "Sheehan, this is Bigart. You have shirt-tailed me. I have a cable here from my employers in New York. They seem to believe that there are 300 dead Viet Cong in the Mekong Delta. Get dressed, we are driving to My Tho . . . And, Sheehan, there better be 300 Viet Cong bodies down there."

When they drove to My Tho, there were twelve bodies, and Bigart's dispatch of May 13, "Raid in Vietnam a Minor Success," said estimates had been "drastically reduced." On the way back from My Tho Sheehan was despairing about his big story and the shame of now writing a denial, talking of suicide. Bigart consoled him. "It happens to all of us. I've done it a few times myself. Don't let it get to you, kid. But just don't do it again while I'm here."

Sheehan, who missed out on the Pulitzer Prize that Halberstam and Malcolm Browne of the Associated Press won for covering the downfall of the Diems, became the man who acquired the Pentagon Papers for the *Times*. He won his Pulitzer for 1988 for a complex history, *A Bright Shining Lie: John Paul Vann and America in Vietnam.* He, Browne, Halberstam, and the late Charles Mohr, who at first covered for *Time* magazine, but who, like the others, eventually worked for the *Times,* viewed themselves as heirs to a vital tradition of skepticism.

Bigart was mortally ill by the time of the Persian Gulf War. It is another book, but it would be valuable for a historian to examine whether it will be possible for citizens to know what goes on in a war as they knew about the wars Bigart covered, because the media of the United States, and their citizen-readers and viewers, have bowed to the rules of totally controlled coverage that the Pentagon promulgated for that brief conflict.

The *Times* columnist Tom Wicker, on April 20, 1991, wrote: "Homer Bigart, one of the best newspaper reporters ever to pound a typewriter, died in New Hampshire this week, at age 83. On the same day, in an irony he might have appreciated, a Federal judge pronounced what may well have been the end of the great tradition of combat correspondents." Federal Judge Leonard B. Sand, on April 16, rebuffed the only legal challenge to the Pentagon restrictions. It was filed before the war by the *Nation* and other publications and news agencies and a few individual reporters and writers.

Wicker quoted Eric Sevareid's letter to the *Times* on the topic:

"Our modern military leadership has put an end to the time-honored role of combat correspondent in American journalism. We are not likely to see, hear or read the work of any future Ed Murrows, Ernie Pyles, Homer Bigarts or Bob Capas. I would settle for that only if future American wars were equally unlikely, which is doubtful."

The headline on Wicker's column was: "End of a Great Era."

Appendix

Homer Bigart Obituary

Homer Bigart, Acclaimed Reporter, Dies

By Richard Severo

Homer Bigart, one of the most accomplished reporters in American journalism, died yesterday at the Edgewood Center in Portsmouth, N.H., where he had been hospitalized for two months. Mr. Bigart, who wrote for both the *New York Herald Tribune* and *The New York Times,* was 83 years old and lived in West Nottingham, N.H.

He died of cancer, his wife, Else, said.

In a calling whose end product tends to be ephemeral and forgettable, in which writers nervously jest that they are only as good as their last story, Mr. Bigart stood as an enduring role model.

During a prize-winning career of nearly four decades, he always seemed to be at the top of his game, much to the dismay of his competitors.

His articles remained taut, witty and astringently understated, even when created under deadline pressure and the appalling working conditions imposed by war and famine; even when they concerned mundane events that lesser reporters regarded as routine. Mr. Bigart knew what counted was not the place but the poetry and that a reporter could create memorable prose from even the most unremarkable happening.

Such pieces became the models of grace by which young reporters measured their own talent, and they were the reality from which a legend was born. In journalism schools and in the drafty city rooms of a town that always prided itself of being the ultimate stop for the nation's most gifted newspaper reporters, Mr. Bigart was regarded with awe.

From *The New York Times,* Wednesday, April 17, 1991

He won most of the major national and local prizes in journalism. There was a Pulitzer Prize, there was an uncommon second Pulitzer. There were an Overseas Press Club award and the George Polk Memorial Award and the Meyer Berger Award and a Page One Award and many others.

All were given for the resourcefulness and courage that Mr. Bigart repeatedly showed in World War II, the Greek civil war, the Korean War and the turbulent years that followed, when he wrote about the civil rights struggle and hunger and the extraordinary changes that were taking place in urban and rural America.

All his articles were written either for the *Herald Tribune,* where he worked from 1927 to 1955, or *The Times,* where he worked from 1955 until his retirement in 1972.

If his reporter friends told him that the encomiums in his stocking approached the indecent level, they were proud that he had won such praise, because they felt he was the best of them. Wherever he went and whatever he did, his copy rose above the moment; no awards judge could resist Mr. Bigart at his best.

Describing History
In the Making

For example, there was the opening of the article he wrote from the battleship *Missouri* on Sept. 2, 1945, telling readers of the *Herald Tribune* that one of the greatest military struggles in world history was finally over:

"Japan, paying for her desperate throw of the dice at Pearl Harbor, passed from the ranks of the major powers at 9:05 a.m. today when Foreign Minister Mamoru Shigemitsu signed the document of unconditional surrender.

"If the memories of the bestialities of the Japanese prison camps were not so fresh in mind, one might have felt sorry for Shigemitsu as he hobbled on his wooden leg toward the green baize-covered table where the papers lay waiting.

"He leaned heavily on his cane and had difficulty seating himself. The cane, which he rested against the table, dropped to the deck of this battleship as he signed."

And there was the time in 1943 that he took a troopship to London and was surprised that it had not been torpedoed, reports of scores of U-boats to the contrary. Three paragraphs from the end of his dispatch he wrote:

"Then you woke up one morning and the ship was very steady, and you knew you had entered the harbor. You had arrived. You had crossed the submarine-infested Atlantic without sighting even a porpoise. A hell of a thing to have to confess to your grandchildren."

War is damaging to the sense of humor of those who are caught up in it, but Mr. Bigart, describing the American Army's pursuit of the Germans in Sicily and noting that civilian conduct had been "exemplary," wrote this on July 25, 1943, as a last paragraph:

"In fact the Sicilians are too friendly. Their attitude strengthens the impression that this island is a forgotten portion of Southern California, instead of a segment of enemy Italy."

But there were times when he had to describe death, as he did on Dec. 15, 1943, from San Pietro, Italy:

"Generally, there is no mistaking the dead—their strange contorted posture leaves no room for doubt. But this soldier, his steel helmet tilted over his face, seemed merely resting in the field. We did not know until we came within a few yards and saw a gray hand hanging limply from a sleeve."

After he joined *The Times,* Mr. Bigart covered such important assignments as the trial of Adolf Eichmann, the Nazi war criminal, in Israel in 1961. The following year Mr. Bigart surveyed the war in Vietnam. He was already in his middle 50's but he had lost none of his ability to understand a situation and report it quickly.

Shy, Private Man,
Insouciant Wit

David Halberstam, who succeeded Mr. Bigart for *The Times,* recalled that Mr. Bigart was one of the first to conclude that contrary to the Pentagon's representations, America was not about to win an easy war, and that the war was in fact a tragedy and a mistake. He advised younger reporters to write that the American effort "just doesn't work."

Mr. Halberstam said Mr. Bigart's irreverence, his "unerring instincts," his willingness to challenge "the official version" and his leadership were the sustenance that younger reporters needed to chronicle an unprecedented American military tragedy.

In 1963, when *The Times* asked him to cover the grim winter confronting unemployed coal miners in Kentucky, it was clear that Mr. Bigart had lost none of his reportorial eye:

"Creeks are littered with garbage, choked with boulders and silt dislodged by strip-mine operations. Hillsides that should be a solid blaze of autumn color are slashed with ugly terraces, where bulldozers and steam shovels have stripped away the forest to get at the coal beneath."

The legend was not built simply on his articles. It rested as much on the man himself.

Mr. Bigart, a shy and private man with a pronounced stammer, was at once retiring and combative, devoted equally, it seemed, to minding his own business and to hoisting a few with friends. It was on these occasions that he told the stories the journalists of the era loved to tell and hear. And he did it as well in bars as in print. His insouciant one-liners about people, places and things were not soon forgotten by colleagues.

At the *Herald Tribune,* for example, one colleague (and rival) was Marguerite Higgins, a determined World War II and Korean War correspondent who won much fame because of the aggressive way she pursued reporting. Miss Higgins was a pioneer in working in a field that men liked to think of as their province and she often outmaneuvered most male rivals, who, in those prefeminist days, would have preferred her to be shy and confined to the society page, or, as they might have put it, barefoot and pregnant.

On one occasion, she did become pregnant. When Mr. Bigart learned of it, he snapped: "Oh, g-good. And wh-who is the mother?" Later, when the baby was born, Mr. Bigart cheerily inquired if the mother had devoured it.

Another competitor in the old days was Clifton Daniel, a correspondent for *The Times* in Jerusalem in the late 1940's when Mr. Bigart covered for the *Herald Tribune.* Years later, Mr. Daniel, who eventually became managing editor of *The Times,* recalled how hard he had to work to avoid being scooped by Mr. Bigart.

"I worked out a system for keeping an eye on him," Mr. Daniel said. "I persuaded him to move into the Eden Hotel, where I lived after the King David was bombed by the Zionist underground. Moreover, I had a car, and Homer didn't; I offered to give him a lift whenever there was a big story to be covered out of town, so I always knew where he was."

But the ploy didn't work. Britain then ran Palestine under a United Nations mandate, and Mr. Daniel said that Mr. Bigart "sneaked out of the press room of the British Office of Information and held a clandestine interview one night with one of the biggest underground leaders."

"I didn't know anything about it until the next day," Mr. Daniel said.

Later, after Mr. Bigart returned to New York, he would occasionally drink martinis at a grungy newspaper bar in the Times Square area where the customers could always see what they were breathing. Taking stock of the environment one night, Mr. Bigart politely inquired of the bartender what day of the week they changed the air.

One evening, late in life, he decided to tell Murray Illson, a reporter friend at *The Times,* that he was marrying again. "I showed her mine, and she showed me hers," Mr. Bigart said. Before Mr. Illson could say anything, Mr. Bigart added, "Our bankbooks."

Like other great reporters of his generation, Mr. Bigart never hesitated to show disdain for his editors and independence from them. One evening late in his career, he was assigned to write about a riot, drawing on information from reporters at the scene.

As one reporter, John Kifner, called in from a phone booth, rioters began shaking it and Mr. Kifner conveyed fright to Mr. Bigart. But Mr. Bigart, busy fending off editors he regarded as hysterical, comforted Mr. Kifner by noting, "At least you're dealing with sane people."

From Architecture to Journalism

Homer William Bigart was born Oct. 25, 1907, in Hawley, Pa., in the Pocono region, the son of Homer S. Bigart, a woolens manufacturer, and Anna Schardt Bigart. He attended public schools there, then ventured to Pittsburgh to enroll in the Carnegie Institute of Technology. He thought he wanted to be an architect. The institute felt otherwise.

"They found I couldn't draw," Mr. Bigart later recalled, "and invited me to find another school."

In 1927, Mr. Bigart complied. He enrolled in the New York University School of Journalism and got a job as a night copy boy on the *Herald Tribune.* N.Y.U. liked him well enough, but Mr. Bigart remained unconvinced that his journalism professors knew much about journalism. He dropped out, and in 1929, as the Great Depression was starting, joined the *Trib* full time.

Since he was neither a college graduate nor adept at office politics, he remained a copy boy for four years. But then the *Trib* decided to give him a chance and made him a general assignment reporter at $25 a week.

At first it seemed he would not make it. He was a painfully slow writer. Editors were amazed at his bizarre typing style, in which he double-spaced between words. He made errors that young reporters are prone to make. Once, assigned to cover the start of a coach railroad service between New York and Florida, he went to the wrong track and wrote about the wrong railroad.

It was in this period that Mr. Bigart found he could use his halting speech to become a more effective reporter. The stammer made it easier for him to pose as a bumbler who was not very smart. He would often say to those he interviewed, "G-g-gee, I d-d-didn't really understand that. C-c-could you repeat it?"

Most of those he interviewed went to extra lengths to be sure he got the story straight, and the result was that Mr. Bigart's articles seemed to be clearer than anyone else's; the quotations were invariably rich.

During the 1930's the paper found ample reason to have more and more confidence in Mr. Bigart's skills, and in 1942 he was asked if he would become a war correspondent. He agreed and went on to cover the London blitz, the bombing of Nazi Germany, the battles of North Africa, Italy and southern France.

When the war was over in Europe, he moved to the Pacific and covered the final months of the war against Japan. He always seemed determined to cover war at the cannon's mouth and was one of the first reporters to enter Hiroshima after the Americans dropped the atomic bomb.

Newsweek called him "the hardest kind of worker and the fairest kind of competitor." Philip Potter of *The Baltimore Sun* said Mr. Bigart "worked over his copy more than any of the rest of us correspondents, who were anxious after a hard day in the field to get our copy written and filed so we could get a drink."

"Homer would be at his portable, crossing off one word because he had thought of a better one," Mr. Potter said. "He observed things that we had missed."

The plaudits kept coming when he covered the war in Korea. In that war, *Newsweek* called him "the best war correspondent of an embattled generation."

The people who ran some of the countries Mr. Bigart visited as a reporter did not entirely agree with that appraisal. Because of the independence of his reporting, he was ordered out of Hungary, Egypt, Syria, Lebanon, Jordan, Saudi Arabia, Oman and Vietnam.

The Vietnamese order was rescinded; the censor admitted he had made a translation error that led him to believe that Mr. Bigart had written something obscene.

When Mr. Bigart left the *Trib* for *The Times,* there was no particular joy in it for him. The *Trib* was a decade away from its demise, and its economic problems were not lost on Mr. Bigart. But it was a paper with a proud tradition of giving writers their head, and Mr. Bigart loved it.

"It seemed to me that he always looked down on the *Times,* even when he worked there," Mr. Daniel said. "Its main fault, in his eyes, was that it wasn't the *Trib*. It was too proud and stiff-necked for his taste. But he knew that if he couldn't work for the *Trib*, the next best thing was the *Times*. He was not disloyal to it; he just wasn't in love with it."

Mr. Bigart's first two wives were Alice Veit, who died in 1959 after they were divorced, and Alice Weel, who died in 1969. The next year he married Else Holmelund Minarik, the author of children's books, who survives him. He is also survived by a sister, Margaret Crowe of Lancaster, Pa., and a step-daughter, Brooke Minarik of Dover, N.H.

No funeral is planned, the family said.

I Worked With Him,
House Organ Obituary

Homer W. Bigart, 83
Reporter, 1955–1972

When Ngo Dinh Diem's Presidential Palace in Saigon was bombed on Feb. 27, 1962, Homer Bigart, the *Times*'s Vietnam correspondent, was, as usual, out of town.* He hated missing the story, but he was furious when he was asked to play catch-up the next day. He filed a lead that sent the editors in New York into a tizzy: "After yesterday's thrilling bombing of the Presidential Palace, Saigon slipped back into its usual state of apathy today."

The lead, which was replaced with a customary second-dayer faster than you could say Gerstenzang and Wade, stuck with me. Fresh from the wire room, it was, more blatant than his puns, a prime example of why you could never take your eye off Homer when you were editing. But now, after a long time retyping Homer's war dispatches from the *Trib* and the *Times* for a book, I bow to its historic validity. However unfit to print, Homer's lead was right.

For him, the story was where the real battle was going on, as far out there as he could get, and he had little tolerance for briefings in cities back in the rear. In March 1944, covering his first war, he wrote from

*In fact, he was in town but asleep, as I learned later from an interview taped in his retirement for the *Times*'s history project. He said he gathered what material he could and tried to file, but the government had thrown a cordon around the telegraph office. It was the "worst day of my career as a journalist," he said, and he was always ashamed of it.

From *Times Talk,* June 1991

Naples: "It is a depressing experience to return from the Anzio beach-head . . . and find in a city 60 miles behind the lines a complacency and lack of realism worse than that prevailing in New York." A response to generals' criticism that correspondents were too pessimistic, this dispatch was carried on Page 1 of the *Trib*.

He could drive you nuts. In November 1961, he was working on a long piece—in those days, called a blockbuster, now called a take-out—about the men on the Bowery—then known as derelicts, now known as the homeless. I was editing it, consulting with Homer all the way. He was irascible: "Why do I always have to write derelict? Why won't the *Times* just use the word 'bum'?" Well, that was all I had to hear. I fought fiercely with the Bull Pen until the word 'bum' was accepted. Homer still had one more take to write on that Sunday afternoon, Nov. 19, when the flash came that Governor Rockefeller's son Michael was missing in New Guinea. The entire machinery of the paper suddenly focused on getting Homer on the plane with the Governor—suitcase, visas, shirts, tickets, money—not easy to do on Sunday. I wrapped up the unfinished story somehow, and it appeared Monday morning.

Homer was a long time getting home, wars and executions required his coverage, and he had some time off due. When he got back, I reported his victory on using the word 'bum' in the long-forgotten Bowery project. "Bum?" Homer said scathingly. "It's unsuitable for the *Times* to use the word bum."

Being a friend of Homer's was likewise demanding and educational. "Would you, could you, come for dinner?" the awed young editor asked the two-time Pulitzer winner. "If you will serve my favorite meal, meat loaf and apple pie with chocolate Dolly Madison ice cream," the reporter said. Well, the editor scrambled and so did her husband and they still had to make do with another brand of ice cream. But the brand of gin was right, and the friendship was established.

At a time when he was not married, Homer frequently joined the reportorial seminars at Gough's. One evening before he was leaving on an overseas assignment, we set a record, closing three saloons—Bleeck's, the Blue Ribbon and Sardi's. As we wobbled out into Times Square at some unearthly hour, it began to snow into the canyons.

Homer gazed up on the city where he had lived since the 20's, and said something I did not learn for myself for years: "New York is never so beautiful as when you're leaving in six hours."

The poet Eve Merriam, who met him at our house, said that she knew the perfect wife for Homer, who was widowed. The prospect, Else Holmelund Minarik, the noted author of *Little Bear* and other children's classics, lived in New Hampshire, but we finally got our two tigers together at the Moon Palace near Columbia. Richard Severo's jewel of an obituary reported that Homer, preparing to marry Else, told Murrary Illson: "I showed her mine and she showed me hers" but before Murray could say a thing, added, "Our bankbooks."

Homer's classic wit to the contrary, it was a wonderful if sometimes stormy marriage and romance, and after they married, Else went with him on his assignments, cooking real meals in motels, until they retired to New Hampshire in 1972.

The obit also mentioned Homer's peculiar style of typing, hitting the space bar while thinking. Here is a sample, from an interview Homer conducted at his home with James Meredith, who had been shot on his freedom march in Mississippi. The insert contains a little nod to the editor, and I saved an unedited carbon for obvious reasons.

```
         teetolaler   and  a   nonsmoker,  Mr. Meredith

also  declined  to interrupt  the  marathon  interview   by taking  coffee.

he said he   had  never  tasted  coffee  in his  life.     H  did  accept

some  grapes and home-made  bread  baked  by   Betsy  Wade.

                   end insert
```

In "Charlotte's Web," E. B. White writes: "It is not often that someone comes along who is a true friend and a good writer." Homer was that rare conjunction.

—Betsy Wade

Technical Notes
and Acknowledgments

—————

These dispatches were in the main transcribed from clipping files maintained by the two newspapers where Homer Bigart worked. In a traditional newspaper clipping collection, the morgue, or library, would file material under subject matter—"Air Disasters," for instance, or "Vietnam War"—and at the same time under the byline of the writer. This made it easier for a reporter to find an earlier story quickly.

The *New York Herald Tribune*'s file of Bigart bylines was given to him when he left the paper by Bob Grayson, the *Trib* librarian, one of the acknowledged greats in this now-defunct field. Bigart lent them for this book. Custody of the *Times* Bigart clips, file B-759,129, was given to the editor of this book when the paper began to shift to an electronic retrieval system. Both of these collections, brittle and brown but mostly intact, are now the property of Else Holmelund Minarik Bigart. She also lent the scrapbook of 1943–45 clippings that Homer's sister Margaret created, which solved riddles about photo dates and filled some unperceived gaps in the *Trib* morgue file.

When clippings were damaged or I learned they were missing, I used microfilm. There is a broken set of *Herald Tribune* microfilm at Columbia University, but no *Trib* index exists for the Bigart period. *Times* microfilm and the *Times Index* are widely available.

The headlines, banks, and subheads in this book are retained as in the original clippings, but all have been rendered in upper and lower case for ease of reading. I have not included the jump (continuation) heads. The datelines are not the date of publication, but the date of filing as printed, with the year added. Other material in the clippings, such as bylines and copyright lines, have generally been dropped. The date of publication of the dispatch has been added in parenthesis at the end of each story.

Some stylistic and spelling peculiarities have been smoothed out for consistency. I have tried to repair obvious typographical errors. Ellipses mark deletions.

Parentheses and brackets in the body of the dispatches are those that appeared in the originals—parentheses are usually the reporter's and brackets the New York editor's. Where there was the rare need to interpose comments within a dispatch, I have added an asterisk and a note at the bottom of the page.

Many people who held Homer Bigart in high esteem brought this book into being and this bare-bones acknowledgment cannot reflect how much they contributed:

Else Bigart; Prof. James Boylan, teacher, editor, and husband; Roy Reed of the University of Arkansas; Edward L. Barlow of the International *Herald Tribune* Corporation, and Dick Wald of ABC News and Kathryn A. Ritchie of Whitney Communications, both formerly of the *Herald Tribune,* all three of whom threw away the red-tape book so this book could be published; Richard Kluger, author of *The Paper, the Life and Death of the* Herald Tribune; I. Reines Skier of Hawley, Pennsylvania, the Bigart family's lawyer; Margaret Bigart Crowe of Lancaster, Pennsylvania, who maintained scrapbooks of her brother's work.

Also, Bigart's fellow Pulitzer Prize winners Harrison E. Salisbury, David Halberstam, Neil Sheehan, and Joseph Lelyveld; Joan Cook, president of the Society of the Silurians; Andy Rooney; Prof. Russell Strong; William Prochnau; Wil Haygood; Pat and Ralph Berens; Helen A. Stephenson of the Authors Guild; Murray Illson; Sydney Gruson; Clifton Daniel; John Kifner; Cathy Byrne; Charles Robinson, head of the *Times* morgue; Ray Paganelli, Ursula Mahoney, and Ed Gross, who understand the *Times* and pictures; Nestor M. Delgado, Bob Glass, Naum Kazhdan, and others in the *Times* photo labs; George V. Mikulec of AP Pictures; Carlo A. Mastricolo of *The Boston Globe;* Kati Marton, William Polk, and Milbry C. Polk; David Binder; Prof. Karen Rothmyer; the staff of the Butler Library microfilm collection at Columbia University; Susan Dryfoos of the *Times* History Project; Mary Marshall Clark of the Columbia Oral History Project, formerly at *The Times;* Nancy Moran; and Debbie Bowen, an editor's editor.

Index

War II in the Pacific, 55–91; Poland, 95–97; Palestine, 98–110; Greek civil war, 110–23; Korean War, 127–52; Guatemala coup, 155–57; shift to *New York Times*, xxii, 161; Middle East, 161–72; Eichmann trial, xxii, 175–82; Vietnam war, 185–217

Binder, David, 123

Bixler, Lieut. Raymond, 128, 130–31

Bleeck's, also known as Artist & Writers, saloon on West 40th Street, xxiv

Borders, Bill, xviii

Boyle, Hal, 152

Bracker, Milton, 50–51

Bragaw, Lieut. Henry C., 33

Braley, Sgt. Karl L., 79

Bremen, Germany, 8, 15

Bridges, Sgt. Corbin H., 142

A Bright Shining Lie: John Paul Vann and America in Vietnam, by Neil Sheehan, 217

Brolo, Sicily, 22–25

Browne, Malcolm, 217

Bulkeley, Lieut. John D., 59

Burgess, Maj. Harry, 64

Burnett, Capt. Alfred S., 141–43

Calley, First Lieut. William L., Jr., trial of, 210–15

Campbell, Lieut. Robert (Soupy), 129

Carey, James W., xxiv–xxv

Carnegie Tech (Carnegie Mellon), 227

Carroceto, Italy, 37

Cassino, 42–47, 50–51

Castillo Armas, Col. Carlos, 155–56

Castro, Fidel, xxii

Catledge, Turner, 161

CBS, xxiv

censorship, at Anzio, 35–37; in Gulf War, 217

Centanni, Capt. Frank D., 61

Central Intelligence Agency, 155

Cherne, Maj. Milton, 194

Cisterna di Littoria, Italy, 36

City of Saco, Maine, B-29 in Kumagaya raid, 76–80

Clark, Mary Marshall, xxiv, 8, 215–16

Clarke, Sgt., tail-gunner, 75

Cleghorn, Lieut. Rufus J., 33–34

Collins, Sgt. Harvie Cecil, 11

Cook, Don, xxiv

Cook, Zeke, 50–51

Coon, Pvt. Bernard, 65

Corbin, Eliza M., 204

Corregidor, 59–61

Cosmopolitan magazine, Willoughby denunciation of Bigart in, 152

Crioli, Mount, Sicily, 22–25

Cronkite, Walter, xiii, 12

Crowe, Margaret Bigart, sister of Bigart, xix, 228

Cu Chi, Vietnam, 205

Cudworth, Capt. William, 146

Dang Duc Khoi, 198–200

Daniel, Clifton, 109–11, 161, 224–25, 227

Dayan, Maj. Gen. Moshe, 162

DDT, in Vietnam, 186, 188–89

Del Valle, Staff Sgt. Rosendo D., Jr., 79

Dewey, Thomas E., xx

Dhala, Western Aden Protectorate, 168–70

Dickerson, Lieut. Col. William, 190

Dixon, Kenneth L., AP, 43

Dodge, Lieut. Col. Howard K., 32–33

Doyle, Rear Adm. James H., 135–36

Drum, Lieut. Gen. Hugh A., 3

Duncan, Spl. 16 Richard L., 191

Eichmann, Adolf, trial of in Jerusalem, xxii, 175–82

Eighth Air Force, U.S., bombing of Europe, xx, 7–15

Eighth Army, U.S., in Italy, 42–47